"Just as I thought it would—it takes a twentysomething media insider to blow the lid off the real workings of today's so-called news media. Holiday shows exactly how a handful of dodgy bloggers control the whole system and turn our collective attention into their own profit."
—Andrew Keen, author of *The Cult of the Amateur* and *Digital Vertigo*

"When playing for high stakes, Ryan Holiday is my secret weapon. His unique stealth manner makes him essential for winning."
—Aaron Ray, partner of the management/production company
The Collective with over 150 million albums sold
and $1 billion in movie revenues

"Ryan Holiday is a man you should listen to. . . . [He] has a truly unique perspective on the seedy underbelly of digital culture. Ignore him at your peril!"
—Matt Mason, director of marketing at BitTorrent and author of
The Pirate's Dilemma: How Youth Culture Is Reinventing Capitalism

---

"In an area where hazy-headed utopianism reigns, Ryan Holiday excels in thinking about the Internet and its future clearly."
—Ethan Brown, author of *Shake the Devil Off*,
a *Washington Post* Critic's Pick

"Ryan Holiday is one of the only people brave enough to peer deep into the murky waters of Internet 'journalism' to see how fabricated and unfounded information can be spun by greedy, unethical Internet overlords—destroying real people's lives. The danger is real—no one is immune from this dystopian world."
—Julia Allison, syndicated columnist and on-air correspondent,
NBC New York

"Ryan Holiday is real. Not only real, but notorious for creating risqué ads online for American Apparel. How could a kid barely legal to buy a drink be the Don Draper of the *Fast Company* crowd?"

—317am.net

"Ryan Holiday is the Machiavelli of the Internet age. Dismiss his message at your own peril: He speaks truths about the dark side of Internet media which no one else dares mention."

—Michael Ellsberg, author of *The Education of Millionaires: It's Not What You Think and It's Not Too Late*

"This primer on how to hack the media zeitgeist is so incredibly accurate, it just might render mainstream media completely useless. As opposed to mostly useless like it is now."

—Drew Curtis, founder Fark.com

TRUST ME
I'M LYING

TRUST ME
I'M LYING

CONFESSIONS OF A MEDIA MANIPULATOR

RYAN HOLIDAY

{ PORTFOLIO / PENGUIN }

PORTFOLIO / PENGUIN
Published by the Penguin Group
Penguin Group (USA) Inc., 375 Hudson Street,
New York, New York 10014, U.S.A.
Penguin Group (Canada), 90 Eglinton Avenue East, Suite 700,
Toronto, Ontario, Canada M4P 2Y3
(a division of Pearson Penguin Canada Inc.)
Penguin Books Ltd, 80 Strand, London WC2R 0RL, England
Penguin Ireland, 25 St. Stephen's Green, Dublin 2, Ireland
(a division of Penguin Books Ltd)
Penguin Books Australia Ltd, 250 Camberwell Road, Camberwell,
Victoria 3124, Australia
(a division of Pearson Australia Group Pty Ltd)
Penguin Books India Pvt Ltd, 11 Community Centre, Panchsheel Park,
New Delhi – 110 017, India
Penguin Group (NZ), 67 Apollo Drive, Rosedale, Auckland 0632,
New Zealand (a division of Pearson New Zealand Ltd)
Penguin Books (South Africa) (Pty) Ltd, 24 Sturdee Avenue,
Rosebank, Johannesburg 2196, South Africa

Penguin Books Ltd, Registered Offices:
80 Strand, London WC2R 0RL, England

First published in 2012 by Portfolio / Penguin,
a member of Penguin Group (USA) Inc.

1   3   5   7   9   10   8   6   4   2

Illustrations by Erin Tyler

LIBRARY OF CONGRESS CATALOGING IN PUBLICATION DATA
Holiday, Ryan.
Trust me, I'm lying : the tactics and confessions of a media manipulator / Ryan Holiday.
p. cm.
Includes bibliographical references.
ISBN 978-1-59184-553-9
1. Marketing—Blogs. 2. Public relations—Blogs. 3. Social media—Economic aspects. I. Title.
HF5415.H7416 2012
659.20285'6752—dc23
2012008773

Printed in the United States of America
Set in Minion Pro
Designed by Pauline Neuwirth

CONTENTS

BOOK ONE
FEEDING THE MONSTER
HOW BLOGS WORK

BOOK TWO

THE MONSTER ATTACKS

WHAT BLOGS MEAN

INTRODUCTION

IF YOU WERE BEING KIND, YOU WOULD SAY MY JOB IS IN marketing and public relations, or online strategy and advertising. But that's a polite veneer to hide the harsh truth. I am, to put it bluntly, a media manipulator—I'm paid to deceive. My job is to lie to the media so they can lie to you. I cheat, bribe, and connive for bestselling authors and billion-dollar brands and abuse my understanding of the Internet to do it.

I have funneled millions of dollars to blogs through advertising. I've given breaking news to blogs instead of *Good Morning America* and, when that didn't work, hired their family members. I have flown bloggers across the country, boosted their revenue by buying traffic, written their stories for them, fabricated elaborate ruses to capture their attention, and courted them with expensive meals and scoops. I've probably sent enough gift cards and T-shirts to fashion bloggers to clothe a small country. Why did I do all this? Because it was the only way. I did it to build them up as sources, sources that I could influence and direct for my clients. I used blogs to control the news.

It's why I found myself at 2:00 A.M. one morning, at a deserted intersection in Los Angeles, dressed in all black. In my hand I had tape and some obscene stickers made at Kinko's earlier in the afternoon. What was I doing here? I was there to deface billboards, specifically billboards I had designed and paid for. Not that I'd expected to do anything like this, but there I was, doing it. My girlfriend, coaxed into being my accomplice, was behind the wheel of the getaway car.

After I finished, we circled the block and I took photos of my work from the passenger window as if I had spotted it from the road. Across the billboards was now a two-foot-long sticker that implied that the movie's creator—my friend, Tucker Max—deserved to have his dick caught in a trap with sharp metal hooks. Or something like that.

As soon as I got home I dashed off two e-mails to two major blogs.

Under the fake name Evan Meyer I wrote, "I saw these on my way home last night. It was on 3rd and Crescent Heights, I think. Good to know Los Angeles hates Tucker Max too," and attached the photos.

One blog wrote back: You're not messing with me, are you?

No, I said. Trust me, I'm not lying.

The vandalized billboards and the coverage that my photos received were just a small part of the deliberately provocative campaign I did for the movie *I Hope They Serve Beer in Hell*. My friend Tucker had asked me to create some controversy around the movie, which was based on his bestselling book, and I did—somewhat effortlessly, it turns out. It is one of many campaigns I have done in my career, and by no means an unusual one. But it illustrates a part of the media system that is hidden from your view: how the news is created and driven by marketers, and that no one does anything to stop it.

In under two weeks, and with no budget, thousands of college students protested the movie on their campuses nationwide, angry citizens vandalized our billboards in multiple neighborhoods, FoxNews.com ran a front-page story about the backlash, Page Six of the *New York Post* made their first of many mentions of Tucker, and the Chicago Transit Authority banned and stripped the movie's advertisements from their buses. To cap it all off, two different editorials railing against the film ran in the *Washington Post* and *Chicago Tribune* the week it was released. The outrage about Tucker was great enough that a few years later, it was written into the popular television show *Portlandia* on IFC.

I guess it is safe to admit now that the entire firestorm was, essentially, fake.

I designed the advertisements, which I bought and placed around the country, and then promptly called and left anonymous complaints about them (and leaked copies of my complaints to blogs for support). I alerted college LGBT and women's rights groups to screenings in their area and baited them to protest our offensive movie at the theater, knowing that the nightly news would cover it. I started a boycott group on Facebook. I orchestrated fake tweets and posted fake comments to articles online. I even won a contest for being the first one to send in a picture of a defaced ad in Chicago (thanks for the free T-shirt, Chicago *RedEye*. Oh, also, that photo was from New York). I manufactured preposterous stories about Tucker's behavior on and off the movie set and reported them to gossip websites, which gleefully repeated them. I paid for anti-woman ads on feminist websites and anti-religion ads on Christian websites, knowing each would write about it. Sometimes I just Photoshopped ads onto screenshots of websites and got coverage for controversial ads that never actually ran. The loop became final when, for the first time in history, I put out a press release to answer my own manufactured criticism: TUCKER MAX RE-SPONDS TO CTA DECISION: "BLOW ME," the headline read.

Hello, shitstorm of press. Hello, number one on the New York Times *bestseller list.*

I pulled this off with no connections, no money, and no footsteps to follow. But because of the way that blogging is structured—from the way bloggers are paid by the pageview to the way blog posts must be written to catch the reader's attention—this was all very easy to do. The system eats up the kind of material I produce. So as the manufactured storm I created played itself out in the press, real people started believing it, and it became true.

My full-time job then and now is director of marketing for American Apparel, a clothing company known for its provocative imagery and un-conventional business practices. But I orchestrate these deceptions for other high-profile clients as well, from authors who sell millions of books to entrepreneurs worth hundreds of millions of dollars. I create and shape the news for them.

Usually, it is a simple hustle. Someone pays me, I manufacture a story for them, and we trade it up the chain—from a tiny blog to *Gawker* to a website of a local news network to the *Huffington Post* to the major news-papers to cable news and back again, until the unreal becomes real.* Some-times I start by planting a story. Sometimes I put out a press release or ask a friend to break a story on their blog. Sometimes I "leak" a document. Sometimes I fabricate a document and leak that. Really, it can be anything, from vandalizing a Wikipedia page to producing an expensive viral video. However the play starts, the end is the same: The economics of the Internet are exploited to change public perception—and sell product.

ω

---

*By "real" I mean that people believe it and act on it. I am saying that the infrastructure of the Internet can be used against itself to turn a manufactured piece of nonsense into widespread outrage and then action. It happens every day. Every single day.

Now I was hardly a wide-eyed kid when I left school to do this kind of PR full time. I'd seen enough in the edit wars of Wikipedia and the politics of power users in social media to know that something questionable was going on behind the scenes. Half of me knew all this but another part of me remained a believer. I had my choice of projects, and I only worked on what I believed in (and yes, that included American Apparel and Tucker Max). But I got sucked into the media underworld, getting hit after publicity hit for my clients and propagating more and more lies to do so. I struggled to keep these parts of me separate as I began to understand the media environment I was working in, and that there was something more than a little off about it.

It worked until it stopped working for me. Though I wish I could pinpoint the moment when it all fell apart, when I realized that the whole thing was a giant con, I can't. All I know is that, eventually, I did.

I studied the economics and the ecology of online media deeply in the pursuit of my craft. I wanted to understand not just how but why it worked—from the technology down to the personalities of the people who use it. As an insider with access I saw things that academics and gurus and many bloggers themselves will never see. Publishers liked to talk to me, because I controlled multimillion-dollar online advertising budgets, and they were often shockingly honest.

I began to make connections among these pieces of information and see patterns in history. In books decades out of print I saw criticism of media loopholes that had now reopened. I watched as basic psychological precepts were violated or ignored by bloggers as they reported the "news." Having seen that much of the edifice of online publishing was based on faulty assumptions and self-serving logic, I learned that I could outsmart it. This knowledge both scared and emboldened me at the same time. I confess, I turned around and used this knowledge against the public interest, and for my own gain.

An obscure item I found in the course of my research stopped me cold. It was a mention of a 1913 editorial cartoon published in the long since defunct *Leslie's Illustrated Weekly Newspaper*. The cartoon, it said, showed a businessman throwing coins into the mouth of a giant fang-bared monster of many arms which stood menacingly in front of him. Each of its tentacle-like arms, which were destroying the city around it, was tattooed with the words like: "Cultivating Hate," "Distorting Facts," and "Slush to Inflame." The man is an advertiser and the mouth belongs to the malicious yellow press that needs his money to survive. Underneath is a caption: THE FOOL WHO FEEDS THE MONSTER.

I knew I had to find this century-old drawing, though I wasn't sure why. As I rode the escalator through the glass canyon of the atrium and into the bowels of the central branch of the Los Angeles Public Library to search for it, it struck me that I wasn't just looking for some rare old newspaper. I was looking for myself. I knew who that fool was. He was me.

In addiction circles, those in recovery also use the image of the monster as a warning. They tell the story of a man who found a package on his porch. Inside was a little monster, but it was cute, like a puppy. He kept it and raised it. The more he fed it, the bigger it got and the more it needed to be fed. He ignored his worries as it grew bigger, more intimidating, demanding, and unpredictable, until one day, as he was playing with it, the monster attacked and nearly killed him. The realization that the situation was more than he could handle came too late—the man was no longer in control. The monster had a life of its own.

The story of the monster is a lot like my story. Except my story is not about drugs or the yellow press but of a bigger and much more modern monster—my monster is the brave new world of new media—one that I often fed and thought I controlled. I lived high and well in that world, and I believed in it until it no longer looked the same to me. Many things went down. I'm not sure where my responsibility for them begins or ends, but I am ready to talk about what happened.

I created false perceptions through blogs, which led to bad conclusions and wrong decisions—real decisions in the real world that had consequences for real people. Phrases like "known rapist" began to follow what were once playfully encouraged rumors of bad or shocking behavior designed to get blog publicity for clients. Friends were ruined and broken. Gradually I began to notice work just like mine appearing everywhere, and no one catching on to it or repairing the damage. Stocks took major hits, to the tune of tens of millions of dollars, on news from the same unreliable sources I'd often trick with fake stories.

In 2008, a *Gawker* blogger published e-mails stolen from my inbox by someone else trying to intimidate a client through the media. It was a

5

humiliating and awful experience. But with some distance I now understand that *Gawker* had little choice about the role they played in the matter. I know that I was as much a part of the problem as they were.

I remember one day mentioning some scandal during a dinner conversation, one that I knew was probably fake, probably a scam. I did it because it was too interesting *not* to pass along. I was lost in the same unreality I'd forced on other people. I found that not only did I not know what was real anymore, but that I no longer cared. To borrow from Budd Schulberg's description of a media manipulator in his classic novel *The Harder They Fall*, I was "indulging myself in the illusions that we can deal in filth without becoming the thing we touch." I no longer have those illusions.

Winston Churchill wrote of the appeasers of his age that "each one hopes that if he feeds the crocodile enough, the crocodile will eat him last." I was even more delusional. I thought I could skip being devoured entirely. It would never turn on me. I was in control. I was the expert. But I was wrong.

WHY I WROTE THIS BOOK

Sitting next to my desk right now is a large box filled with hundreds of articles I have printed over the last several years. The articles show all the trademarks of the fakes and scams I myself have run, yet they involve many of biggest news and entertainment stories of the decade. The margins are filled with angry little notes and question marks. The satirist Juvenal wrote of "cramming whole notebooks with scribbled invective" amid the corrupt opulence of Rome; that box and this book are my notebooks from my own days inside such a world. Collectively, it was this process that opened my eyes. I hope it will have the same effect for you.

Lately I have slowed my contributions to the pile of evidence, not because the quality of the content has improved, but because hope for anything different would be silly. I'm not so foolish as to expect bloggers to know what they are talking about. I no longer expect to be informed—not when manipulation is so easy for bloggers and marketers to profit from. I can't shake the constant suspicion that others are baiting, tricking, or cheating me, just as I did to them. It's hard to browse the Internet when you are haunted by the words of A. J. Daulerio, the editor of the popular sports blog *Deadspin*: "It's all professional wrestling."[1]

Some of you, by the time you are done with this book, will probably hate me for ruining it for you too. Or call me a liar. Or accuse me of exaggerating. You may not want me to expose the people behind your favorite websites as the imbeciles, charlatans, and pompous frauds they are. But it is a world of many hustlers, and you are the mark. The con is to build a brand off the backs of others. Your attention and your credulity are what's stolen.

This book isn't structured like typical business books. Instead of extended chapters, it is split into two parts, and each part is made up of short, overlapping, and reinforcing vignettes. In the first part I explain why blogs matter, how they drive the news, and how they can be manipulated. In the second I show what happens when you do this, how it backfires, and the dangerous consequences of our current system.

What follows are the methods used to manipulate bloggers and reporters at the highest levels, broken down into nine simple tactics.

Every one of these tactics reveals a critical vulnerability in our media system. I will show you where they are and what can be done with them, and help you recognize when they're being used on you. Sure, I am explaining how to take advantage of these weaknesses, but mostly I am saying that *these vulnerabilities exist.* It is the first time that these gaps have ever been exposed, by a critic or otherwise. Hopefully, once in the open they'll no longer work as well. I understand that there is some contradiction in this position, as there has long been in me. My dis-integration wasn't always healthy, but it does allow me to explain our problems from a unique perspective.

This book is my experience behind the scenes in the worlds of blogging, PR, and online machinations—and what those experiences say about the dominant cultural medium. I'm speaking personally and honestly about what I know, and I know this space better than just about anyone.

I didn't intend to, but I've helped pioneer a media system designed to trick, cajole, and steal every second of the most precious resource in the world—people's time. I'm going to show you every single one of these tricks, and what they mean.

What you choose to do with this information is up to you.

BOOK ONE

FEEDING THE MONSTER

HOW BLOGS WORK

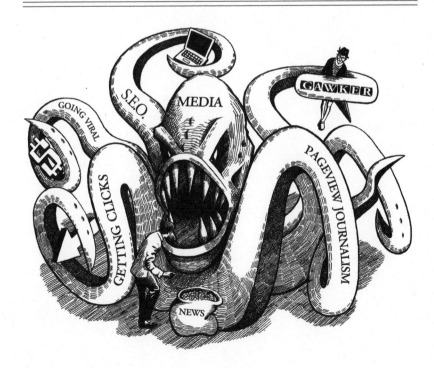

BLOGS MAKE
THE NEWS

{ We play by their rules long enough and it becomes
our game.

—ORSON SCOTT CARD, *ENDER'S GAME* }

I CALL TO YOUR ATTENTION AN ARTICLE IN THE *NEW York Times* written at the earliest of the earliest junctures of the 2012 presidential election, nearly two years before votes would be cast.[1]

It told of a then obscure figure, Tim Pawlenty, the governor of Minnesota. Pawlenty was not yet a presidential candidate. He had no campaign director, no bus, few donors, and little name recognition. In fact, he did not even have a campaign. It was January 2011, after all. What he did have was a beat reporter from the blog *Politico* following him from town to town with a camera and a laptop, reporting every moment of his noncampaign.

It's a bit peculiar, if you think about it. Even the *New York Times*, the newspaper that spends millions of dollars a year for a Baghdad bureau, which can fund investigative reports five or ten years in the making, didn't have a reporter covering Pawlenty. Yet *Politico*, a blog with only a fraction of the resources of a major newspaper, did. The *Times* was covering *Politico* covering a noncandidate.

It was a little like a Ponzi scheme, and like all such schemes, it went from boom to bust. Pawlenty became a candidate, coverage of him generated millions of impressions online, then in print, and finally on television, before he flamed out and withdrew from the race. Despite all of this, his candidacy's impact on the election was significant and real enough that the next Republican front-runner courted Pawlenty's endorsement.

There's a famous twentieth-century political cartoon about the Associated Press that was, at the time, the wire service responsible for supplying news to the majority of the newspapers in the United States. In it an AP agent is pouring different bottles into a city's water supply. The bottles are labeled "lies," "prejudice," "slander," "suppressed facts," and "hatred." The image reads: "The News—Poisoned At Its Source."

I think of blogs as today's newswires.

BLOGS MATTER

By "blog," I'm referring collectively to all online publishing. That's everything from Twitter accounts to major newspaper websites to web videos to group blogs with hundreds of writers. I don't care whether the owners consider themselves blogs or not. The reality is that they are all subject to the same incentives, and they fight for attention with similar tactics.*

Most people don't understand how today's information cycle really works. Many have no idea of how much their general worldview is influenced by the way news is generated online. What begins online ends offline.

Although there are millions of blogs out there, you'll notice some mentioned a lot in this book: *Gawker, Business Insider, Politico, BuzzFeed, Huffington Post, Drudge Report,* and the like. This is not because they are the most widely read, but instead because they are mostly read by the media elite, and their proselytizing owners, Nick Denton, Henry Blodget, Jonah Peretti, and Arianna Huffington, have an immense amount of influence. A blog isn't small if its puny readership is made up of TV producers and writers for national newspapers.

Radio DJs and news anchors once filled their broadcasts with newspaper headlines; today they repeat what they read on blogs—certain blogs more than others. Stories from blogs also filter into real conversations and rumors that spread from person to person through word of mouth. In short, blogs are vehicles from which mass media reporters—and your most chatty and "informed" friends—discover and borrow the news. This hidden cycle gives birth to the memes that become our cultural references, the budding stars who become our celebrities, the thinkers who become our gurus, and the news that becomes our news.

When I figured this out early in my career in public relations I thought what only a naive and destructively ambitious twentysomething would have: If I master the rules that govern blogs, I can be the master of all they determine. It was, essentially, access to a fiat over culture.

It may have been a dangerous thought, but it wasn't hyperbole. In the

---

*I have never been a fan of the word "blogosphere" and will use it only sparingly.

Pawlenty case, the guy could have become the president of the United States of America. One early media critic put it this way: We're a country governed by public opinion, and public opinion is largely governed by the press, so isn't it critical to understand what governs the press? What rules over the media, he concluded, rules over the country. In this case, what rules over *Politico* literally almost ruled over everyone.

To understand what makes blogs act—why *Politico* followed Pawlenty around—is the key to making them do what you want. Learn their rules, change the game. That's all it takes to control public opinion.

SO, WHY *DID POLITICO* FOLLOW PAWLENTY?

On the face of it, it's pretty crazy. Pawlenty's phantom candidacy wasn't newsworthy, and if the *New York Times* couldn't afford to pay a reporter to follow him around, *Politico* shouldn't have been able to.

It wasn't crazy. Blogs need things to cover. The *Times* has to fill a newspaper only once per day. A cable news channel has to fill twenty-four hours of programming 365 days a year. But blogs have to fill an *infinite* amount of space. The site that covers the most stuff wins.

Political blogs know that their traffic goes up during election cycles. Since traffic is what they sell to advertisers, elections equal increased revenue. Unfortunately, election cycles come only every few years. Worse still, they end. Blogs have a simple solution: change reality through the coverage.

With Pawlenty, *Politico* was not only manufacturing a candidate, they were manufacturing an entire leg of the election cycle purely to profit from it. It was a conscious decision. In the story about his business, *Politico*'s executive editor, Jim VandeHei, tipped his hand to the *New York Times*: "We were a garage band in 2008, riffing on the fly. Now we're a 200-person production, with a precise feel and plan. We're trying to take a leap forward in front of everyone else."

When a blog like *Politico* tried to leap in front of everyone else, the person they arbitrarily decided to cover was turned into an actual candidate. The campaign starts gradually, with a few mentions on blogs, moves on to "potential contender," begins to be considered for debates, and is then included on the ballot. Their platform accumulates real supporters who donate real time and money to the campaign. The campaign buzz is reified by the mass media, who covers and legitimizes whatever is being talked about online.

Pawlenty's campaign for elected office may have failed, but for blogs and other media, it was profitable success. He generated millions of page-views for blogs, was the subject of dozens of stories in print and online, and had his fair share of television time. When *Politico* picked Pawlenty they made the only bet worth making—where they had the power to control the outcome.

In case you didn't catch it, here's the cycle again:

➡ Political blogs need things to cover; traffic increases during election

➡ Reality (election far away) does not align with this

➡ Political blogs create candidates early; move up start of election cycle

➡ The person they cover, by nature of coverage, becomes actual candidate (or president)

➡ Blogs profit (literally), the public loses

You'll see this cycle repeated again and again in this book. It's true for celebrity gossip, politics, business news, and every other topic blogs cover. The constraints of blogging create artificial content, which is made real and impacts the outcome of real world events.

The economics of the Internet created a twisted set of incentives that make traffic more important—and more profitable—than the truth. With the mass media—and today, mass culture—relying on the web for the next big thing, it is a set of incentives with massive implications.

Blogs need traffic, being first drives traffic, and so entire stories are created out of whole cloth to make that happen. This is just one facet of the economics of blogging, but it's a critical one. When we understand the logic that drives these business choices, those choices become predictable.

And what is predictable can be anticipated, redirected, accelerated, or controlled—however you or I choose.

Later in the election, *Politico* moved the goalposts again to stay on top. Speed stopped working so well, so they turned to scandal to upend the race once more. Remember Herman Cain, the preposterous, media-created candidate who came after Pawlenty? After surging ahead as the lead contender for the Republican nomination, and becoming the subject of an exhausting number of traffic-friendly blog posts, Cain's candidacy was utterly decimated by a sensational but still strongly denied scandal reported by . . . you guessed it: *Politico*.

I'm sure there were powerful political interests that could not allow Cain to become anything more than a sideshow. So his narrative was changed, and some suspect it was done by a person just like me, hired by another candidate's campaign—and the story spread, whether it was true or not. If true, from the looks of it whoever delivered the fatal blow did it exactly the way I would have: painfully, untraceably, and impossible to recover from.

And so another noncandidate was created, made real, and then taken out. Another one bit the dust so that blogs could fill their cycle.

II

HOW TO TURN NOTHING INTO SOMETHING IN THREE WAY-TOO-EASY STEPS

> Some people in the press, I think, are just lazy as hell. There are times when I pitch a story and they do it word for word. That's just embarrassing. They're adjusting to a time that demands less quality and more quantity. And it works to my advantage most of the time, because I think most reporters have liked me packaging things for them. Most people will opt for what's easier, so they can move on to the next thing. Reporters are measured by how often their stuff gets on Drudge. It's a bad way to be, but it's reality.
>
> **— KURT BARDELLA, FORMER PRESS SECRETARY FOR REPUBLICAN CONGRESSMAN DARRELL ISSA**

IN THE INTRODUCTION I EXPLAINED A SCAM I CALL
"trading up the chain." It's a strategy I developed that manipulates the
media through recursion. I can turn nothing into something by placing a
story with a small blog that has very low standards, which then becomes
the source for a story by a larger blog, and that, in turn, for a story by
larger media outlets. I create, to use the words of one media scholar, a
"self-reinforcing news wave." People like me do this everyday.

The work I do is not exactly respectable. But I want to explain how it
works without any of the negatives associated with my infamous clients.
I'll show how I manipulated the media for a good cause.

A friend of mine recently used some of my advice on trading up the
chain for the benefit of the charity he runs. This friend needed to raise
money to cover the costs of a community art project, and chose to do it
through Kickstarter, the crowdsourced fund-raising platform. With just
a few days' work, he turned an obscure cause into a popular Internet
meme and raised nearly ten thousand dollars to expand the charity inter-
nationally.

Following my instructions, he made a YouTube video for the Kickstarter page showing off his charity's work. Not a video of the charity's
best work, or even its most important work, but the work that exaggerated
certain elements aimed at helping the video spread. (In this case, two or
three examples in exotic locations that actually had the least amount of
community benefit.) Next, he wrote a short article for a small local blog
in Brooklyn and embedded the video. This site was chosen because its
stories were often used or picked up by the New York section of the *Huffington Post*. As expected, the *Huffington Post* did bite, and ultimately featured the story as local news in both New York City and Los Angeles.
Following my advice, he sent an e-mail from a fake address with these
links to a reporter at CBS in Los Angeles, who then did a television piece

on it—using mostly clips from my friend's heavily edited video. In anticipation of all of this he'd been active on a channel of the social news site Reddit (where users vote on stories and topics they like) during the weeks leading up to his campaign launch in order to build up some connections on the site.

When the CBS News piece came out and the video was up, he was ready to post it all on Reddit. It made the front page almost immediately. This score on Reddit (now bolstered by other press as well) put the story on the radar of what I call the major "cool stuff" blogs—sites like *BoingBoing, Laughing Squid, FFFFOUND!*, and others—since they get post ideas from Reddit. From this final burst of coverage, money began pouring in, as did volunteers, recognition, and new ideas.

With no advertising budget, no publicist, and no experience, his little video did nearly a half million views, and funded his project for the next two years. It went from nothing to something.

This may have all been for charity, but it still raises a critical question: *What exactly happened?* How was it so easy for him to manipulate the media, even for a good cause? He turned one exaggerated amateur video into a news story that was written about independently by dozens of outlets in dozens of markets and did millions of media impressions. It even registered nationally. He had created and then manipulated this attention entirely by himself.

Before you get upset at us, remember: We were only doing what Lindsay Robertson, a blogger from *Videogum, Jezebel*, and *New York* magazine's *Vulture* blog, taught us to do. In a post explaining to publicists how they could better game bloggers like herself, Lindsay advised focusing "on a lower traffic tier with the (correct) understanding that these days, content filters *up* as much as it filters down, and often the smaller sites, with their ability to dig deeper into the [I]nternet and be more nimble, act as farm teams for the larger ones."[*1]

Blogs have enormous influence over other blogs, making it possible to turn a post on a site with only a little traffic into posts on much bigger sites, if the latter happens to read the former. Blogs compete to get stories

---

*Proving this theory unnervingly correct, *Newsweek* picked up the Lindsay's advice from her tiny personal blog and reposted it on the the official *Newsweek Tumblr*.

first, newspapers compete to "confirm" it, and then pundits compete for airtime to opine on it. The smaller sites legitimize the newsworthiness of the story for the sites with bigger audiences. Consecutively and concurrently, this pattern inherently distorts and exaggerates whatever they cover.

THE LAY OF THE LAND

Here's how it works. There are thousands of bloggers scouring the web looking for things to write about. They *must* write several times each day. They search Twitter, Facebook, comments sections, press releases, rival blogs, and other sources to develop their material.

Above them are hundreds of mid-level online and offline journalists on websites and blogs and in magazines and newspapers who use those bloggers below them as sources and filters. They also have to write constantly—and engage in the same search for buzz, only a little more developed.

Above them are the major national websites, publications, and television stations. They in turn browse the scourers below them for their material, grabbing their leads and turning them into truly national conversations. These are the most influential bunch—the *New York Times*, the *Today Show*, and CNN—and dwindling revenues or not, they have massive reach.

Finally, between, above, and throughout these concentric levels is the largest group: *us*, the audience. We scan the web for material that we can watch, comment on, or share with our friends and followers.

It's bloggers informing bloggers informing bloggers all the way down. This isn't anecdotal observation. It is fact. In a media monitoring study done by Cision and George Washington University, *89 percent of journalists* reported using blogs for their research for stories. Roughly half reported using Twitter to find and research stories, and more than two thirds use other social networks, such as Facebook or LinkedIn, in the same way.[2] The more immediate the nature of their publishing mediums (blogs, then newspapers, then magazines), the more heavily a journalist will depend on sketchy online sources, like social media, for research.

Recklessness, laziness, however you want to categorize it, the attitude is openly tolerated and acknowledged. The majority of journalists surveyed admitted to knowing that their online sources were less reliable than traditional ones. Not a single journalist said they believed that the information gathered from social media was "a lot more reliable" than traditional media! Why? Because it suffers from a "lack of fact-checking, verification or reporting standards."[3]

For the sake of simplicity, let's break the chain into three levels. I know these levels as one thing only: beachheads for manufacturing news. I don't think someone could have designed a system easier to manipulate if they wanted to.

Level 1: The Entry Point

At the first level, small blogs and hyperlocal websites that cover your neighborhood or particular scene are some of the easiest sites to get traction on. Since they typically write about local, personal issues pertaining to a contained readership, trust is very high. At the same time, they are cash-strapped and traffic-hungry, always on the lookout for a big story that might draw a big spike of new viewers. It doesn't have to be local, though; it can be a site about a subject you know very well, or it can be a site run by a friend.

What's important is that the site is small and understaffed. This makes it possible to sell them a story that is only loosely connected to their core message but really sets you up to transition to the next level.

Level 2: The Legacy Media

Here we begin to see a mix of online and offline sources. The blogs of newspapers and local television stations are some of the best targets. For starters, they share the same URL and often get aggregated in Google News. Places like the *Wall Street Journal*, *Newsweek*, and CBS all have sister sites like SmartMoney.com, Mainstreet.com, BNet.com, and others that feature the companies' logos but have their own editorial standards not always as rigorous as their old media counterparts'. They seem legitimate, but they are, as Fark.com founder Drew Curtis calls them, just

"Mass Media Sections That Update More Often but with Less Editorial Oversight."

Legacy media outlets are critical turning points in building up momentum. The reality is that the bloggers at Forbes.com or the *Chicago Tribune* do not operate on the same editorial guidelines as their print counterparts. However, their final output can be made to look like they carry the same weight. If you get a blog on Wired.com to mention your startup, you can smack "'A revolutionary device'—*Wired*" on the box of your product just as surely as you could if *Wired* had put your CEO on the cover of the magazine.

These sites won't write about just anything, though, so you need to create chatter or a strong story angle to hook this kind of sucker. Their illusion of legitimacy comes at the cost of being slightly more selective when it comes to what they cover. But it is worth the price, because it will grant the bigger websites in your sights later the privilege of using magic words like: "NBC is reporting . . ."

Level 3: National

Having registered multiple stories from multiple sources firmly onto the radar of both local and midlevel outlets, you can now leverage this coverage to access the highest level of media: the national press. Getting to this level usually involves less direct pushing and a lot more massaging. The sites that have already taken your bait are now on your side. They desperately want their articles to get as much traffic as possible, and being linked to or mentioned on national sites is how they do that. These sites will take care of submitting your articles to news aggregator sites like Digg, because making the front page will drive tens of thousands of visitors to their article. Mass media reporters monitor aggregators for story ideas, and often cover what is trending there, like they did with the charity story after it made the front page of Reddit. In today's world even these guys have to think like bloggers—they need to get as many pageviews as possible. Success on the lower levels of the media chain is evidence that the story could deliver even better results from a national platform.

You just want to make sure that such reporters notice the story's gaining traction. Take the outlet where you'd ultimately like to receive coverage and observe it for patterns. You'll notice that they tend to get their story ideas from the same second-level sites, and by tailoring the story to those smaller sites (or site), it sets you up to be noticed by the larger one. The blogs on *Gawker* and *Mediabistro*, for instance, are read very heavily by the New York City media set. You can craft the story for those sites and automatically set yourself up to appeal to the other reporters reading it—without ever speaking to them directly. An example: Katie Couric claims she gets many story ideas from her Twitter followers, which means that getting a few tweets out of the seven hundred or so people she follows is all it takes to get a shot at the nightly national news.

News anchors aren't the only people susceptible to this trick. Scott Vener, the famous hit maker responsible for picking the songs that go into HBO's trendiest shows, like *Entourage* and *How to Make It in America*, has a reputation for discovering "unknown artists." Really, he admits, most of the music he finds is just "what is bubbling up on the Internet."[4] Since Vener monitors conversations on Twitter and the comments on trendy music blogs, a shot at a six-figure HBO payday and instant mainstream exposure is just a few manufactured bubbles away.

It's a simple illusion: Create the perception that the meme already exists and all the reporter (or the music supervisor or celebrity stylist) is doing is popularizing it. They rarely bother to look past the first impressions.

LEVELS 1, 2, 3:
HOW I TRADED UP THE CHAIN

My campaign for *I Hope They Serve Beer in Hell* began by vandalizing the billboards. The graffiti was designed to bait two specific sites, *Curbed Los Angeles* and *Mediabistro*'s *FishbowlLA*. When I sent them photos of my work under the fake name Evan Meyer, they both quickly picked it up.[5] (For his contributions as a tipster, Evan earned his own *Mediabistro* profile, which still exists. According to the site he has not been "sighted" since.)

Curbed LA began their post by using my e-mail verbatim:

23

A reader writes: "I saw these on my way home last night. It was on 3rd and Crescent Heights, I think. Good to know Los Angeles hates him too." Provocateur Tucker Max's new movie "I Hope They Serve Beer in Hell" opens this weekend *[emphasis mine].*

Thanks for the plug!

In creating outrage for the movie, I had a lot of luck getting local websites to cover or spread the news about protests of the screenings we had organized through anonymous tips.* They were the easiest place to get the story started. We would send them a few offensive quotes and say something like "This misogynist is coming to our school and we're so fucking pissed. Could you help spread the word?" Or I'd e-mail a neighborhood site to say that "a controversial screening with rumors of a local boycott" was happening in a few days.

Sex, college protesters, Hollywood—it was the definition of the kind of local story news producers love. After reading about the growing controversy on the small blogs I conned, they would often send camera crews to the screenings. The video of the story would get posted on the station's website, and then get covered again by the other, larger blogs in that city, like those hosted by a newspaper or companies like the *Huffington Post.* I was able to get the story to register, however briefly, by using a small site with low standards of newsworthiness. Other media outlets might be alerted to this fact, and in turn cover it, giving me another bump. At this point I now have something to work with. Three or four links are the makings of a trend piece, or even a controversy—that's all major outlets and national website need to see to get excited. Former Slate.com media critic Jake Shafer called such manufactured online controversy "frovocation"—a portmanteau of faux provocation. It works incredibly well.

The key to getting from the second to the third level is the soft sell. I couldn't very well e-mail a columnist at the *Washington Post* and say, "Hey, will you denounce our movie so we can benefit from the negative

---

*It is standard practice in journalism that the identity of anonymous sources must be shared with the editor so that they know the person is real and the writer hasn't been tricked. I have been used as an anonymous source for blogs dozens of times. No one has ever asked my identity, I've never been verified, and I have never spoken to an editor.

PR?" So I targeted the sites that those kinds of columnists were likely to read. *Gawker* and *Mediabistro* are very media-centric, so we tailored stories to them to queue ourselves up for outrage from their audiences— which happen to include reporters at places like the *Washington Post*.* And when I want to be direct, I would register a handful of fake e-mail addresses on Gmail or Yahoo and send e-mails with a collection of all the links gathered so far and say, "How have you not done a story about this yet?" Reporters rarely get substantial tips or alerts from their readers, so to get two or even three legitimate tips about an issue is a strong signal.

So I sent it to them. Well, kind of. I actually just did more of the same fake tips from fake e-mail addresses that worked for the other sites—only this time I had a handful of links from major blogs that made it clear that everyone was talking about it. At this point something amazing happened: The coverage my stunts received began helping the twenty-thousand-dollar-a-month publicist the movie had hired. Rejections from late-night television, newspaper interviews, and morning radio turned into callbacks. Tucker did Carson Daly's NBC late-night show for the first time. By the end of this charade, hundreds of reputable reporters, producers, and bloggers had been swept up into participating. Thousands more had eagerly gobbled up news about it on multiple blogs. Each time they did, views of the movie trailer spiked, book sales increased, and Tucker became more famous and more controversial. If only people had known they were promoting the offensive Tucker Max brand for us, just as we'd planned.

With just a few simple moves, I'd taken his story from level 1 to level 3—not just once but several times, back and forth. Ultimately the movie did not do nearly as well at release as we'd hoped—this supplementary guerrilla marketing ended up being the entirety of the movie's advertising efforts rather than a small part of it for reasons outside of my control—but the attention generated by the campaign was overwhelming and incredibly lucrative. Eventually the movie became a cult hit on DVD.

Once you get a story like this started it takes on a life of its own. That's

---

*In fact, a few years later one of the sites we exploited repeatedly while promoting the movie wrote a post titled: "Are traditional news media stealing scoops from bloggers?," which accused the *Chicago Tribune* of stealing article ideas from her blog *Chicago Now*. She was right, they were stealing, and that's exactly how we got coverage into the editorial page of the *Tribune*.

what happened after I vandalized Tucker's billboards. Exactly one week later, inspired by my example, sixteen feminists gathered in New York City late at night to vandalize *I Hope They Serve Beer in Hell* posters all over Manhattan.[6] Their campaign got even more coverage than my stunt, including a 650-word, three-picture story on a *Village Voice* blog with dozens of comments (I posted some comments under fake names to get people riled up, but looking at them now I can't tell which ones are fake and which are real). From the fake came real action.

THE MEDIA: DANCING WITH ITSELF

Trading up the chain relies on a concept created by crisis public relations expert Michael Sitrick. When attempting to turn things around for a particularly disliked or controversial client, Sitrick was fond of saying, "We need to find a lead steer!" The media, like any group of animals, gallops in a herd. It takes just one steer to start a stampede. The first level is your lead steer. The rest is just pointing everyone's attention to the direction it went in.

Remember: Every person (with the exception of a few at the top layer) in this ecosystem is under immense pressure to produce content under the tightest of deadlines. Yes, you have something to sell. But more than ever they desperately, desperately need to buy. The flimsiest of excuses is all it takes.

It freaked me out when I began to see this sort of thing happen *without* the deliberate prodding of a promoter like myself. I saw media conflagrations set off by internal sparks. In this networked, interdependent world of blogging, misinformation can spread even when no one is consciously pushing or manipulating it. The system is so primed, tuned, and ready that often it doesn't need people like me. The monster can feed itself.

Sometimes just a single quote taken out of context can set things off. In early 2011, a gossip reporter for an AOL entertainment blog asked former quarterback Kurt Warner who he thought would be the next ex-athlete to join the show *Dancing with the Stars*. Warner jokingly suggested Brett Favre, who was then embroiled in a sexual harassment scandal. Though the show told him they wanted nothing to do with Favre, the reporter still titled the post "Brett Favre Is Kurt Warner's Pick to Join 'Dancing': 'Controversy Is Good for Ratings,'" and tagged it as an exclusive. The post made it clear that Warner was just goofing around.

Two days later the blog *Bleacher Report* linked to the piece but made it sound as though Warner was seriously urging Favre to join the show (which, remember, had just told AOL they wanted nothing to do with Favre).

After their story, the rumor started to multiply rapidly. A reporter from a local TV-news website, KCCI Des Moines, caught the story and wrote a sixty-two-word piece titled "Brett Favre's Next Big Step?" and mentioned the "rumors" discussed on *Bleacher Report*. From there the piece was picked up by *USA Today*—"Brett Favre Joining 'Dancing With the Stars' Season 12 Cast?"—*ProFootballTalk*, and others, making the full transition to the national stage.[7]

To recap what happened: a gossip blog manufactured a scoop by misrepresenting, deliberately or not, a joke. That scoop was itself misrepresented and misinterpreted as it traveled up the chain, going from a small entertainment blog to a sports site to a CBS affiliate in Iowa and eventually to the website of one of the biggest newspapers in the country.* What spread was not even a rumor, which at least would have been logical. It was just an empty bit of nothing.

The fake Favre meme spread almost exactly along the lines of my fake outrage campaign for Tucker's movie—only there was no me involved! The media is hopelessly interdependent. Not only is the web susceptible to spreading false information, but it can also be the source of it.

For a gossip story, it's not a big deal. But the same weakness creates the opportunity for dangerous, even deadly, abuses of the system.

A TRUE FOOL FEEDING THE MONSTER

I am obviously jaded and cynical about trading up the chain. How could I not be? It's basically possible to run anything through this chain, even

---

*This was excellently caught and detailed by *Quickish* in its post "'Brett Farve on Dancing With the Stars?' No. Not Even a Rumor"; their research was promptly stolen and reposted by the oft-guilty *Deadspin* for an easy twenty-five thousand pageviews.

utterly preposterous and made-up information. But for a long time I thought that fabricated media stories could only hurt feelings and waste time. I didn't think anyone could *die* because of it.

I was wrong. Perhaps you remember Terry Jones, the idiotic pastor whose burning of the Koran in March 2011 led to riots that killed nearly thirty people in Afghanistan. Jones's bigotry happened to trade up the chain perfectly, and the media unwittingly allowed it.

Jones first made a name for himself in the local Florida press by running offensive billboards in front of his church. Then he stepped it up, announcing that he planned to stage a burning of the Koran. This story was picked up by a small website called Religion News Service. Yahoo linked to their short article, and dozens of blogs followed, which led CNN to invite Jones to appear on the network. He was now a national story.

Yet the media and the public, aware of the potential implications of airing video of his act, began to push back. Many decided they would not air such a video. Some five hundred people attended a protest in Kabul where they burned Jones in effigy. At the last second Jones, under pressure, backed down, and the crisis was averted.

But Terry Jones was back a few months later, announcing for the second time that he planned to burn the Koran. Each blog and outlet that covered the lead-up to the burning made the story—and the media monster that was Terry Jones—that much bolder and bigger. Reporters asked if a direct request from President Obama would stop him, which of course meant that the president of the United States of America would have to negotiate with a homegrown terrorist (he traded up the chain to the *most powerful man in the world*).

This circus was what finally pushed Jones over the edge. In March 2011, he went through with the burning, despite the threatened media blackout.

He called their bluff and it worked. The blackout fell apart when a college student named Andrew Ford, freelancing for the wire service Agence France-Presse, took advantage of a story too dirty and dangerous for many journalists to touch in good conscience.*

---

*This happens in politics all the time, as Democratic consultant Christian Grantham told *Forbes,* "Campaigns understand that there are some stories that regular reporters won't print. So they'll give those stories to the blogs." (Daniel Lyons, "Attack of the Blogs," last modified November 14, 2005, http://www.forbes.com/forbes/2005/1114/128_3.html).

Agence France-Presse, Ford's publisher, is syndicated on Google and Yahoo! News. They immediately republished his article. The story began to go up the chain, getting bigger and bigger. Roughly thirty larger blogs and online news services had picked up Ford's piece or linked to it in the first day. It made the story too big for the rest of the media—including the foreign press—to continue to resist. So the news of Jones's Koran burning, a calculated stunt to extract attention from a system that could not prevent itself from being exploited, became known to the world. And it was a deadly monster of a story.

Within days, twenty-seven people were killed during riots in Afghanistan, including seven UN workers; forty more were injured. Christians were specifically targeted, and Taliban flags were flown in the streets of the Kabul. "It took just one college student to defeat a media blackout and move a story halfway around the globe within twenty-four hours," the Poynter Institute wrote in an analysis of the reporting. This was, as *Forbes* journalist Jeff Bercovici put it, truly an example of "when Journalism 2.0 kills."[8]

One kook, one overeager young journalist, unintentionally show why trading up the chain—feeding the monster—can be so dangerous (though for Jones, very effective). They weren't just turning nothing into something. The beast these blogs built up was set off needless bloodshed.

You can trade up the chain for charity or you can trade up it to create funny fake news—or you can do it to create violence, hatred, and even incidentally, death. I've done the first two, while others, out of negligence or malice, have done the latter. At the end of the day, intentions are not a justification I'm going to hide behind. There is more than enough blame to go around.

III

THE BLOG CON

HOW PUBLISHERS MAKE MONEY ONLINE

Media companies can very much be in a race against time for growth. Investors want a return on their money and, given the economics of web news, that almost always requires exponential growth in uniques and pageviews.

—RYAN MCCARTHY, REUTERS

Picture a galley rowed by slaves and commanded by pirates.

—TIM RUTTEN, *LOS ANGELES TIMES*, ON THE *HUFFINGTON POST* BUSINESS MODEL

STRIPPED BARE, THE ECONOMICS OF ONLINE NEWS—the way blogging really works—is a shocking thing. I've never been desperate enough to need to work inside the system as a lowly (un-) paid blogger, but as an outsider (a press agent and a media buyer), I saw plenty. What I learned is the ways that sites such as AOL, the *Huffington Post*, and even the website of the *New York Times* make their money, and how much money they actually make.

This matters, because as businesses designed to make money, the way in which they do business is the main filter for how they do the news. Every story they produce must contort itself to fit this mold—whatever the topic or subject. I will show you this by explaining exactly how I have exploited these economics for my own personal gain. You're free to view these lessons as opportunities or as loopholes that must be closed. I see them as both.

TRAFFIC IS MONEY

On the face of it, blogs make their money from selling advertisements. These advertisements are paid for by the impression (generally a rate per thousand impressions). A site might have several ad units on each page; the publisher's revenue equals the cumulative CPM (cost per thousand) multiplied by the number of pageviews. Advertisement × Traffic = Revenue. An ad buyer like me buys this space by the millions—ten million impressions on this site, five million on another, fifty million through a network. A few blogs produce a portion of their revenue through selling extras—hosting conferences or affiliate deals—but, for the most part, this is the business: Traffic is money.

A portion of the advertising on blogs is sold directly by the publisher, a portion is sold by sales reps who work on commission, and the rest is sold by advertising networks that specialize in the remaining inventory. Regardless of who sells it or who buys it, what matters is that every ad impression on a site is monetized, if only for a few pennies. Each and every pageview is money in the pocket of the publisher.

Publishers and advertisers can't differentiate between the types of impressions an ad does on a site. A perusing reader is no better than an accidental reader. An article that provides worthwhile advice is no more valuable than one instantly forgotten. So long as the page loads and the ads are seen, both sides are fulfilling their purpose. A click is a click.

Knowing this, blogs do everything they can to increase the latter variable in the equation (traffic, pageviews). It's how you must understand them as a business. Every decision a publisher makes is ruled by one dictum: *traffic by any means.*

Scoops Are Traffic

One of the biggest shocks to the online world was the launch of *TMZ*. The blog was developed by AOL in 2005, and revenues skyrocketed to nearly $20 million a year almost immediately, paving the way for its now famous television program. This was all accomplished through a handful of major scoops. Or at least, *TMZ*'s special definition of "scoops."

The blog's founder, Harvey Levin, once said in an interview that *TMZ* is "a serious news operation that has the same rigid standards that any news operation in America has." This is the same site that once published, at 4:07 A.M., an exclusive scoop: a blurry, never-before-seen photo of future president John F. Kennedy on a boat filled with naked women. This EXCLUSIVE scoop was headlined "The JFK Photo That Could Have Changed History." Only it couldn't have altered world events for one simple reason: The man in the photo wasn't JFK. In fact, it turned out to be a spread from a 1967 issue of *Playboy*.[1] Oops!

Despite missteps like this, *TMZ* turned scoop-getting into a science. They broke the story of Mel Gibson's anti-Semitic outbursts during his DUI arrest. And then got video of Michael Richards's racist onstage meltdown, posted the bruised Rihanna police photo, and announced the news of Michael Jackson's death. *TMZ* originated four of the biggest stories to come from the Internet and captured a substantial audience from these enormous surges of traffic.* They didn't always use the most reputable or reliable means off getting their scoops, but nevertheless, today when people think celebrity news, they think of *TMZ*. (They don't think of *Defamer*, *Gawker*'s predecessor to *TMZ*, which was shuttered because it couldn't deliver any scoops and they don't like Perez Hilton's silly little drawings anymore either.)

It sent a very clear message to publishers: Exclusives build blogs. Scoops equal traffic.

The thing is, exclusive scoops are rare, and at the very least, they require some effort to obtain. So greedy blogs have perfected what is called the "pseudo-exclusive." In a private memo to his employees, Nick Denton, founder and publisher of the Gawker Media blog empire, asked the writers to use this technique, because it allows them "to take ownership of a story even if it isn't a strict exclusive."[2] In other words, *pretend they have a scoop*. The strategy works well, because many readers will see the story in only one place; they have no idea that it was actually broken or originally reported elsewhere.

One of *Gawker*'s biggest scoops early on in the race—certainly a *TMZ*-level story—was a collection of Tom Cruise Scientology videos. It is a good example of a pseudo-exclusive, since the work wasn't done by the site who eventually got all the pageviews from it. Since I witnessed the story unfold behind the scenes, I know that tapes were actually unearthed by Hollywood journalist Mark Ebner, whose blog I was advising at the time. Ebner called me, very excited with news of a potentially huge scoop and said that he'd bring over the materials. A few hours later, he gave me some DVDs in an envelope marked confidential, which I watched later that night with a friend. Our stupid reaction: "Tom Cruise being crazy; how is that new?"

Gawker had a different reaction. See, Ebner had also shown the clips to his friends at *Gawker*, who turned around and immediately posted a story featuring the videos before Mark or anyone else had a chance to. I don't know whether *Gawker* promised Mark they'd give him credit. All I know is that

---

*Exclusives, as they are called, are important for another reason. Advertising a story as an exclusive by extension takes a dig at a publication's competitors: "We got this story and they didn't—because we're better." This is partly why a site would rather post a weak exclusive on its front page than a more interesting story they've been forced to share with others.

what happened was shitty: Their post went on to do 3.2 million views and bring their site a whole new audience. Mark received nothing, because *Gawker* didn't link back to his site—which would have been the right thing to do. By doing this, *Gawker* owned a story that was not theirs. Only after did I begin to understand how blog fortunes were made: off the backs of others.

When all it takes is one story to propel a blog from the dredges of the Internet to mainstream notoriety, it shouldn't come as a surprise that sites will do anything to get their shot, even if it means manufacturing or stealing scoops (and deceiving readers and advertisers in the process).

Established media doesn't have this problem. They aren't anxious for name recognition, because they already have it. Instead of bending the rules (and the truth) to get it, their main concern for their business model is to protect their reputations. This is a critical difference. Media was once about protecting a name; on the web it is about building one.

Using Names to Build a Name

Blogs are built on scoops and traffic, and this is made possible by big names. The economics of the Internet values consistent hitters, and so one of the safest bets a site can make is to lock up an all-star or A-list blogger to helm their business. Like so much of the history of blogging, this trend begins with *Gawker* . . . sort of.

In 2004, Jason Calacanis, the found of Weblogs, Inc., poached editor Pete Rojas away from *Gizmodo*, at the time the dominant gadget blog owned by *Gawker*. He gave Rojas a small equity stake in his company, and together they founded *Engadget*, which quickly surpassed *Gizmodo* as the reigning champion of scoops and big stories. After founding *Engadget*, Rojas created another site for Calacanis, this time a video game blog called *Joystiq*, which became another enormously popular site.

Next, there is Andrew Sullivan, who makes Rojas look like a minor league player. Sullivan's name and blog, *The Dish*, is one of the most sought-after to build a site around. His now decade-old site was first leased by *Time* magazine's website and spent several years under their domain. He was then stolen away from Time.com by TheAtlantic.com to bring digital life to the faltering print publication. Sullivan delivered; his Daily Dish would eventually draw more than one million visitors a month to *The Atlantic*. Like any franchise athlete, they were able to build a team around him, using his name to attract writers and influential readers. In 2011, Sullivan left for *The Daily Beast*, in order to start the cycle all over again—but the bump in traffic and prestige stayed at *The Atlantic*. *The Daily Beast*, fresh from its merger with *Newsweek*, was equally desperate for traffic and name recognition and was willing to pay serious money for a shot of Sullivan's brand-building power.

Bringing in big (online) names is now a go-to move for sites trying to build traffic. The *New York Times* brought the *Freakonomics* blog under their umbrella in 2007, and later did the same with Nate Silver's FiveThirtyEight.com. B5Media launched Crushable.com and TheGloss.com under the charge of notorious *Gawker* founding editor Elizabeth Spiers. The *Huffington Post* built most of its original cache by having celebrities blog on the site, a rarer feat then than it is now. The list goes on and on.

All these bloggers, from Sullivan to Rojas to Spiers, got their high-paying gigs (and often a percentage of a site's revenue) because they built big names for themselves. Their strategy is the same as their publisher's: Build a brand by courting controversy, breaking big scoops, driving comments, and publishing *constantly*. And their big deals with sites like the *New York Times* or *The Daily Beast* make these questionable tactics all the more necessary. The big names have to stay big to stay on top.

THE BLOG CON: NAMES, SCOOPS, AND TRAFFIC CREATE AN EXIT

I've written about how sites engage in an endless chase for revenue through pageviews, and that *is* what they do. However, blogs are not intended to be profitable and independent businesses. The tools they use to build traffic and revenue are part of a larger play.

Blogs are built to be sold. Though they make substantial revenues from advertising, the real money is in selling the entire site to a larger company for a multiple of the traffic and earnings. Usually to a rich sucker.

Weblogs, Inc. was sold to AOL for $25 million. The *Huffington Post* was sold to AOL for $315 million in cash, with its owner, Arianna Huffington, deliberately eschewing the opportunity to wait and build for an IPO. *TechCrunch* was also sold to AOL for $30 million. Discovery bought the blog *TreeHugger* for $10 million. *Ars Technica* was sold to Condé Nast for more than $20 million. *Know Your Meme* was acquired by Cheezburger Media for seven figures. FOX Sports Interactive purchased the sports blog network *Yardbarker*. I worked on an acquisition like this myself when The Collective, a talent management company I advise, bought *Bloody Disgusting*, a blog about horror films, with an eye on potentially selling it to someone bigger down the line.

Blogs are built and run with an exit in mind. This is really why they need scoops and acquire marquee bloggers—to build up their names for investors and to show a trend of rapidly increasing traffic. The pressure for this traffic in a short period of time is intense. And desperation, as a media manipulator knows, is the greatest quality you can hope for in a potential victim. Each blog is its own mini-Ponzi scheme, for which traffic growth is more important than solid financials, brand recognition more important than trust, and scale more important than business sense. Blogs are built so someone else will want it—one stupid buyer cashing out the previous ones—and millions of dollars are exchanged for essentially worthless assets.

ANYTHING GOES IN THE DEN OF THIEVES

It doesn't surprise me at all that shady business deals and conflicts of interest abound in this world. My favorite example, of course, is myself. I am regularly the online ad buyer and the publicist or PR contact for the clients I represent. So the same sites that snarkily cover my companies also depend on me for large six- or even seven-figure checks each year. On the same day a writer for a blog might be e-mailing me for information about a rumor they heard, their publisher is calling me on the phone asking if I want to increase the size of my ad buy. Later in this book I'll write about how difficult it is to get bloggers to correct even blatantly inaccurate stories—this conflict of interest was one of the only effective tools I could use to combat that. Naturally, nobody minded what I was doing, because they were too busy lining their own pockets to care.

Michael Arrington, the loudmouth founder and former editor in chief of *TechCrunch*, is famous for investing in the start-ups that his blogs would then cover. Although he no longer runs *TechCrunch*, he was a partner in two investment funds during his tenure and now manages his own, CrunchFund. In other words, even when he is not a direct investor he has connections or interests in dozens of companies on his beat, and his insider knowledge helps turn profits for the firm.

When criticized for these conflicts he responded by saying that his competitors were simply jealous because he was—I'm not kidding—"a lot better than them." So when Arrington blew the lid off a secret meeting of angel investors in Silicon Valley in 2011—later known as "Angelgate"—it's hard to say whose interests he was serving, his readers' or his own. Or maybe he was upset not because collusion is wrong but because the group had declined to invite him and—again, not kidding—treated him rudely when he showed up anyway. He ultimately left *TechCrunch* after a highly publicized fight with the new owners, AOL, who dared to question this conflict of interest.

Nick Denton of *Gawker* is also a prolific investor in his own space, often putting money in companies founded by employees who left his company or were fired. He has stakes in several local blog networks, such as *Curbed*, that are often linked to or written about on his larger sites. By shuffling users around to two sites he can charge advertisers twice. Denton also invested in the site Cityfile, which he was able to pump up with traffic from his other blogs before acquiring it outright and rolling it back into *Gawker*.

Influence is ultimately the goal of most blogs and blog publishers, because that influence can be sold to a larger media company. But, as Arrington and Denton show, influence can also be abused for profit through strategic investments—be it in the companies they write about or where they decide to send monetizeable traffic. And, of course, these are only the conflicts of interest blatant enough to be discovered by the public. Who knows what else goes on behind the curtain?

ENTER: THE MANIPULATOR

Bloggers eager to build names and publishers eager to sell their blogs are like two crooked businessmen colluding to create interest in a bogus investment opportunity—building up buzz and clearing town before anyone gets wise. In this world, where the rules and ethics are lax, a third player can exert massive influence. Enter: the media manipulator.

The assumptions of blogging and their owners present obvious vulnerabilities that people like me exploit. They allow us to control what is in the media, because the media is too busy chasing profits to bother trying to stop us. They are not motivated to care. Their loyalty is not to their audience but to themselves and their con. While ultimately this is reason to despair, I have found one small solace: Conning the conmen is one of life's most satisfying pleasures. And it's not even hard.

In the next chapters I will outline how to do this and how it is being done. I have broken down the manipulation of blogs into nine effective tactics. Each exposes a pathetic vulnerability in our media system—each, when wielded properly, levels the playing field and gives you free rein to control the flow of information on the web.

IV

TACTIC #1

BLOGGERS ARE POOR; HELP PAY THEIR BILLS

> The writings by which one can live are not the writings which themselves live, and are never those in which the writer does his best. . . . Those who have to support themselves by their pen must depend on literary drudgery, or at best on writings addressed to the multitude.
>
> —JOHN STUART MILL, *AUTOBIOGRAPHY*

THERE ARE MANY WAYS TO GIVE SOMEONE A BRIBE. Very rarely does it mean handing them a stack of bills. You use this logic and the criteria that bloggers' employers use to determine the size of their paycheck—the stuff bloggers are paid for—can be co-opted and turned into an indirect bribe. These levers were easy enough for me to find, and properly identified and wielded, they turned out to be as effective as any overt payoff.

It begins with how these bloggers are hired. Put aside any notion that applicants are chosen based on skill, integrity, or a love of their craft. Ben Parr, editor at large at the popular technology blog *Mashable*, was once asked what he looked for when he hired writers for his blogs. His answer was one word: quickness. "Online journalism is fast-paced," he explained. "We need people that can get the story out in minutes and can compose the bigger opinion pieces in a couple hours, not a couple of days." As to any actual experience in journalism, that would be considered only "a definite plus."[1]

The payment structure of blogging reflects this emphasis on speed over other variables, such as quality, accuracy, or how informative the content might be. Early on blogs tended to pay their writers a rate per post or a flat rate with a minimum number of posts required per day. *Engadget, Slashfood, Autoblog*, and other sites run by Weblogs, Inc. paid bloggers a reported five hundred dollars a month in 2005 for 125 posts—or four dollars a post, four per day.[2] *Gawker* paid writers twelve dollars a post as late as 2008. And of course these rates don't include the other duties bloggers are stuck with, such editing, responding to e-mails, and writing comments. Professional blogging is done in the boiler room, and it is brutal.

Gawker set the curve for the industry again when they left the pay-per-post model and switched to a pageview-based compensation system that gave bonuses to writers based on their monthly traffic figures. These bonuses came on top of a set monthly pay, meaning that bloggers were eligible for payments that could effectively double their salary once they hit their monthly quota. You can imagine what kind of results this led to. I recall a post from a *Gawker* writer whining about how he didn't know how much money he'd make that month—and getting seventeen thousand views for it.

The bonus system was so immediately rewarding for *Gawker* bloggers that the company tweaked their ratio to deemphasize the bonus slightly. The system remains, however, and today the company has a big board in its offices that shows the stats for all the writers and their stories. When writers aren't fighting for bonuses, all they have to do is look up to be reminded: If you're at the bottom of the board, you might get fired.

This is now the standard model for blogs. Forbes.com was relaunched with hundreds of blogger contributors who are paid per visitor. Seeking Alpha, a network of financial writers (arguably worth a lot to its investor-type readers), launched a payment platform in 2010 that pays writers based on the traffic their posts generate. The average payment per article turned out to be only fifty-eight dollars for the first six months. A writer needs to rack up roughly one hundred thousand views to make even one thousand dollars—a tough fight when you're jostling for share of voice against the thousand-plus writers who publish there each month. The blog *The Awl* announced it would also start paying its writers using a similar model two years after its founding. A dozen or so bloggers split a small pool of revenue generated by advertisements on the site. The more traffic the site does, the larger the pool. It's the same incentive—desperately dependent on big hits—but instead of fighting each other for pageviews, they're all in on the hustle together.[3]

Business Insider, run by Henry Blodget, is barely breaking even, so they don't have much to pay their writers. Earlier experiments with highly paid, experienced journalists failed to work. When he does pay his writers, Blodget has a fairly simple rule of thumb: Writers need to generate three times the number of pageviews required to pay for their own salary and benefits, as well as a share of the overhead, sales, hosting, and Blodget's cut. In other words, an employee making $60,000 a year needs to produce 1.8 million pageviews a month, every month, or they're out.[4] This is no easy task.

Google and YouTube pay their video bloggers solely on how many views they get, once they have been verified as a "quality" producer. In other cases Google will green-light just one hit video from an account and allow that to be monetized. YouTube sells and serves the ads, takes a substantial cut, and passes the rest on. Most of these figures are not public, but a decent account can hope to make about one penny per view, or one dollar for every thousand.

I remember working with the very popular multiplatinum rock band Linkin Park and realizing their account, which had done over one hundred million views, would earn them barely six figures—to be split among six guys, a manager, a lawyer, and a record label. These kinds of rates force channels big and small to churn out videos constantly to make money. Every view is only a penny in their pocket.

Twitter users are straight-up mercenary. Through various ad networks you can actually pay influential accounts to tweet a message of your choosing. And by message, I mean that they will tweet *anything*.

In order to promote one of Tucker's books I got a Twitter account with more than four hundred thousand followers to say: "FACT: People will do anything for money"—for twenty-five dollars. For a few hundred dollars more I tricked dozens of other accounts into posting humiliating promotional messages that pushed the book to a number two debut on the *New York Times* bestseller list. One blog headline summed it up well: "Tucker Max Proves You Can Pay Celebrities To Tweet Whatever You Want."[5]

Other companies, such as Demand Media, Associated Content, and examiner.com, have revived the earlier payment model and typically pay their writers on a per post and per video basis. The figure for text tends to hover around eight dollars, and slightly more for video.

If all these numbers sound small—and they do to me—it isn't simply because bloggers are getting shafted. It's because what they produce isn't worth all that much. Political analyst Nate Silver estimated that the median user-contributed article on the *Huffington Post* is worth only three dollars in revenue to the company.[6] So even if they were paid fairly for their contributions, it wouldn't be much of a paycheck. Silver looked at high-profile articles by former U.S. secretary of labor Robert Reich that did 547 comments and 27,000 pageviews and concluded that they'd be worth only about two hundred dollars—an amount for which a man like

that usually wouldn't get out of bed. Most articles from the currently unpaid contributors generate significantly less revenue than that.

RIPE FOR EXPLOITATION

All this means that if bloggers want to get rich—or even cover their rent—
they've got to find other ways to get paid. That's where people like me
come in—with boatloads of free stuff.

One of the quickest ways to get coverage for a product online is to give
it away for free to bloggers (they'll rarely disclose their conflict of interest).
At American Apparel I have two full-time employees whose job it is to
research fashion bloggers—girls who post photos of their outfits each day
to thousands of readers who imitate them—and send them our newest
garments. I would offer an affiliate ad deal to the most popular girls that
would pay them a commission each time someone bought something
from our site after seeing their photos. I'm sure you're shocked to read
how often their posts featured something from American Apparel.

When I promoted movies, tours of the set or invitations to the pre-
miere worked wonders in getting blog coverage. When I worked with
bands, concert tickets, or even just an e-mail from the artist, can make
most blogs star-struck enough to give you what you need. And that's
nothing compared to what Samsung did: As an advertiser on *Business
Insider*, Samsung paid for a *Business Insider* staffer to go to Barcelona to
cover the Mobile World Congress. Thankfully, the writer disclosed this
relationship. But in that very disclosure, he cops to feeling "pretty warm
and fuzzy about Samsung" as a result of the generous offer. In my line of
work, it's all about encouraging those feelings however possible.[7]

But this is just free swag and perks. The easiest way for bloggers to
make *real* money is to transition to a job with an old media company or a
tech company. They can build a name and sell it to a sucker, just like their
owners and investors are trying to do. Once a blogger builds a personal
brand—through scoops or controversy or major stories—they can expect
a cushy job at a magazine or start-up desperate for the credibility and
buzz that these attributes offer. These lagging companies can then tell
shareholders, "See, we're current!" or "We're turning things around!"

Tony Pierce, a founding editor of *LAist*, a local blog about Los Angeles, left it to head up the digital efforts for the *Los Angeles Times*. *CNET* blogger Caroline McCarthy turned in her blogging gig for a job at Google as a trend analyst. Yahoo!, in its days as a media company, hired a whole slew of bloggers away from their website, including reporters from *Defamer* and Movieline.com, *The Awl*, and others. Reporter John Cook left the *Chicago Tribune* to join *Gawker*, left *Gawker* to join Yahoo!, and then left Yahoo! to return to *Gawker*, all in less than two years. A former editor of *Engadget*, Joshua Topolsky, is a regular guest on *Late Night with Jimmy Fallon* and a weekly columnist for the *Washington Post*. The founding editor of *Wonkette*, Ana Marie Cox, is the queen of the revolving door; she turned her few years as a blogging celebrity into stints editing or reporting for Time.com, MSNBC, Air America, and *Playboy*.

This revolving door has a peculiar influence on coverage, as is to be expected. What blogger is going to do real reporting on companies like Google, Facebook, or Twitter when there is the potential for a lucrative job down the road? They'd prefer to play it safe and build their name through any means but being a reliable journalist.

For my part, I've lost track of the bloggers whose names I have helped make by giving them big stories (favorable and to my liking) and watched transition into bigger gigs at magazines, newspapers, and editorships at major blogs. In fact, the other day I was driving in Los Angeles and noticed a billboard on La Cienega Boulevard with nothing but a large face on it: the face of a video blogger who I'd started giving free clothes to back when his videos did a few thousand views apiece. Now his videos do millions of views, and he has a show on HBO. If you invest early in a blogger, you can buy your influence very cheaply.

In most cases, they know what I am doing and don't care. If blog publishers are constantly looking for an exit, then their bloggers are too. They both want money from the same big media companies. They don't care if the scandals they write about are real or made up, or if their sources are biased or self-serving—as long as the blogger gets something out of it.

THE *REAL* CONFLICT OF INTEREST

We take it as self-evident that journalists shouldn't be paid off by people they write about or have financial investments (like owning a stock they're reporting on) in their field. The conflict would shape the coverage and corrupt their writing. So for a second I was pleasantly surprised to read pretty much that exact sentiment in a post by *Gawker* writer Hamilton Nolan titled "New Rules for Media Ethics." He said it plainly: "Media people—reporter, commentator, or otherwise—shouldn't have a financial stake in what they're reporting on."

But then I realized how hypocritical it *all* was, since Nolan is being paid by how many views his posts do. His financial interest isn't in *what* he writes about but in *how* he writes. In the pay-per-pageview model, every post is a conflict of interest. It's why I've never bought influence directly. *I've never had to.* Bloggers have a direct incentive to write bigger, to write simpler, to write more controversially or, conversely, more favorably, to write without having to do any work, to write more often than is warranted. Their paycheck depends on it. It's no wonder they are vicious, irresponsible, inaccurate, and dishonest.

They call it a "digital sweatshop" for good reason. "Ceaseless fight for table scraps" might be another phrase for it. Or in the immortal words of Henry Kissinger: The reason the knives are so sharp online is because the pie is so small.

47

TACTIC #2

TELL THEM WHAT THEY WANT TO HEAR

> Even though credibility is all you have to sell, it's not enough anymore. Credibility is not working as a business model. Credibility of journalism is at an all-time low, anyway.
>
> —KELLY McBRIDE, POYNTER INSTITUTE

THE PROBLEM OF JOURNALISM, SAYS EDWARD JAY Epstein in his book *Between Fact and Fiction*, is simple. Journalists are rarely in a position to establish the truth of an issue themselves, since they didn't witness it personally. They are "entirely dependent on self-interested 'sources'" to supply their facts. Every part of the news-making process is defined by this relationship; everything is colored by this reality.

Who are these self-interested sources? Well, anyone selling a product, a message, or an agenda. People like me.

When the *New York Times* publishes leaked documents there is an implicit understanding that they have at least attempted to verify their validity. The same goes for the identity of the source who gave it to them. Online, anonymous means something else entirely. Quotes and tips are drawn from unsolicited, untraced e-mails or angry comments pulled from comments sections, or sent in by people who have something to gain from it. I know, because I have been this kind of source dozens of times, and it was never for anything important. My identity is never verified.

Today, the online-driven news cycle is going a million miles a minute in a million directions. The *New York Times* may still *try* to verify their sources, but it hardly matters, because no one else does. This creates endless opportunities for people like me to slip in and twist things to my liking. As Epstein said, the discrepancy between what actually happened and the version of what happened provided by sources is an enormous gray area. Of all such areas, it's where I have the most fun and direct influence.

THE DELIBERATE LEAK

Once during a lawsuit I needed to get some information into the public discussion of it, so I dashed off a fake internal memo, printed it out, scanned it, and sent the file to a bunch of blogs as if I were an employee leaking a "memo we'd just gotten from our boss." The same bloggers who were uninterested in the facts when I informed them directly gladly put up EXCLUSIVE! and LEAKED! posts about it. They could tell my side of the story because I told it to them in words they wanted to hear. More people saw it than ever would have had I issued an "official statement."

Another time I had some promotional images for a Halloween campaign I also couldn't use, because of copyright concerns. I still wanted them seen, so I had one of my employees e-mail them to *Jezebel* and *Gawker* and write, "I shouldn't be doing this but I found some secret images on the American Apparel server and here they were." The post based on this lie did ninety thousand views. The writer wrote back a helpful tip: No need to leak me info from your company e-mail address; you might get caught. I thought, but how else could she be sure they were real?

It was funny at the time. Then a few months later, a U.S. congressman allegedly exchanged e-mails with a girl on craigslist and sent her a shirtless photo of himself. The girl forwarded this photo and the incriminating e-mail correspondence that supposedly occurred along with them to *Gawker* (which owns *Jezebel*). *Gawker* posted it, and the congressman immediately resigned.

Knowing now that an anonymous tip to *Gawker* has the power to end the career of a United States congressman took a little of the fun out of it for me. Scratch that—now my personal knowledge of *Gawker*'s sourcing standards scares me shitless.

PRESS RELEASE 2.0

When I first started in PR all of the leading web gurus were proclaiming the death of the press release. Good riddance, I thought. Journalists *should* care too much about what they write to churn out articles and posts based on press releases.

I could not have been more wrong. Before long I came to see the truth: Blogs love press releases. It does every part of their job for them: The material is already written; the angle laid out; the subject newsworthy; and, since it comes from an official newswire, they can blame someone else if the story turns out to be wrong.

As a 2010 study by Pew Research Center's Project for Excellence in Journalism found:

> As news is posted faster, often with little enterprise reporting added, the official version of events is becoming more important. We found official press releases often appear word for word in first accounts of events, though often not noted as such.[1] [emphasis mine]

So I started putting out press releases all the time. Open a new store? Put out a press release. Launch a new product? Put out a press release. Launch a new *color* of a new product? Press release. A blogger might pick it up. And even if no outlets do, press releases through services like PRWeb are deliberately search-engine optimized to show up well in Google results indefinitely. Most important, investing sites like Google Finance, CNN Money, Yahoo! Finance, and Motley Fool all automatically syndicate the major release wires. If you're a public company with a stock symbol, the good news in any release you put out shows up right in front of your most important audience: stockholders. Minutes after you put it out, it's right there on the company's stock page in the "Recent News" section, eagerly being read by investors and traders.

I quickly learned that not everyone saw this as harmless, low-hanging media fruit. My instinct is not illegal profit, but for those who have it, blogs' blind faith in press releases presents opportunities. It did for New York stockbroker Lambros Ballas: He was charged by the Securities and Exchange Commission for issuing fake online press releases about the stocks of companies like Google, Disney, and Microsoft and seeding them on blogs and finance forums. On the fake news of an acquisition offer from Microsoft, shares of Local.com jumped 75 percent in one day, after which he and other traders dumped all their shares and moved on to pumping other stocks on fake news.[2]

It's stunning how much news is now driven by such releases—reputable or otherwise. A LexisNexis search of major newspapers for the words "in a press release" brings back so many results that the service actually attempts to warn you against trying, saying, "This search has been interrupted because it will return more than 3,000 results. If you continue with this search it may take some time to return this information." Same goes for the phrase "announced today" and "told reporters." In other words, newspapers depended on marketing spam literally too many times to count in the last year.

A Google blog search for "said in a press release" (meaning they quoted directly from a release) brings back 307,000 results for the same period as the LexisNexis search, and more than 4 million for all time. "Announced today" brings up more than 32,000 articles for a single week. If you get specific, an internal search of *TechCrunch* brings up more than 5,000 articles using "announced today" and 7,000 attributed citations to press releases. This pales in comparison to the *Huffington Post*, whose bloggers have written the words "announced today" more than 50,000 times and cited press releases more than 200,000 times. And, of course, there is also talkingpointsmemo.com, whose name unintentionally reveals what most blogs and newspapers carelessly pass on to their readers: prewritten talking points from the powers that be.

Anyone can now be that power. Anyone can give blogs their talking points. To call it a sellers' market is an understatement. But it's the only thing I can think of that comes close to describing a medium in which dominant personalities like tech blogger Robert Scoble can nostalgically repost things on his Google+ account like the "original pitch" for publicity that the iPad start-up Flipboard had sent him.[3] It's a great time to be a media manipulator when your marks actually love receiving PR pitches.

NOT EVEN NEEDING TO BE THE SOURCE

Bloggers are under incredible pressure to produce, leaving little time for research or verification, let alone for speaking to sources. In some cases, the story they are chasing is so crazy that they don't want to risk doing research, because the whole facade would collapse.

From my experience, bloggers operate by some general rules of thumb: If a source can't be contacted by e-mail, they probably can't be a source. I've talked to bloggers on the phone only a few times, ever—but thousands of times over e-mail. If background information isn't publicly or easily available, it probably can't be included. Writers are at the mercy of official sources, such as press releases, spokesmen, government officials, and media kits. And these are for the instances they even bother to check anything.

Most important, they're at the mercy of Wikipedia, because that's where they do their research. Too bad people like me manipulate that too. Nothing illustrates this better than the story of a man who, as a joke, changed the name of comedian and actor Russell Brand's mother on Wikipedia from Barbara to Juliet. When Brand took his mother as his date to the Academy Awards shortly after, the *Los Angeles Times* ran the online headline over their picture: "Russell Brand and His Mother Juliet Brand . . ."

I remember sitting on the couch at Tucker Max's house one January a few years ago when something occurred to me about his then on-and-off-again bestseller. "Hey Tucker, did you notice your book made the *New York Times* list in 2006, 2007, and 2008?" (Meaning the book had appeared on the list at least once in all three years, *not* continuously.) So I typed it up, sourced it, and added it to Wikipedia, delineating each year.* Not long after I posted it, a journalist cribbed my "research" and did us the big favor of having poor reading comprehension. He wrote: "Tucker Max's book has spent over 3 years on the *New York Times* Bestseller List." Then we took this and doubled up our citation on Wikipedia to use this new, more generous interpretation.

This is a cycle I have watched speed up but also descend into outright plagiarism. I can't divulge my specifics, but I commonly see uniquely worded or selectively edited facts that paid editors inserted into Wikipedia show up later in major newspapers and blogs with the exact same wording (you'll have to trust me on when and where).

Wikipedia acts as a certifier of basic information for many people, including reporters. Even a subtle influence over the way that Wikipedia frames an issue—whether criminal charges, a controversial campaign, a lawsuit, or even a critical reception—can have a major impact on the way

---

*On occasion I have instructed a client to say something in an interview, knowing that once it is covered we can insert it into Wikipedia, and it will become part of the standard media narrative about them. We seek out interviews in order to advance certain "facts," and then we make them doubly real by citing them on Wikipedia.

bloggers write about it. It is the difference between "So-and-so released their second album in 2011" and "So-and-so's first album was followed by the multiplatinum and critically lauded hit . . ." You change the descriptors on Wikipedia and reporters and readers change their descriptors down the road.

A complete overhaul of one high-profile starlet's Wikipedia page was once followed less than a week later by a six-page spread in a big tabloid that so obviously used our positive and flattering language from Wikipedia that I was almost scared it would be its own scandal.

It's why you have to control your page. Or you risk putting yourself in the awkward position a friend found himself in when profiled by a reporter at a national newspaper, who asked: "So, according to Wikipedia you're a failed screenwriter. Is that true?"

TRUST ME, I'M AN EXPERT

It's not a stretch to convince anyone that it's easy to become a source for blogs. Cracking the mainstream media is much harder, right? Nope. There's actually a tool designed expressly for this purpose.

It's called HARO (Help a Reporter Out), and it is a site that connects hundreds of "self-interested sources" to willing reporters every day. The service, founded by PR man Peter Shankman, is a wildly popular tool that connects journalists working on stories with people to quote in them. It is the de facto sourcing and lead factory for journalists and publicists. According to the site, nearly thirty thousand members of the media have used HARO sources, including the *New York Times*, the Associated Press, the *Huffington Post*, and everyone in-between.

What do these experts get out of offering their services? Free publicity, of course. In fact, "Free Publicity" is HARO's tagline. I've used it myself to con reporters from ABC News to Reuters to the *Today Show*, and yes, even the vaunted *New York Times*. Sometimes I don't even do it myself. I just have an assistant pretend to be me over e-mail or on the phone.

The fact that my eyes light up when I think of how to use HARO's services to benefit myself and my clients should be illustrative. If I was tasked with building someone's reputation as an "industry expert," it would take nothing but a few fake e-mail addresses and speedy responses to the right bloggers to manufacture the impression. I'd start with using HARO to get quoted on a blog that didn't care much about credentials, then use that piece as a marker of authority to justify inclusion in a more reputable publication. It wouldn't take long to be a "nationally recognized expert who has been featured in _____, _____, and _____." The only problem is that it wouldn't be real.

Journalists say HARO is a research tool, but it isn't. It is a tool that manufactures self-promotion to look like research. Consider alerts like

> URGENT: [E-mail redacted]@aol.com needs NEW and LITTLE
> known resources (apps, Websites, etc.) that offer families unique
> ways to save money.*

This is not a noble effort by a reporter to be educated but an all too common example of a lazy blogger giving a marketer an opportunity to insert themselves into their story. Journalists also love to put out bulletins asking for sources to support stories they are already writing.

> [E-mail Redacted]@gmail.com needs horror story relating to
> mortgages, student loans, credit reports, debt collectors, or
> credit cards.

> URGENT: [E-mail Redacted]@abc.com is looking for a man who
> took on a new role around the house after losing his job.

There you have it—how your bogus trend-story sausage is made. In fact, I even saw one HARO request by a reporter hoping "to speak with an expert about how fads are created." I hope whoever answered it explained that masturbatory media coverage from people like her has a lot to do with it.

What HARO encourages—and the site is filled with thousands of posts asking for it—is for journalists to look for sources who simply confirm

---

*Ten days later the reporter generously gave a second marketer a chance at the same story, with this request: "URGENT: [E-mail redacted]@aol.com needs NEW or LITTLE known app or website that can help families with young kids save money."

what they were already intending to say. Instead of researching a topic and communicating their findings to the public, journalists simply grab obligatory—but artificial—quotes from "experts" to validate their pageview journalism. To the readers it appears as legitimate news. To the journalist, they were just reverse engineering their story from a search engine–friendly premise.

HARO also helps bloggers create the false impression of balance. Nobody is speaking to sources on both sides. They're providing token space to the opposition and nothing else. It is a sham. I constantly receive e-mails from bloggers and journalists asking me to provide "a response" to some absurd rumor or speculative analysis. They just need a quote from me denying the rumor (which most people will skip over) to justify publishing it.

Most stories online are created with this mind-set. Marketing shills masquerade as legitimate experts, giving advice and commenting on issues in ways that benefit their clients and trick people into buying their products. Blogs aren't held accountable for being wrong or being played, so why should they avoid it?

FORGETTING MY OWN BULLSHIT

As I was gathering up press done on me personally over the years, I came across an article I'd forgotten. I'd posted a question on my blog: "What is the classic book of the '80s and '90s?" It was a discussion I'd had with several friends; we were wondering what book teachers would assign to students to learn about this era fifty years from now. This discussion was picked up and featured by *Marginal Revolution*, a blog by the economist Tyler Cowen, which does about fifty thousand pageviews a day. His post said:

What is the classic book of the '80s and '90s?

BY TYLER COWEN ON SEPTEMBER 3, 2008 AT 6:42 PM IN BOOKS | PERMALINK

That's Ryan Holiday's *query*. This is not about quality, this is about "representing a literary era" or perhaps just representing the era itself. I'll cite *Bonfire of the Vanities* and *Fight Club* as the obvious picks. Loyal **MR** reader Jeff Ritze is thinking of Easton Ellis ("though not *American Psycho*"). How about you? Dare I mention John Grisham's *The Firm* as embodying the blockbuster trend of King, Steele, Clancy, and others? There's always Harry Potter and graphic novels.

Coming across this struck me not only because I am a big Tyler Cowen fan but because I am *also* Jeff Ritze. Or was, since that's one of the fake names I used to use, and had apparently e-mailed my post as a tip to *Marginal Revolution*. Of course Jeff Ritze was thinking about Bret Easton Ellis—he's one of my favorite authors. I even answered a variant of that question as me—Ryan Holiday—a few years later for a magazine that was interviewing me.

I had been the source of this article and totally forgotten about it. I wanted traffic for my site, so I tricked Tyler, and he linked to me. (Sorry, Tyler!) It paid off too. A blog for the *Los Angeles Times* picked up the discussion from Cowen's blog and talked positively about "twentysomething Ryan Holiday." *Marginal Revolution* is a widely read and influential blog, and I never would have popped up on the *Los Angeles Times*'s radar without it. Best of all, now, when I write my bio, I get to list the *Los Angeles Times* as one of the places I've gotten coverage. Score.

VI

TACTIC #3

GIVE THEM WHAT SPREADS, NOT WHAT'S GOOD

Study the top stories at Digg or MSN.com and you'll notice a pattern: the top stories all polarize people. If you make it threaten people's 3 Bs—behavior, belief, or belongings—you get a huge virus-like dispersion.

—TIM FERRISS, #1 *NEW YORK TIMES* BESTSELLING AUTHOR

THE ADVICE THAT MIT MEDIA STUDIES PROFESSOR
Henry Jenkins gives publishers and companies is blunt: "If it doesn't
spread, it's dead." With social sharing comes traffic, and with traffic
comes money. Something that isn't shared isn't worth anything.

For someone tasked with advancing narratives in the media, the flip
side of this advice is equally straightforward: If it spreads, you're golden.
Blogs don't have the resources to advertise their posts, and bloggers certainly don't have the time to work out a publicity launch for something
they've written. Every blog, publisher, and oversharer in your Facebook
feed is constantly looking to post things that will take on a life of their
own and get attention, links, and new readers with the least work possible.
Whether that content is accurate, important, or helpful doesn't even register on their list of priorities.

If the quality of their content doesn't matter to bloggers, do you think
it's going to matter to marketers? It's never mattered to me. So I design
what I sell to bloggers based on what I know (and they think) will spread.
I give them what they think will go viral online—and make them money.

A TALE OF TWO CITY SLIDE SHOWS

If you're like me, you've sat and stared in fascination at the pictures of the
ruins of Detroit that get passed around the Internet. We've all gaped at the
stunning shots of the cavelike interior of the decaying United Artists Theater and the towering Michigan Central Station that resembles an abandoned Gothic cathedral. These beautiful high-res photo slideshows are
impressive pieces of online photojournalism . . . or so you think.

Like everyone else, I ate up these slideshows, and I even harbored a
guilty desire to go to Detroit and walk through the ruins. My friends

know this and send me the newest ones as soon as they come out. When I see the photos I can't help thinking of this line from *Fight Club*:

> In the world I see, you're stalking elk through the damp canyon forests around the ruins of Rockefeller Center. . . . You'll climb the wrist-thick kudzu vines that wrap the Sears Tower. And when you look down, you'll see tiny figures pounding corn, laying strips of venison on the empty car pool lane of some abandoned superhighway.

To see a broken, abandoned American city is a moving, nearly spiritual experience, one you are immediately provoked to share with everyone you know.

A slideshow that generates a reaction like that is online gold. An ordinary blog post is only one page long, so a thousand-word article about Detroit would get one pageview per viewer. A slideshow about Detroit gets twenty per user, hundreds of thousands of times over, while premium advertising rates are charged against the photos. A recent twenty-picture display posted by the *Huffington Post* was commented on more than four thousand times and liked twenty-five thousand times on Facebook. And that was the second time they'd posted it. The *New York Times*'s website has two of their own, for a total of twenty-three photos. The *Guardian*'s website has a sixteen-pager. Time.com's eleven-pager is the top Google result for "Detroit photos." We're talking about millions of views combined.

One would think that any photo of Detroit would be an instant hit online. Not so. A series of beautiful but sad photographs of foreclosed and crumbling Detroit houses and their haggard residents was posted on Magnum Photos's site in 2009, well before most of the others. It shows the same architectural devastation, the same poverty and decline. While the slideshow on the *Huffington Post* received four thousand comments within days, these photos got twenty-one comments over *two years*.[1]

ONE SPREADS, THE OTHER DOESN'T

In an article in the *New Republic* called "The Case Against Economic Disaster Porn," Noreen Malone points out that one thing stands out about the incredibly viral photographs of Detroit: Not a single one of the popular photos of the ruins of Detroit has a person in it. That was the difference between the *Huffington Post* slideshows and the Magnum photos—Magnum dared to include human beings in their photos of Detroit. The photos that spread, on the other hand, are deliberately devoid of any sign of life.[2]

Detroit has a homeless population of nearly twenty thousand, and in 2011, city funding for homeless shelters was cut in half. Thousands more live in foreclosed houses and buildings without electricity or heat, the very same structures in the pictures. These photos don't just omit people. Detroit is a city overrun by stray dogs, which roam the city in packs hunting and scavenging for food. Conservative figures estimate that there are as many as 50,000 wild dogs living in Detroit and something like 650,000 feral cats. In other words, you can't walk a block in Detroit without seeing heartbreaking and deeply wounded signs of life.

You'd have to try not to. And that's exactly what these slideshow photographers do. Why? Because all that is depressing. As Jonah Peretti, the virality expert behind both the *Huffington Post* and *BuzzFeed,* believes, "if something is a total bummer, people don't share it." And since people wouldn't share it, blogs won't publish it. Seeing the homeless and drug addicts and starving, dying animals would take away all the fun.* It'd make the viewers feel uncomfortable, and unsettling images are not conducive to sharing. Why, Peretti asks, would anyone—bloggers or readers—want to pass along bad feelings?[3]

The economics of the web make it impossible to portray the complex situation in Detroit accurately. It turns out that photos of Detroit that spread do so precisely *because they are dead.* Simple narratives like the haunting ruins of a city spread and live, while complicated ones like a city filled with real people who desperately need help don't.

One city. Two possible portrayals. One is a bummer, one looks cool. Only one makes it into the *Huffington Post* slideshow. Only one is worth trying to sell the bloggers.

---

*Another photo for a much more popular *New York Times* slideshow says it all. The picture is of the abandoned Michigan Central Station, and in the snow on the floor are dozens of crisscrossing footprints and a door. There are no people. "Don't worry," it seems to say. "There's no reason to feel bad. Everybody left already. Keep gawking."

THE DNA OF THE VIRUS

Only a certain style of video, article, or tweet has the ability to rise above the overwhelming noise and make an impression. But the web is not some fair or positive meritocracy, and the first comprehensive study on why this is bears this out. In 2010, two researchers at the Wharton School looked at seven thousand articles that made it onto the *New York Times* Most E-mailed List. (A story from the *Times* is shared on Twitter once every four seconds, making the list one of the biggest media platforms on the web.) The researchers' results confirm almost everything we see when content like the sensational ruin porn of Detroit goes viral. For me it confirmed every intuition behind my manipulations.[4]

According to the story, "the most powerful predictor of virality is *how much anger an article evokes*" [emphasis mine]. I will say it again: *The most powerful predictor of what spreads online is anger.* No wonder the outrage I created for Tucker's movie worked so well. Anger has such a profound effect that one standard deviation increase in the anger rating of an article is the equivalent of spending an additional three hours as the lead story on the front page of NYTimes.com.

Again, extremes in any direction have a large impact on how something will spread, but certain emotions do better than others. For instance, an equal shift in the positivity of an article is the equivalent of spending about 1.2 hours as the lead story. It's a significant but clear difference. The angrier an article makes the reader, the better.

The researchers found that while sadness is an extreme emotion, it is a wholly unviral one. Sadness, like what one might feel to see a stray dog shivering for warmth or a homeless man begging for money, is typically a low-arousal emotion. Sadness depresses our impulse for social sharing. It's why nobody wanted to share the Magnum photos but gladly shared the ones on the *Huffington Post*. The HuffPo photos were *awe*-some; they made us angry, or they surprised us. Such emotions trigger a desire to act—they are arousing—and that is exactly the reaction a publisher hopes to exploit.

In turn, it's what marketers exploit as well. A powerful predictor of whether content will spread online is valence, or the degree of positive or negative emotion a person is made to feel. Both extremes are more desirable than anything in the middle. Regardless of the topic, the more an article makes someone feel good *or* bad, the more likely it is to make the Most E-mailed list. No marketer is ever going to push something with the stink of reasonableness, complexity, or mixed emotions.

Yet information is rarely clearly good or bad. It tends to have elements of both, or none of either. It just *is*. Navigating this quandary forces marketers and publishers to conspire to distort this information into something that will register on the emotional spectrum of the audience. To turn it into something that spreads and to drive clicks. Behind the scenes I work to crank up the valence of articles, relying on scandal, conflict, triviality, titillation, and dogmatism. Whatever will ensure transmission.

The media is in the evil position of needing to go negative and play tricks with your psyche in order to drive you to share their material online. For instance, in studies where subjects are shown negative video footage (war, an airplane crash, an execution, a natural disaster), they become more aroused, can better recall what happened, pay more attention, and engage more cognitive resources to consume the media than nonnegative footage.[5] That's the kind of stuff that will make you hit "share this." They push your buttons so you'll press theirs.

Things must be negative but not too negative. Hopelessness, despair—these drive us to do nothing. Pity, empathy—those drive us to do something, like get up from our computers to act. But anger, fear, excitement, or laughter—these drive us to spread. They drive us to do something that makes us feel as if we are doing something, when in reality we are only contributing to what is probably a superficial and utterly meaningless conversation. Online games and apps operate on the same principles and exploit the same impulses: be consuming without frustrating, manipulative without revealing the strings.

For those who know what levers provoke people to share, media manipulation becomes simply a matter of packaging and presentation. All it takes is the right frame, the right angle, and millions of readers will willingly send your idea or image or ad to their friends, family, and coworkers on your behalf. Bloggers know this, and want it badly. If I can hand them a story that may be able to deliver, who are they to refuse?

GIVING THE BASTARDS
WHAT THEY WANT

When I design online ads for American Apparel, I almost always look for an angle that will provoke. Outrage, self-righteousness, and titillation all work equally well. Naturally, the sexy ones are probably those you remember most, but the formula worked for all types of images. Photos of kids dressed up like adults, dogs wearing clothes, ad copy that didn't make any sense—all high-valence, viral images. If I could generate a reaction, I could propel the ad from being something I had to pay for people to see (by buying ad inventory) to something people would gladly post on the front page of their highly trafficked websites.

I once ran a series of completely nude (not safe for work, or NSFW) advertisements featuring the porn star Sasha Grey on two blogs. They were very small websites, and the total cost of the ads was only twelve hundred dollars. A naked woman with visible pubic hair + a major U.S. retailer + blogs = a massive online story.

The ads were picked up online by *Nerve*, *BuzzFeed*, *Fast Company*, *Jezebel*, *Refinery29*, NBC New York, *Fleshbot*, the *Portland Mercury*, and many others. They eventually made it into print as far away as *Rolling Stone* Brazil, and they're still being passed around online. The idea wasn't ever to sell products directly through the ads themselves, since the model wasn't really wearing any of it—and the sites were too small, anyway. I knew that just the notion of a company running pornographic advertisements on legitimate blogs would be too arousing (no pun intended) for share-hungry sites and readers to resist. I'm not sure if I was the first person to ever do this, but I certainly told reporters I was. Some blogs wrote about it in anger, some wrote about it in disgust, and others loved it and wanted more. The important part was that they wrote about it at all. It ended up being seen millions of times, and almost none of those views was on the original sites where we paid for the ads to run.

I wasn't trying to create controversy for the sake of controversy. The publicity from the spectacle generated tens of thousands of dollars in sales, and that was my intention all along. I had substantial data to back up the fact that chatter correlated with a spike in purchases of whatever product was the subject of the conversation. Armed with this information, I made it my strategy to manufacture chatter by exploiting emotions of high valence: arousal and indignation. I'd serve ads in direct violation of the standards of publishers and ad networks, knowing that while they'd inevitably be pulled, the ads would generate all sorts of brand awareness in the few minutes users saw them. A slight slap on the wrist or pissing off some prudes was a penalty well worth paying for, for all the attention and money we got.

In the case of American Apparel, this leveraged advertising strategy I developed was responsible for taking online sales from forty million dollars to nearly sixty million dollars in three years—with a minuscule ad budget.

HIDDEN CONSEQUENCES

I use these tactics to sell products, and they work—lots of product gets sold. But I have come to know that the act of constantly provoking and fooling people has a larger cost. Nor am I the only one doing it.

You probably don't remember what happened on February 19, 2009, and that's because nothing notable happened—at least by any normal standard. But to those who make their living by "what spreads," it was an incredibly lucrative day, and for our country, it was a costly one.

During what was supposed to be a standard on-camera segment, CNBC correspondent Rick Santelli had a somewhat awkward meltdown on the floor of the Chicago Mercantile Exchange. He went off script and started ranting about the Obama administration and the then recently passed stimulus bill. Then he started yelling about homeowners who bit off bigger mortgages than they could chew, and Cuba, and a bunch of other ridiculous stuff. Traders on the floor began to cheer (and jeer), and he ended by declaring that he was thinking about having a "Chicago Tea Party" to dump derivatives into Lake Michigan. The whole thing looked like a shit show.

CNBC was smart. They recognized from the reaction of their anchors—which ranged from horror to mild bemusement—that they had something valuable on their hands. Instead of waiting for the video to be discovered by bloggers, news junkies, message boards, and mash-up artists, CNBC posted it on their own website immediately. While this might seem like a strange move for a serious media outlet to make, it wasn't. The Drudge Report linked to the clip, and it immediately blew up. This was, as Rob Walker wrote for *The Atlantic* in an analysis of the event, a core principle of our new viral culture: "Humiliation should not be suppressed. It should be monetized." Instead of being ashamed of this crappy television journalism, CNBC was able to *make extra money* from the millions of views it generated.

The real reason the Santelli clip spread so quickly was a special part of toying with the valance of the web. Originally the clip spread as a joke, with the degree of amusement being determined by where the viewers fit on the political spectrum. But where some saw a joke, others saw a truth teller. An actual Chicago Tea Party was organized. Disaffected voters genuinely agreed with what he said. Santelli wasn't having a meltdown, some thought; he was just as angry as they were. On the other end of the spectrum, not only were people *not* laughing, they were horribly offended. To them this was proof of CNBC's political bias. Some were so serious that they endorsed a conspiracy theory (launched by a blog on Playboy .com, of all places) that alleged the meltdown was a deliberately planned hoax funded by conservative billionaires to energize the right wing.

Regardless of how they interpreted Santelli's rant, *everyone's* reactions were so extreme that few of them were able see it for what it truly was: a mildly awkward news segment that should have been forgotten.

Of all the political and financial narratives we needed in 2009, this was surely not it. Reasoned critiques of leveraged capitalism, solutions that required sacrifice—these were things that did not yield exciting blog posts or spread well online. But the Santelli clip did. CNBC fell ass first into the perfect storm of what spreads on the web—humiliation, conspiracy theories, anger, frustration, humor, passion, and possibly the interplay of several or all of these things together.

As Chris Hedges, the philosopher and journalist, wrote, "In an age of images and entertainment, in an age of instant emotional gratification, we neither seek nor want honesty or reality. Reality is complicated. Reality is boring. We are incapable or unwilling to handle its confusion."

As a manipulator, I certainly encourage and fuel this age. So do the content creators. CNBC doesn't care how they come off as long as they can sell ads against the traffic it brings. And the audience says they're okay with it too—voting clearly with their clicks. We're all feeding that monster.

This may seem like nothing. It's just people having fun, right? Sure, my deliberately provocative ads, once caught, quickly do disappear and awareness subsides—just like all viral web content. Roughly 96 percent of the seven thousand articles that made the Most E-mailed list in the *New York Times* study did so only once. In almost no cases did an article make the list, drop off, and then return. They had a brief, transitory existence and then disappeared. But though viral content may disappear, its consequences do not—be it a toxic political party or an addiction to cheap and easy attention.

The omission of humanity from the popular slideshows of Detroit is not a malicious choice. There was no person like me behind the scenes hoping to mislead you. There was no censorship. In fact, there are thousands of the other, more realistic photos out there. Yet, all the same, the public is misinformed about a situation that we desperately need to solve. But heartbreaking sadness does not spread well. Through the selective mechanism of what spreads—and gets traffic and pageviews—we get suppression not by omission but by transmission.

The web has only one currency, and you can use any word you want for it—valence, extremes, arousal, powerfulness, excitement—but it adds up to false perception. Which is great if you're a publisher but not if you're someone who cares about the people in Detroit. What thrives online is not the writing that reflects anything close to the reality in which you and I live. Nor does it allow for the kind of change that will create the world we wish to live in.

It does, however, make it possible for me to do what I do. And people like me will keep doing it as long as that is true.

VII

TACTIC #4

HELP THEM TRICK THEIR READERS

1. "Is Sitting a Lethal Activity?"

2. "How Little Sleep Can You Get Away With?"

3. "Is Sugar Toxic?"

4. "What's the Single Best Exercise?"

5. "Do Cellphones Cause Brain Cancer?"

—SCREENSHOT OF THE MOST POPULAR
ARTICLES BOX, *NEW YORK TIMES
MAGAZINE*, APRIL 16, 2011

ARE LOADED-QUESTION HEADLINES POPULAR? YOU bet. As Brian Moylan, a *Gawker* writer, once bragged, the key is to "get the whole story into the headline but leave out just enough that people will want to click."

Nick Denton knows that being evasive and misleading is one of the best ways to get traffic and increase the bottom line. In a memo to his bloggers he gave specific instructions on how to best manipulate the reader for profit:

> *When examining a claim, even a dubious claim, don't dismiss with a skeptical headline before getting to your main argument. Because nobody will get to your main argument. You might as well not bother. . . . You set up a mystery—and explain it after the link. Some analysis shows a good question brings twice the response of an emphatic exclamation point.*

I have my own analysis: When you take away the question mark, it usually turns their headline into a lie. The reason bloggers like to use them is because it lets them get away with a false statement that no one can criticize. After the reader clicks, they soon discover that the answer to the "question" in their headline is obviously, "No, of course not." But since it was posed as a question, the blogger wasn't *wrong*—they were only asking. "Did Glenn Beck Rape and Murder a Young Girl in 1990?" Sure, I don't know, whatever gets clicks.

Bloggers tell themselves that they are just tricking the reader with the headline to get them to read their nuanced, fair-er articles. But that's a lie. (I actually read the articles, and they're rarely any better than the headline would suggest.) This lie is just one bloggers tell to feel better about themselves, and you can exploit it. So give them a headline, it's what they want. Let them rationalize it privately however they need to.

When I want *Gawker* or other blogs to write about my clients I intentionally exploit their ambivalence about deceiving people. If I am giving them an official comment on behalf of a client, I leave room for them to speculate by not fully addressing the issue. If I am creating the story as a fake tipster, I ask a lot of rhetorical questions: Could [some preposterous misreading of the situation] be what's going on? Do you think that [juicy scandal] is what they're hiding? And then I watch as the writers pose those very same questions to their readers in a click-friendly headline. The answer to my questions is obviously, "No, of course not," but I play the skeptic about my own clients—even going so far as to say nasty things— so the bloggers will do it on the front page of their site.

I trick the bloggers, and they trick their readers. This arrangement is great for the traffic-hungry bloggers, for me, and for my attention-seeking clients. Readers might be better served by posts that inform them about things that really matter. But, as you saw in the last chapter, stories with useful information are less likely to be shared virally than other types of content.

For example: Movie reviews, in-depth tutorials, technical analysis, and recipes are typically popular with the initial audience and occasionally appear on most e-mailed lists. But they tend not to draw significant amounts of traffic from other websites. They are less fun to share and spread less as a result. This may seem counterintuitive at first, but it makes perfect sense according to the economics of online content. Commentary on top of someone else's commentary or advice is cumbersome and often not very interesting to read. Worse, the writer of the original material may have been so thorough as to have solved the problem or proffered a reasonable solution—two very big dampers on a getting a heated debate going.

For blogs, practical utility is often a liability. It is a traffic killer. So are other potentially positive attributes. It's hard to get trolls angry enough to comment while being fair or reasonable. Waiting for the whole story to unfold can be a surefire way to eliminate the possibility for follow-up posts. So can pointing out that an issue is frivolous, Being the voice of reason does also. No blogger wants to write about another blogger who made him or her look bad.

To use an exclamation point, to refer back to Denton's remark, is to be final. Being final, or authoritative, or helpful, or any of these obviously positive attributes is avoided, because they don't bait user engagement. And engaged users are where the money is.

GETTING ENGAGED WITH CONTENT

Before objecting that "user engagement" is a good thing, let's look at it in practice. Pretend for a second that you read an article on the blog *Politico* about an issue that makes you angry. Angry enough that you *must* let the author know how you feel about it: You go to leave a comment.

Here's how it went for me the other day:

You must be logged in to comment, the site tells me. Not yet a member? Register now. When I click, a new page comes up with ads all across it. I fill out the form on the page, handing over my e-mail address, gender, and city, and hit Submit. Damn it, I didn't type the CAPTCHA right, so the page reloads with another ad. Finally I get it right and get the confirmation page (another page, another ad). Now I check my e-mail. Welcome to *Politico!*, it tells me: Click this link to validate your account. (Now they can spam me later with e-mails with more ads!) Registration is now complete, it says: another page and another ad. I'm asked to log in, so I do. More pages, more ads, but now I can finally share my opinion with the author. I am "engaged."

This is how it is everywhere. It might take as many as ten pageviews to leave a comment on a blog the first time. The *Huffington Post* makes a big show of asking users to rate its articles on a scale from one to ten. What happens when you do that? It shows you another page and another ad. Or when you see a mistake in an article and fill out the Send Corrections form? Well, first they'll need your e-mail address, and then they ask if you want to receive daily e-mails from them.

When you do this, you are the sucker. The site doesn't care about your opinion; it cares that, by eliciting it, they score free pageviews. I just got tired of being toyed with and decided to use this system to my advantage.

The best way to get online coverage is to tee a blogger up with a story that will obviously generate comments (or votes, or shares, or whatever). This impossible maze of pageviews is so lucrative that bloggers can't help but try to lure readers into it. Following that logic, when I whisper to a blog about something disgusting that Tucker Max supposedly did, what I am really doing is giving the writer a chance to invite the readers to comment with "Eww!!!" or "What a misogynist!" I'm also giving Tucker's fans a chance to hear about it and come to his defense. Nobody involved actually cares what any of these people think or are feeling—not even a little bit. But I am giving the blog a way to make money at their expense.

YOU ARE BEING PLAYED

A click is a click and a pageview is a pageview. A blogger doesn't care how they get it. Their bosses don't care. They just want it.*

The headline is there to get you to view the article, end of story. Whether you get anything out of it after is irrelevant—the click already happened. The Comments section is meant to be used. So are those Share buttons at the bottom of every post. The dirty truth, as Venkatesh Rao, the entrepreneur in residence at Xerox, pointed out, is that

> social media isn't a set of tools to allow humans to communicate with humans. It is a set of embedding mechanisms to allow technologies to use humans to communicate with each other, in an orgy of self-organizing. . . . The Matrix had it wrong. You're not the battery power in a global, human-enslaving AI, you are slightly more valuable. You are part of the switching circuitry.[1]

As a user, the fact that blogs are not helpful, deliberately misleading, or unnecessarily incendiary might exhaust and tire you, but Orwell reminded us in 1984: "The weariness of the cell is the vigor of the organism."

So goes the art of the online publisher: To string the customer along as long as possible, to deliberately *not* be helpful, is to turn simple readers into pageview-generating machines. Publishers know they have to make

---

*As Richard Greenblatt—maybe the greatest hacker who has ever lived—told *Wired* in 2010, "There's a dynamic now that says, let's format our web page so people have to push the button a lot so that they'll see lots of ads. Basically, the people who win are those who manage to make things the most inconvenient for you."

each new headline even more irresistible than the last, the next article even more inflammatory or less practical to keep getting clicks. It's a vicious cycle in which, by screwing the reader and getting screwed by me, they must screw the reader harder next time to top what they did before.

And sure, sometimes people get mad when they realize they've been tricked. Readers don't like to learn that the story they read was baseless. Bloggers don't like it when they discover I played them. But this is a calculated risk bloggers and I both take, mostly because the consequences are so low. In the rare cases we're caught red-handed, it's not like we have to give the money we made back. As Juvenal joked, "What's infamy matter if you can keep your fortune?"

VIII

TACTIC #5

SELL THEM SOMETHING THEY CAN SELL (EXPLOIT THE ONE-OFF PROBLEM)

I'M NO MEDIA SCHOLAR, BUT IN MY FANATICAL SEARCH for what makes bloggers tick, I turned to every media historian I could find and devoured their work. Through these experts I started to see that the very way that blogs get their articles in front of readers predetermines what they write. Just like the yellow press of a century ago, blogs are at the mercy of unrelenting pressures that compel them to manipulate the news, and be manipulated in turn.

History lessons can be boring but trust me, in this case, a brief one is worth it because it unlocks a new angle of media control. Once you know how the newsmen sell their product, it becomes easier to sell them yours.

There are three distinct phases of the newspaper (which have been synonymous with "the news" for most of history). It begins with the Party Press, moves to the infamous Yellow Press, and ends finally with the stable period of the Modern Press (or press by subscription). These phases contain surprising parallels to where we are today with blogs—old mistakes made once more, manipulations made possible again for the first time in decades.

THE PARTY PRESS

The earliest forms of newspapers were a function of political parties. These were media outlets for party leaders to speak to party members, to give them the information they needed and wanted. It's a part of news history that is often misunderstood or misused in discussions about media bias.

These papers were not some early version of Fox News. They usually were one-man shops. The editor-publisher-writer-printer was the dedicated steward of a very valuable service to that party in his town. The service was the ability to communicate ideas and information about important issues. These political papers sold the service to businessmen, politicians, and voters.

It was sold on a subscription model, typically about ten dollars a year. A good paper might have only a thousand or so subscribers, but they were almost always mandatory for party members in certain areas, which was a kind of patronage.

This first stage of journalism was limited in its scope and impact. Because of the size and nature of its audience, the party press was not in the *news* business. They were in the editorial business. It was a different time and style, one that would be eclipsed by changes in technology and distribution.

THE YELLOW PRESS

Newspapers changed the moment that Benjamin Day launched the *New York Sun* in 1833. It was not so much his paper that changed everything but his way of selling it: on the street, one copy at a time. He hired the unemployed to hawk his papers and immediately solved a major problem that had plagued the party presses: unpaid subscriptions. Day's "cash and carry" method offered no credit. You bought and walked. The *Sun*, with this simple innovation in distribution, invented the news and the newspaper. A thousand imitators followed.

These papers weren't delivered to your doorstep. They had to be exciting and loud enough to fight for their sales on street corners, in barrooms, and at train stations.* Because of the change in distribution methods and the increased speed of the printing press, newspapers truly became *newspapers*. Their sole aim was to get new information, get it to print faster, get it more exclusively than their competition. It meant the decline of the editorial. These papers relied on gossip. Papers that resisted failed and went out of business—like abolitionist Horace Greeley's disastrous attempt at a gossip-free cash-and-carry paper shortly before Day's.

---

*Day invented the Help Wanted and Classifieds sections around this time. It was a highly effective way to drive daily sales.

In 1835, shortly after Day began, James Gordon Bennett, Sr. launched the *New York Herald*. Within just a few years the *Herald* would be the largest circulation daily in the United States, perhaps in the world. It would also be the most sensational and vicious.

It was all these things not because of Bennett's personal beliefs but because of his business beliefs. He knew that the newspaper's role was "not to instruct but to startle." His paper was anti-black, anti-immigrant, and anti-subtlety. These causes sold papers—to both people who loved them for it and people who hated them for it. And they bought and they bought.

Bennett was not alone. Joseph Pulitzer, a sensationalist newsmonger long before his name was softened by years of association with the prestigious Pulitzer Prize, enforced a similar dictum with his paper: The *World* would be "not only cheap but bright, not only bright but large." It *had* to be, in order to sell thousands of papers every morning to busy people in a busy city.

The need to sell every issue anew each day creates a challenge I call the "One-Off Problem." Bennett's papers solved it by getting attention however they could.

The first issue of Bennett's *Herald* looked like this: First page—eye-catching but quickly digestible miscellany; Second page—the heart of the paper, editorial and news; Third page—local; Fourth page—advertising and filler. There was something for everyone. It was short, zesty. He later tried to emphasize quality editorial instead of disposable news by swapping the first two pages. The results were disastrous. He couldn't sell papers on the street that way.

The One-Off Problem shaped more than just the design and layout of the newspaper. When news is sold on a one-off basis, publishers can't sit back and let the news come to them. There isn't enough of it, and what comes naturally isn't exciting enough. So they must create the news that will sell their papers. When reporters were sent out to cover spectacles and events, they knew that their job was to cover the news when it was there and to make it up when it was not.*

---

*In other words, we've been tearing down public figures on bogus charges for more than a century. Do yourself a favor and look up the Fatty Arbuckle scandal for a sobering look at One-Off consequences.

This is exactly the same position blogs are in today. Just as blogs are fine with manipulators easing their burden, so too were the yellow papers.

Yellow papers paid large sums to tipsters and press agents. Fakes and embellishments were so pervasive that the noted diarist and lawyer George Templeton Strong almost didn't believe the Civil War had commenced. In April 1861 he wrote in his diary that he and his friends had deliberately ignored noise they heard—the streets "vocal with newsboys" shouting "Extra!—a *Herald*. Get the bombardment of Fort Sumter!!!"—for nearly four blocks, because they were convinced it was a "sell." That Fort Sumter issue, which Strong broke down and bought, sold 135,000 copies in a single day. It was the most printed issue in the history of the *Herald*. The success of that war was what drove yellow papers to clamor for (and some say create) the Spanish-American War. As Benjamin Day put it: "We newspaper people thrive best on the calamities of others."

Media historian W. J. Cambell once identified the distinguishing markers of yellow journalism as follows:

- Prominent headlines that screamed excitement about ultimately unimportant news

- Lavish use of pictures (often of little relevance)

- Impostors, frauds, and faked interviews

- Color comics and a big, thick Sunday supplement

- Ostentatious support for the underdog causes

- Use of anonymous sources

- Prominent coverage of high society and events

Besides the Sunday supplement, does any of that sound familiar? Perhaps you should pull up *Gawker* or the *Huffington Post* for a second to jog your memory.

This realization was a common occurrence during the writing of this book. I often felt I could take media criticism written one hundred years ago, change a few words, and describe exactly how blogs work. Knowing the trademarks of yellow journalism from this era made it possible for me to know how to give blogs what they "want" in this era. But more on that later.

As the daily sales of these papers soared, they become incredibly attractive opportunities for advertisers, particularly with the advent of large corporations and department stores. The rates these new advertisers paid propelled newspapers to boost readership even more.

Master promoters like Bennett, Pulitzer, and William Randolph Hearst delivered. Their skyrocketing circulations were driven by one thing: escalating sensationalism. Welcome to the intersection of the One-Off Problem and ad-driven journalism.

THE MODERN STABLE PRESS (BY SUBSCRIPTION)

Just as James Gordon Bennett embodied the era of sensational yellow journalism, another man, Adolph S. Ochs, publisher of the *New York Times*, ushered in the next iteration of news.

Ochs, like most great businessmen, understood that doing things differently was the way to great wealth. In the case of his newly acquired newspaper and the dirty, broken world of yellow journalism, he made the pronouncement that "decency meant dollars."

He immediately set out to change the conditions that allowed the Bennett, Hearst, Pulitzer, and their imitators to flourish. He was the first publisher to solicit subscriptions via telephone. He offered contests to his salesman. He gave them quotas and goals for the number of subscribers they were expected to bring in.

He understood that people bought the yellow papers because they were cheap—and they didn't have any other options. He felt that if they had a choice, they'd pick something better. He intended to be that option. First, he would match his competitors' prices, and then he would deliver a paper that far surpassed the value implied by the low price.

It worked. When he dropped the price of the *Times* to one cent, circulation tripled in the first year. He would compete on content. He came up with the phrase "All the News That's Fit to Print" as a mission statement for the editorial staff, two months after taking over the paper. The less known runner-up says almost as much: "All the World's News, But Not a School for Scandal."

I don't want to exaggerate. The transition to a stable press was by no means immediate, and it didn't immediately transform the competition. But subscription did set forth new conditions in which the newspaper and the newspaperman had incentives more closely aligned with the needs of their readers. The end of that wave of journalism meant that papers were sold to readers by subscriptions, and all the ills of yellow journalism have swift repercussions in a subscription model: Readers who are misled unsubscribe; errors must be corrected in the following day's issue; and the needs of the newsboys no longer drove the daily headlines.

A subscription model—whether it's music or news—offers necessary subsidies to the nuance that is lacking in the kind of stories that flourish in one-off distribution. Opposing views can now be included. Uncertainty can be acknowledged. Humanity can be allowed. Since articles don't have to spread on their own, but rather as part of the unit (the whole newspaper or album or collection), publishers do not need to exploit valence to drive single-use buyers.

With Ochs's move, reputation began to matter more than notoriety. Reporters started social clubs, where they critiqued one another's work. Some began talk of unionizing. Mainly they began to see journalism as a profession, and from this they developed rules and codes of conduct. The professionalization of journalism meant applying new ideas to how stories were found, written, and presented. For the first time, it created a sense of obligation, not just to the paper and circulation, but also to the audience.

Just as Bennett had his imitators, so did Ochs. In fact, the press has imitated the principles he built into the *New York Times* since he took it over. Even now, when someone buys a paper at a newsstand, they don't survey the headlines and buy the most sensational. They buy the paper they trust—the same goes for what radio stations they listen to and television news they watch. This is the subscription model, the brand model, invented by Ochs, internalized. It is selling on subscription and not by the story.

I'm not saying it is a perfect system by any means. I don't want to imply that newspapers in the twentieth century were paragons of honesty or accuracy or embraced change immediately. As late at the 1970s, papers like the New Orleans *Times-Picayune* were still heavily dependent on street and newsstand sales, and thus continued to play up and sensationalize crime stories.

The subscription model may have been free of the corruptive influence of the masses, but that didn't spare it from corruption from the top. As the character Philip Marlowe observed in Raymond Chandler's novel *The Long Goodbye*:

> *Newspapers are owned and published by rich men. Rich men all belong to the same club. Sure, there's competition—hard tough competition for circulation, for newsbeats, for exclusive stories. Just so long as it doesn't damage the prestige and privilege and position of the owners.*

This was incisive media criticism (in fiction, no less) that was later echoed with damning evidence by theorists such as Noam Chomsky and Ben Bagdikian. A friend put it more bluntly: "Each generation of media has a different cock in its mouth."

At least there was once an open discussion about the problems of the media. Today, the toxic economics of blogs are not only obscured, but tech gurus on the take actually defend them. We have the old problems *plus* a host of new ones.

THE DEATH OF SUBSCRIPTION, REBIRTH OF MEDIA MANIPULATION

For most of the last century, the majority of journalism and entertainment was sold by subscription (the third phase). It is now sold again online à la carte—as a one-off. Each story must sell itself, must be heard over all the others, be it in Google News, on Twitter, or on your Facebook wall. This One-Off Problem is exactly like the one faced by the yellow press a century or more ago, and it distorts today's news just as it did then—only now it's amplified by millions of blogs instead of a few hundred newspapers. As Eli Pariser put it in *The Filter Bubble*, when it comes to news on the Internet:

Each article ascends the most-forwarded lists or dies an ignominious death on its own. . . . The attention economy is ripping the binding, and the pages that get read are the pages that are frequently the most topical, scandalous, and viral.

People don't read one blog. They read a constant assortment of many blogs, and so there is little incentive to build trust. Competition for readers is on a per-article basis, taking publishers right back to the (digital) street corner, yelling, "War Is Coming!" to sell papers. It takes them back to making things up to fill the insatiable need for new news.

Instead of being a nineteenth-century press agent manipulating newspapers, I am a twenty-first-century press agent manipulating blogs. The tactics are the same, but I ply my trade with more influence, less oversight, and faster results than ever imagined. I got all sorts of great inspiration (and ideas) for the job by reading old books like *The Harder They Fall* and *All the King's Men*, which are about press agents and media fixers for powerful politicians and criminals of many years ago. You want to know how to con bloggers today? Look at media hoaxes from before your grandparents were born. The same things will play. They may even play better now.

Think about how we consume blogs. It is *not* by subscription. The only viable subscription method for blogs, RSS, is dead. For some of you who still religiously use an RSS reader, it might feel strange to hear me speak about it in the past tense, but RSS has died.* And so has the concept of subscribing.

Just look at the top referring sources of traffic to major websites and blogs. Cumulatively, these referring sources almost always account for more visitors than the site's direct traffic (i.e., people who typed in the URL). Though it varies from site to site, the biggest sources of traffic are, usually, in this order: Google, Facebook, Twitter. The viewers were sent directly to a specific article for a disposable purpose: they're not subscribers; they are seekers or glancers.

83

---

*RSS readers Bloglines and NewsGator are in the deadpool. Apple's Mountain Lion OS X doesn't include RSS, and Google no longer features Reader in its top-level navigation. The latest versions of the Firefox browser don't even have RSS buttons. Twitter and Facebook both stopped supporting direct RSS feeds. And the death of RSS has been heralded in a million headlines.

This is great news for a media manipulator, bad news for everyone else. The death of subscription means that instead of attempting to provide value to you, the longtime reader, blogs are constantly chasing Other Readers—the mythical reader out in viral land. Instead of providing quality day in and day out, writers chase big hits like a sexy scandal or a funny video meme. Bloggers aren't interested in building up consistent, loyal readerships via RSS or paid subscriptions, because what they really need are the types of stories that will do hundreds of thousands or millions of pageviews. They need stories that will sell.

A popular article on the technology blog *Ars Technica* blares the headline: "Why keeping up with RSS is poisonous to productivity, sanity."[1] Poisonous? What sounds poisonous to me is the writer's newly RSS-free life, which included scanning social media and new aggregators at constant intervals throughout the day, because she knew "if something *truly important or controversial blew up*, I'd hear about it instantly via Twitter and our loyal readers" [emphasis mine].

Blogs must fight to be that story. You can provide them the ammunition. Getting something "controversial" to blow up is easy, and it's the tactic I prefer to use over doing something "important." With limited resources and the constraints of a tight medium, there are only a handful of options: sensationalism, extremism, sex, scandal, hatred. The media manipulator knows that bloggers know that these things sell—so that's what we sell them.

Whereas subscriptions are about trust, single-use traffic is all immediacy and impulse—even if the news has to be distorted to trigger it. Our news is what rises, and what rises is what spreads, and what spreads is what makes us angry or makes us laugh. Our media diet is quickly transformed into junk food, fake stories engineered by people like me to be consumed and passed around. It is the refined and processed sugars of the information food pyramid—out of the ordinary, unnatural, and deliberately sweetened.

Inside the chaos, it is easy to mislead. Only the exciting, sensational stuff finds readers—the stories that "blow up." Reporters don't have time for follow-ups or reasoned critiques, only quick hits. Blogs are all chasing the same types of stories, the mass media chase blogs, and the readers are following both of them—and everyone is led astray.

The reason subscription (and RSS) was abandoned was because in a subscription economy the users are in control. In the one-off model, the competition might be more vicious, but it is on the terms of the publisher. Having followers instead of subscribers—where readers have to check back on sites often and are barraged with a stream of refreshing content laden with ads—is much better for their bottom line.

RSS never became truly mainstream for this reason. It's antithetical to the interests of the people who would need to push readers toward using it. It comes as no surprise that despite glowing reports from satisfied readers and major investments from Google and others that it would not be able to make it. So today, as RSS buttons disappear from browsers and blogs, just know that this happened on purpose, so that readers could be deceived more easily.

85

IX

TACTIC #6

MAKE IT ALL ABOUT THE HEADLINE

A [*Huffington Post*] story . . . headlined: "Obama Rejects Rush Limbaugh Golf Match: Rush 'Can Play With Himself.'" It's digital nirvana: two highly searched proper nouns followed by a smutty entendre, a headline that both the red and the blue may be compelled to click, and the readers of the site can have a laugh while the headline delivers great visibility out on the web.

—DAVID CARR, *NEW YORK TIMES*

FOR MEDIA THAT LIVES AND DIES BY CLICKS (THE ONE-Off Problem) it all comes down to the headline. It's what catches the attention of the public—yelled by a newsboy or seen on a search engine. In a one-off world there is nothing more important than the pitch to prospective buyers. And they need many exciting new pitches every day, each louder and more compelling than the last. Even if reality is not so interesting.

That's where I come in. I make up the news; blogs make up the headline.

Although it seems easy, headline writing is an incredibly difficult task. The editor has to reduce an entire story down to just a few units of text—turning a few hundred- or thousand-word piece into just a few words, period. In the process it must express the article's central ideas in an exciting way.

According to Gabriel Snyder, the former managing editor of Gawker Media and now an editor at the traffic powerhouse TheAtlantic.com, blog headlines are "naked little creatures that have to go out into the world to stand and fight on their own." Readers and revenue depend on the headline's ability to win this fight.

In the days of the yellow press the front pages of the *World* and the *Journal* went head to head every day, driving each other to greater and greater extremes. As a publisher, William Randolph Hearst obsessed over his headlines, tweaking their wording, writing and rewriting them, riding his editors until they were perfect. Each one, he thought, could steal another one hundred readers away from another paper.[1]

It worked. As a young man Upton Sinclair remembered hearing the newsboys shouting "Extra!" and saw the headline "War Declared!" splashed across the front page of Hearst's *New York Evening Journal.* He parted with his hard-earned pennies and read eagerly, only to find something rather different between what he'd thought and what he'd bought. It was actually: "War (may be) Declared (soon)."[2]

They won, he lost. That same hustle happens online every day. Each blog is competing not just to be *the* leader on a particular story but against all the other topics a reader could potentially commit to reading about (and also against checking e-mail, chatting with friends, and watching videos, or even pornography). So here we are in 2012, on our fancy MacBooks and wireless Internet, stuck again with the same bogus headlines we had in the nineteenth century.

From today:*

Naked Lady Gaga Talks Drugs and Celibacy

Hugh Hefner: I Am Not a Sex Slave Rapist in a Palace of Poop

The Top Nine Videos of Babies Farting and/or Laughing with Kittens

How Justin Bieber Caught a Contagious Syphilis Rumor

WATCH: Heartbroken Diddy Offers to Expose Himself to Chelsea Handler

Little Girl Slaps Mom with Piece of Pizza, Saves Life

Penguin Shits on Senate Floor

---

*My favorite: The *Washington Post* accidentally published a headline to an article about weather preparedness: "SEO Headline Here" (SEO stands for search engine optimization).

Now compare those to some of these classic headlines from 1898 to 1903:

WAR WILL BE DECLARED IN FIFTEEN MINUTES

AN ORGY OF GRAY-HAIRED MEN, CALLOW YOUTHS, GAMBLERS, ROUGHS, AND PAINTED WOMEN—GENERAL DRUNKENNESS—FIGHTS AT INTERVALS—IT WAS VICE'S CARNIVAL.

COULDN'T SELL HIS EAR, OLD MAN SHOOTS HIMSELF

OWL FRIGHTENS WOMAN TO DEATH IN HOSPITAL

BULLDOG TRIES TO KILL YOUNG GIRL HE HATES

CAT GAVE TENANTS NIGHTLY "CREEPS"

As magician Ricky Jay once put it, "People respond to and are deceived by the same things they were a hundred years ago." Only today the headlines aren't being yelled on busy street corners but on noisy news aggregators and social networks.

In a subscription model the headlines of any one article compete only with the other articles included in the publication. The articles on the front page compete with those on the inside pages, and perhaps with the notion of putting down the paper entirely, but they do not, for the most part, compete head to head with the front pages of other newspapers. The subscription takes care of that—you already made your choice. As a result, the job of the headline writer for media consumed by subscription is relatively easy. The reader has already paid for the publication, so they'll probably read the content in front of them.

The predicament of an online publisher today is that it has no such buffer. Its creative solution, as it was one hundred years ago, is exaggeration and lies and bogus tags like EXLUSIVE, EXTRA, UNPRECEDENTED,[*] and PHOTOS in the requisite CAPITAL LETTERS. They overstate their stories, latching on to the most compelling angles and parading themselves in front of the public like a prostitute. They are more than willing for PR people and marketers to be their partners in crime.

PICK ME, PICK ME!

In 1971, the *New York Times*, a subscription paper, had a big story on their hands. A disillusioned government analyst named Daniel Ellsberg leaked thousands of documents, now known as the Pentagon Papers, proving that the United States had systematically deceived the public and the world to go to war with Vietnam.

Could a one-off paper have gotten away with this headline: "Vietnam Archive: A Consensus to Bomb Developed Before '64 Election, Study Says"?

Because that's what the *New York Times* ran, still successfully reaching everyone in the country with the big news. They could afford to be reasoned, calm, and circumspect while still aggressively pursuing the story, despite the shameful efforts of the U.S government to block its publication. The truth and significance of the Pentagon Papers were enough.

Compare this to a headline I conned *Jezebel* into writing for a non-event: "Exclusive: American Apparel's Rejected Halloween Costume Ideas (American Appalling)."[3] It did nearly one hundred thousand pageviews. Not only was the headline overstated, the leak was *fake*. I just had one of my employees send over some extra photos I couldn't use for legal reasons.

---

[*]This one is my favorite, because the thing always happens to be not only *not* unprecedented but hilariously pedestrian.

Outside of the subscription model, headlines are not intended to represent the contents of articles but to *sell them*—to win the fight for attention against an infinite number of other blogs or papers. It must so captivate the customer that they click or plunk down the money to buy it. Each headline competes with every other headline. On a blog, every page is the front page. It's no wonder that the headlines of the yellow press and the headlines of blogs run to such extremes. It is a desperate fight. Life or death.

Newspapers from the stable period not only had plainly stated headlines, but they also had a tradition of witty headlines. Readers had time to get subtle jokes. Things are a little different now. As they say, Google doesn't laugh. According to CEO Eric Schmidt, Google News sends more than a billion clicks a month to newspapers and another three billion clicks through its search and other services. In other words, Google's sense of humor matters the most.[4]

Follow a story through Google News and you'll see. The service begins by displaying twenty or so main news stories from which a reader may choose. I may read one article, or I may read five, but I likely will not read all, so each one vies for my attention—to scream, in so many words, "Pick Me! Pick Me! Pick Me!" Google News displays the story from a handful of outlets under each of those bold headlines. If the main headline is from CNN, the smaller headlines underneath may be from Fox News or the *Washington Post* or Wikipedia or TalkingPointsMemo. Each outlet's headline screams "Pick Me! Pick Me!" and Google alludes to the rest of the iceberg lurking beneath under these chosen few: "All 522 news articles." How does one stand out against five hundred other articles? Its scream of "No, Pick Me! Pick Me!" must be the loudest and most extreme.

Andrew Malcolm, creator of the *Los Angeles Times*'s massive *Top of the Ticket* political blog (thirty-three million readers in two years), specifically asks himself before writing a headline, "How can we make our item stick out from all the other ones?" And from this bold approach to editorial ethics comes proud headlines such as: "Hillary Clinton Shot a Duck Once" and "McCain Comes Out Against Deadly Nuclear Weapons, Obama Does Too." I'm not cherry-picking: *That's what he chose to brag about in a book of advice to aspiring bloggers.*

"We do ironic headlines, smart headlines, and work hard to make very serious stories as interesting as we can," Arianna Huffington told the *New York Times*.[5] "We pride ourselves on bringing in our community on which headlines work best."

They also do their headlines in a massive thirty-two-point font. By best, Huffington does not mean the one that represents the story better. The question is not "Was this headline accurate?" but "Was it clicked more than the others?" The headlines must work for the publisher, not the reader. Yahoo!'s homepage, for example, tests more than forty-five thousand unique combinations of story headlines and photos every five minutes.[6] They too pride themselves in how they display the best four main stories they can, but I don't think their complicated, four-years-in-the-making algorithm shares any human's definition of that word.

SPELLING IT OUT FOR THEM

It should be clear what types of headlines blogs are interested in. It's not pretty, but if that's what they want, give it to them. You don't really have a choice. They aren't going to write about you, your clients, or your story unless it can be turned into a headline that will drive traffic.

You figured out the best way to do this when you were twelve years old and wanted something from your parents: Come up with the idea and let them think they were the ones who came up with it. Basically, write the headline—or hint at the options—in your e-mail or press release or whatever you give to the blogger and let them steal it. Make it so obvious and enticing that there is no way they can pass it up. Hell, make them tone it down. They'll be so happy to have the headline that they won't bother to check whether it's true or not.

Their job is to think about the headline above all else. The medium and their bosses force them to. So that's where you make the sale. Only the reader gets stuck with the buyer's remorse.

TACTIC #7

KILL 'EM WITH PAGEVIEW KINDNESS

> A status update that is met with no likes (or a clever tweet that isn't retweeted) becomes the equivalent of a joke met with silence. It must be rethought and rewritten. And so we don't show our true selves online, but a mask designed to conform to the opinions of those around us.
>
> —NEIL STRAUSS, *WALL STREET JOURNAL*

THE BREAKTHROUGH FOR BLOGGING AS A BUSINESS was the ability to track what gets read and what doesn't. From *Gawker* to *The Guardian*, sites of all sizes are open about their dependence on pageview statistics for editorial decisions.

Editors and analysts know what spreads, what draws traffic, and what doesn't, and they direct their employees accordingly. The *Wall Street Journal* uses traffic data to decide which articles will be displayed on its homepage and for how long. Low-tracking articles are removed; heat-seeking articles get moved up. A self-proclaimed web-first paper like the *Christian Science Monitor* scours Google Trends for story ideas that help the paper "ride the Google wave." Places like Yahoo! and Demand Media commission their stories in real time based on search data. Other sites take topics trending on Twitter and Techmeme and scurry to get a post up in order to be included in the list of articles for a particular event. Even tiny one-person blogs eagerly check their stat counters for the first sign of a spike.

Bloggers publish constantly in order to hit their pageview goals or quotas, so when you can give them something that gets them even one view closer to that goal, you're serving their interests while serving yours. To ignore these numbers in an era of pageview journalism is business suicide for bloggers and media manipulators. And anything that pervasive presents opportunities for abuse.

I see it like this: The Top 10 "Most Read" or "Most Popular" section that now exists on most large websites is a compass for the editors and publishers. Mess with the magnet inside the compass and watch as its owner goes wildly off track.

As economists love to say: incentives matter. What makes the Most Popular or Most E-mailed leaderboard on Salon.com or the *New York Times* is a clear directive that tells writers what kinds of stories to head toward. It doesn't matter that the stories suck or if they have nothing to do with the publisher's mission. This is about getting pageviews—by whatever means.

THE DISTURBING SCIENCE

Yellow papers had their own circulation dragons; instead of celebrity slideshows, these papers had staples like hating black people, preposterous Wall Street conspiracies, and gruesome rape and murder stories. But while in the past decisions were guided by an editor's intuitive sense of what would pander to their audience, today it is a science.

Sites employ full-time data analysts to ensure that the absolute worst is brought out of the audience. *Gawker* displays its stats on a big screen in the middle of their newsroom. The public can look at it too at Gawker.com/stats. Millions of visitors and millions of dollars are to be had from content and traffic analysis. It just happens that these statistics become the handles by which manipulators can pick up and hijack the news.

It's too transparent and simple for that not to be the case. For some blog empires, the content-creation process is now a pageview-centric checklist that asks writers to think of everything *except* "Is what I am making any good?" AOL is one of these organizations, as it emphatically (and embarrassingly) outlined in a memo titled "The AOL Way." If writers and editors want to post something on the AOL platform they must ask themselves:

> *How many pageviews will this content generate? Is this story SEO-winning for in-demand terms? How can we modify it to include more terms? Can we bring in contributors with their own followers? What CPM will this content earn? How much will this content cost to produce? How long will it take to produce?*[1]

And other such stupid questions.

Even the famed *New Yorker* writer Susan Orlean has admitted her gravitational pull toward the stories on the Most Popular lists, as a reader and as writer. "Why, I wonder, should the popularity of a news story matter to me?" she writes.

Does it mean it's a good story or just a seductive one? Isn't my purpose on this earth, at least professionally, precisely to read the most unpopular stories? Shouldn't I ignore this list? Shouldn't I roam through the news unconcerned and maybe even uninformed of how many other people read this same news and "voted" for it?[2]

But in the end these guilty pangs cannot win out. Amid the clutter and chaos of a busy site, the lists pop. The headlines scream out to be clicked. Those articles seem more interesting than everything else. Plus, hey, they appear to be vetted by the rest of the world. That can occasionally be a good thing, as Orlean points out, but is it worth it?

Sometimes they contain a nice surprise, a story I might not have noticed otherwise. Sometimes they simply confirm the obvious, the story you know is in the air and on everybody's mind. Never do they include a story that is quiet and ordinary but wonderful to read. *[emphasis mine]*

That great insight is often buried in material that seems quiet and ordinary does not matter to blogging. That wouldn't get clicks.

I'm fond of a line by Nicolas Chamfort, a French writer, who believed that popular public opinion was the absolute worst kind of opinion. "One can be certain," he said, "that every generally held idea, every received notion, will be idiocy because it has been able to appeal to the majority." To a marketer, it's just as well, because idiocy is easier to create than anything else.

THEIR METRICS, YOUR ADVANTAGE

What gets measured gets managed, or so the saying goes. So what do publishers measure? Out of everything that can possibly be measured, blogs have picked a handful of the most straightforward and cost-effective metrics to rely on (wonderfulness is not one of them). They choose to measure only what can be clearly communicated to their writers as goals. Like officers in Vietnam ordered to report body counts back to Washington as indicators of success or failure, these ill-conceived metrics—based on simplicity more than anything else—make bloggers do awful things.

To understand bloggers, rephrase the saying as: "Simplistic measurements matter." Like, did a shitload of people see it? Must be good. Was there a raging comments section going? Awesome! Did the story get picked up on *Gawker*? It made the *Drudge Report*? Yes! In practice, this is all blogs really have time to look for, and it's easy to give it to them.

I exploit these pseudo-metrics all the time. If other blogs have covered something, competitors rush to copy them, because they assume there is traffic in it. As a result, getting coverage on one site can simply be a matter of sending those links to an unoriginal blogger. That those links were scored under false pretenses hardly matters. How could anyone tell? Showing that a story you want written is connected to a popular or search engine–friendly topic (preferably one the site already has posts about) does the same thing. However tenuous the connection, it satisfies the pageview impulse and gives the blogger excuse to send readers to their stories. You've done something that gets them paid.

Remember, some bloggers have to churn out as many as a dozen posts a day. That's not because twelve is some lucky number but because they need to meet serious pageview goals for the site. Not every story is intended to be a home run—a collection of singles, doubles, and triples adds up too. Pageview journalism is about scale. Sites *have* to publish multiple stories every few minutes to make a profit, and why shouldn't your story be one of them?

Once your story has gotten coverage, one of the best ways to turn yourself into a favorite and regular subject is to make it clear your story is a reliable traffic draw. If you're a brand, then post the story to your company Twitter and Facebook accounts and put it on your website. This inflates the stats in your favor and encourages more coverage down the road. There are also services that allow you to "buy traffic," sending thousands of visitors to a specific page. At the penny-per-click rates of StumbleUpon and Outbrain, one hundred dollars means a rush of one thousand people or more—illusory confirmations to the blogger that you are newsworthy. The stat counters on these sites make no distinctions between fake and real views, nor does anyone care enough to dig deep into the sources of traffic. The lure of the indirect bribe is all that matters.

But be careful: This beast can bite you back if it feels like it. Once sites see there is traffic in something, they do not stop—often falling to new lows in the process. Companies enjoy the spotlight at first, until the good news runs out and the blog begins to rely on increasingly spurious sources to keep the high-traffic topic on their pages. What begins as positive press often ends in the fabrication of scandals or utter bullshit. As Brandon Mendelson wrote for *Forbes*, the lure of pageviews takes blogs to places they otherwise never should have gone:

> *A couple of years ago, I quit blogging for Mashable after they had posted the suicide note to the guy who flew a helicopter into a government building in Texas. Pete's [the publisher] response to me quitting over the suicide note was, pretty much, "Other blogs were doing it." He never explained why a Web / Tech / Social Media guide would post a crazy person's suicide note.*
>
> *"Who wants to say 'I did it for the page views' out loud?"*[3]

The answer to that question is "almost every blogger."

Why do you think the *Huffington Post* once ran a front-page story about what time the Super Bowl would start? The query was a popular one on game day, and the post generated incredible amounts of traffic. It may have been a pointless story for a political and news blog like the *Huffington Post* to write, but the algorithm justified it—along with the rest of their "the world is round" stories and well-timed celebrity slideshows.

This content is attractive to blogs because the traffic it does is both measurable and predictable. Like a fish lure, it is not difficult to mimic the appearance of these kinds of stories and for unthinking writers to fall for it. They are looking to eat. They know what key words are lucrative, what topics get links, and what type of writing gets comments, and they'll bite without asking themselves whether the version of events you've presented is just a barbed trick.

Metrics and measurements are a comfort to publishers. It takes the uncertainty out of their business. What can't be measured—or requires true editorial judgment—is scary and requires financial risk.

CAN'T STAND THE SILENCE

"I posted something but nobody responded. What does it mean?" It's a question you've probably asked yourself after nobody liked the Facebook status with your big news, or no friends commented on your new Facebook photo album. Maybe you thought that tweet you wrote was hilarious, and you're not sure why it wasn't retweeted—not even once. This innocent little question is just about hurt feelings for you, but for pageview-hungry publishers, it's what keeps them up at night.

Early Usenet users called this Warnock's Dilemma, after its originator, Bryan Warnock. The dilemma began with mailing lists but now applies to message boards (why is no one responding to the thread), blogs (why hasn't anyone commented?), and websites (why isn't this generating any chatter?). The answer to any of these questions could just as easily be satisfaction as apathy, and publishers want to know which it is.

This dilemma was actually predicted by Orson Scott Card in the 1985 book *Ender's Game*. Peter Wiggin creates the online persona of a demagogue named Locke and began to test the waters by posting deliberately inflammatory comments. Why write this way? his sister asked. Peter replied: "We can't hear how our style of writing is working unless we get responses—and if we're bland, no one will answer."

Card understood that it is incredibly difficult to interpret silence in a constructive way. Warnock's Dilemma, for its part, poses several interpretations:

1. The post is correct, well-written information that needs no follow-up commentary. There's nothing more to say except, "Yeah, what he said."
2. The post is complete and utter nonsense, and no one wants to waste the energy or bandwidth to even point this out.
3. No one read the post, for whatever reason.
4. No one understood the post but won't ask for clarification, for whatever reason.
5. No one cares about the post, for whatever reason.[4]

If you're a publisher, this checklist causes more headaches than it cures. It's all bad. Possibility number one is unprofitable: We know that practical utility doesn't spread, and posts that don't generate follow-up commentary are dead in the link economy. Possibility number two is embarrassing and damaging to the brand. Possibility number three is bad for obvious reasons. Possibility number four means the post was probably too ambitious, too academic, and too certain for anyone to risk questions. Possibility number five means somebody chose the wrong topic.

Whatever the cause, the silence all means the same thing: no comments, no links, no traffic, *no money*. It lands the publisher firmly in a territory labeled "utterly unprofitable." Jonah Peretti, for his part, has his bloggers at *BuzzFeed* track their failures closely. If news doesn't go viral or get feedback, then the news needs to be changed. If news does go viral, it means the story was a success—whether or not it was accurate, in good taste, or done well.

That is where the opportunity lies: Blogs are so afraid of silence that the flimsiest of evidence can confirm they're on the right track. You can provide this by leaving fake comments to articles about you or your company from blocked IP addresses—good and bad to make it clear that there is a hot debate. Send fake e-mails to the reporter, positive and negative. This rare kind of feedback cements the impression that you or your company make for high-valence material, and the blog should be covering you. Like Peter Wiggin, publishers don't care what they say as long as it isn't bland or ignored. But by avoiding the bad kind of silence prompted by poor content, they avoid the good kind that results from the type of writing that makes people think but not say, "Yeah, what he said. I'm glad I read this article."

Professional bloggers understand this dilemma far better than the casual or amateur one, according to an analysis done by Nate Silver of unpaid versus paid articles on the *Huffington Post*. Over a three-day period, 143 political posts by amateurs received 6,084 comments, or an average of just 43 comments per article (meaning that many got zero). Over that same period, Huffington Post published 161 *paid* political articles (bought from other sites, written by staff writers, or other copyrighted content) that accumulated more than 133,000 comments combined. That amounts to more than 800 per article, or twenty times what the unpaid bloggers were able to accomplish.[5]

According to *Huffington Post*'s pageview strategy, the paid articles are indisputably better, because they generated more comments and traffic (like a 2009 article about the Iranian protests that got *96,281 comments*). In a sane system, a political article that generated thousands of comments would be an indicator that something went wrong. It means the conversation descended into an unproductive debate about abortion or immigration, or devolved into mere complaining. But in the broken world of the web, it is the mark of a professional.

A blog like the *Huffington Post* is not going to *pay* for something that is met with silence, even the good kind. They're certainly not going to promote it or display it on the front page, since it would reduce the opportunity to generate pageviews. The *Huffington Post* does not wish to be the definitive account of a story or inform people—since the reaction to that is simple satisfaction. Blogs deliberately do not want to help.

You're basically asking for favors if you try to get blogs to cover something that isn't going to drive pageviews and isn't going to garner clear responses. Blogs are not in the business of doing favors—even if all you're asking is for them to print the truth. Trust me, I have tried. I have shown them factories of workers whose jobs are at risk because of inaccurate online coverage. I have begged them to be fair for these poor people's sake. If that didn't make a difference, nothing will.

BREAKING THE NEWS

I don't know if blogs enjoy being tricked. All I know is that they don't care enough to put a stop to it. The response to sketchy anonymous tips, in my experience, is Thanks, a lot more often than Prove it.

Nobody is fooling anyone. That's not the game—because sites don't have any interest in what they post, as long as it delivers pageviews. Samuel Axon, formerly an editor at *Mashable* and *Engadget*, complained that the rules by which blogs get "traffic, high impressions, and strong ad revenues betray journalists and the people who need them at every turn." This is only partially true. They betray the *ethical* journalists and earnest readers. As far as bloggers and publishers looking to get rich or manipulators eager to influence the news are concerned, the system is just fine.

Pageview journalism puffs blogs up and fattens them on a steady diet of guaranteed traffic pullers of a mediocre variety that require little effort to produce. It pulls writers and publishers to the extremes, and only to the extremes—the shocking and the already known. Practicing pageview journalism means that a publisher never has to worry about seeing "(0) Comments" at the bottom of a post. With tight deadlines and tight margins, any understanding of the audience is helpful guidance. For marketers, this is refreshingly predictable.

It just happens that this metric-driven understanding breaks the news. The cynicism is self-fulfilling and self-defeating; as the quip famously attributed to Henry Ford points out, if he'd listened to what his customers "said" they wanted, all "we'd have ended up with was a faster horse."

Pageview journalism treats people by what they *appear* to want—from data that is unrepresentative to say the least—and gives them this and only this until they have forgotten that there could be anything else. It takes the audience at their worst and makes them worse. And then, when criticized, publishers throw up their hands as if to say, "We wish people liked better stuff too," as if they had nothing to do with it.

Well, they do.

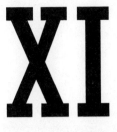

XI

TACTIC #8

USE THE TECHNOLOGY
AGAINST ITSELF

{ Actions are constrained by income, time, imperfect
memory and calculating capacities, and other
limited resources, and also by the available
opportunities in the economy and elsewhere. . . .
Different constraints are decisive for different
situations, but the most fundamental constraint is
limited time.

—GARY BECKER, NOBEL PRIZE–WINNING
ECONOMIST }

SOMETIMES I SEE A PREPOSTEROUSLY INACCURATE blog post about a client (or myself) and I take it personally, thinking that it was malicious. Or I wonder why they didn't just pick up the phone and call me to get the other side of the story. I occasionally catch myself complaining about sensational articles or crummy writing, and place the blame on an editor or a writer. It's hard for me to understand the impulse to reduce an important issue to a stupid quote or unfunny one-liner.

This is an unproductive attitude. It forgets the structure and constraints of blogging as a medium and how these realities explain almost everything blogs do. Where there is little volition, there should be little bitterness or blame. Only understanding, which, I have learned, can be turned to advantage

The way news is found online more or less determines what is found. The way the news must be presented—in order to meet the technical constraints of the medium and the demands of its readers—determines the news itself. It's basically a cliché at this point, but that doesn't change the fact that Marshall McLuhan was right: The medium *is* the message.

Think about television. We're all tired of the superficiality of cable news and its insistence on reducing important political issues into needless conflict between two annoying talking heads. But there's a simple reason for this, as media critic Eric Alterman explained in *Sound and Fury: The Making of the Punditocracy*. TV is a visual medium, he said, so to ask for the audience to think about something it cannot see would be suicide. If it were possible to put an abstract idea to film, producers would happily show that instead of pithy soundbites. But it isn't, so conflict, talking heads, and b-roll footage are all you'll get. The values of television, Alterman realized, behave like a dictator, exerting their rule over the kind of information that can be transmitted across the channels.

Blogs aren't any different. The way the medium works essentially predetermines what bloggers can publish and how exactly they must do it. Blogs are just as logical as the television producers Alterman criticized; it's just a matter of understanding their unique logic.

To know what the medium demands of bloggers is to be able to predict, and then co-opt, how they act.

HEMMED IN ON ALL SIDES

Why do blogs constantly chase new stories? Why do they update so much? Why are posts so short? A look at their development makes it clear: Bloggers don't have a choice.

Early bloggers, according to Scott Rosenberg in his book on the history of blogging, *Say Everything: How Blogging Began, What It's Becoming, and Why It Matters,* had to answer one important question: How do our readers know what's new?

To solve this, programmers first tried "New!" icons, but that didn't work. It was too difficult to tell what the icons meant across many blogs— on one site "New!" might mean the latest thing published and on another it could be anything written within the last month. What they needed was a uniform way to organize the content that would be the same across the web. Tim Berners-Lee, one of the founders of the web, set a procedure in motion that would be copied by almost everyone after him: New stuff goes at the top.

The reverse chronological order on one of the web's first sites—called "stacking" by programmers—became the de facto standard for blogging. Because the web evolved through imitation and collaboration, most sites simply adopted the form of their predecessors and peers. Stacking developed as an implicit standard, and that has had extraordinary implications. When content is stacked, it sets a very clear emphasis on the present. For the blogger, the time stamp is like an expiration date. It also creates considerable pressure to be short and immediate.

In 1996, three years before the word "blogger" was even invented, protoblogger Justin Hall wrote to his readers at Links.net that he'd been criticized at a party for not posting enough, and for not putting his posts right on the front page. "Joey said he used to love my pages," Hall wrote,

107

"but now there's too many layers to my links. At Suck(.com) you get sucked in immediately, no layers to content."[1]

It's really an illustrative moment, if you think about it. In one of of the first data-stamped posts on a blog ever, Hall was already alluding to the pressures the medium was putting on content. His post was ninety-three words and basically a haiku. This was not a man of too many "layers." But Suck.com had just sold for thirty thousand dollars, so who was Hall to argue? So he resolved to put "a little somethin' new" at the top of his website every single day.

We can trace a straight line from this conversation in 1996 to the post-per-day minimums of blogs like *Gizmodo* and *Engadget* in 2005, and to today, when authors of guides like *Blogger Bootcamp* tell prospective bloggers that the experience of publishing more than twenty thousand blog posts taught them that "Rule #1" is "Always Be Blogging," and that the best sites are "updated daily, if not hourly."

Since content is constantly expiring, and bloggers face the Sisyphean task of trying to keep their sites fresh, creating a newsworthy event out of nothing becomes a daily occurrence. The structure of blogging warps the perspective of everyone who exists in this space—why would a blogger spend much time on a post that will very shortly be pushed below view? Understandably, no one wants to be the fool who wasted his or her time working on something nobody read. The message is clear: The best way to get traffic is to publish as much as possible, as quickly as possible, and as simply as possible.

The Huffington Post Complete Guide to Blogging has a simple rule of thumb: Unless readers can see the end of your post coming around eight hundred words in, they're going to stop. Scrolling is a pain, as is feeling like an article will never end. This gives writers around eight hundred words to make their point—a rather tight window. Even eight hundred words is pushing it, the *Huffington Post* says, since a block of text that big on the web can be intimidating. A smart blogger, they note, will break it up with graphics or photos, and definitely some links.

In a retrospective of his last ten years of blogging, publisher Om Malik of *GigaOM* bragged that he'd written over eleven thousand posts and 2 million words in the last decade. Which, while translating into three posts a day, means the average post was just 215 words long. But that's nothing compared to the ideal *Gawker* item. Nick Denton told a potential hire in 2008 that it was "one hundred words long. Two hundred, max. Any good idea," he said, "can be expressed at that length."[2]

Preposterously faulty intuition like this can be seen across the web, on blogs and sites of all types. The pressure to keep content visually appealing and ready for impulse readers is a constant suppressant on length, regardless of what is cut to make it happen. In a University of Kentucky study of blogs about cancer, researchers found that a full 80 percent of the blog posts they analyzed contained fewer than five hundred words.[3] The average number of words per post was 335, short enough to make the articles on the *Huffington Post* seem like lengthy manuscripts. I don't care what Nick Denton says; I'm pretty sure that the complexities of *cancer* can't be properly expressed in 100 words. Or 200, or 335, or 500, for that matter.

Even the most skilled writer would have trouble conveying the side effects of chemotherapy or discussing the possibility of death with your children in just a handful of words. Yet here they are—the majority of posts barely filling it three pages, doubled spaced, in a twelve-point font. They wouldn't even take three minutes to read.

People are busy, and computers are wrought with distraction. It would be crazy to think that blogs don't adapt their content around these facts. The average time users spend on a site like *Jezebel* is a little over a minute. On the technology and personal efficiency blog *Lifehacker*, they can average less than ten seconds. The common wisdom is that the site has one second to make the hook. *One second.* The bounce rate on blogs, or the percentage of people who leave the site immediately, without clicking anything, is incredibly high. Analysis of news sites has the average bounce rate pushing well north of 50 percent. When the statistics show a medium to be so fickle that half the audience starts leaving as soon as they get there, there is no question that this dynamic is going to seriously impact content choices.

Studies that have tracked the eye movements of people browsing the web show the same fickleness. The biggest draw of eyeballs is the headline, of which viewers usually see only the first few words before moving on. After users break off from the headline their glance tends to descend downward along the left hand column, scanning for sentences that catch their attention. If nothing does, they leave. What slows this dismissive descent is the form of the article—small, short paragraphs (one to two sentences versus three to five) seem to encourage slightly higher reading rates, as does a bolded introduction or subheadline (occasionally called a deck). What blogger is going to decide they're above gimmicks such as bulleted lists when it's precisely those gimmicks that seem to keep readers on the page for a few priceless seconds longer?

Jakob Nielsen, the reigning guru of web usability, according to *Fortune* magazine, and the author of twelve books on the subject, advises sites to follow a simple rule: Forty percent of every article must be cut.[4] But despair not, because according to his calculations, when chopped thus the average article loses only 30 percent of its value. *Oh, only 30 percent!* It's the kind of math publishers go through every day. As long as the equation works out in their favor, it's worth doing. What does it matter if the readers get stuck with the losses?

Once at a lunch meeting with an editor of *Racked NY*, a blog about retail shopping in New York City, the incredibly influential blogger told me that she did all her shopping online. "So you wear our clothes but you never go in our stores?" I asked, since she was wearing American Apparel at the meeting. "I just don't have time to go shopping anymore." There was a store within blocks of her office and two others on her way home. This was *literally* her beat. I guess it doesn't matter anyway; where would she put personal observations in a two-hundred-word post even if she had them?

I once watched as blogger doing a story on me for the site *Mediagazer* tried to do her fact-checking by simply tweeting out into the universe. After watching her hilarious attempts to "verify [my] credibility" by asking people I've never worked with and never met, I finally logged onto Twitter to send my first message in years: "@LyraMckee Have you thought about emailing me? ryan.holiday@gmail.com."

Why would she? Though I'd actually be able to answer her questions, tweeting out loud was easier than e-mailing me, and it meant she didn't have to wait for my response. Plus, I'm boring and would have rained all over her speculation parade.

When Nielsen talks about cutting 40 percent of an article, actually knowing anything about what they're talking about is what bloggers leave on the cutting-room floor. As a manipulator, that's fine with me. It makes it easier to spin or even to lie. It's not like I have to worry about them verifying it. They don't have time for anything like that. A writer has minimums they must hit, and chasing a story that won't make it on the site is an expensive error. So it's not surprising that bloggers stick to eight hundred or fewer word posts about stories they *know* will generate traffic.

Jack Fuller, a former editor and publisher of the *Chicago Tribune*, once admonished a group of newspaper editors by saying, "I don't know about your world, but the one I live in does not shape itself so conveniently to anybody's platform."[5] For bloggers it would be nice if life was all exciting headlines and a clean eight hundred words, and happened to self-organize all its juicy bits down the left-hand column. The world is far too messy, too nuanced and complicated, and frankly far less exciting for that to be the case. Only a fool addicted to his laptop would fail to see that the material demanded by the constraints of their medium and the one reality gives them rarely match.

On the other hand, I quite like these fools.

MAKING LEMONADE

Let's just say Fuller's advice does not have a wide following online, particularly his reminder that reporters owe a "duty to reality, not to platforms."

In fact, bloggers believe the opposite. And that sucks for everyone—except me, when I am doing my job. Because once you understand the limitations of the platform, the constraints can be used against the people who depend on it. The technology can be turned on itself.

I remember promoting one author whose book had just spent five weeks on the *New York Times* bestseller list (meaning people were willing to *pay* for it in one medium). When I was trying to post material from the book on various popular blogs, it became clear that it was just too long. So we got rid of the thoroughness and the supporting arguments and reduced it down to the most basic, provocative parts. One chapter—the same chapter people enjoyed fully in book form—had to be split up into *eight* separate posts. To get attention we had to cut it up into itty-bitty bites and spoon-feed it to readers and bloggers like babies.

If a blogger isn't willing or doesn't have the time to get off their ass to visit the stores they write about, that's their problem. It makes it that much easier to create my own version of reality. I will come to them with the story. I'll meet them on their terms, but their story will be filled with my terms. They won't take the time or show the interest to check with anyone else.

Blogs must—economically and structurally—distort the news in order for the format to work. As businesses, blogs can see the world through no other lens. The *format* is the problem. Or the perfect opportunity, depending on how you look at it.

XII

TACTIC #9

JUST MAKE STUFF UP (EVERYONE ELSE IS DOING IT)

> Those who have gone through the high school of reporterdom have acquired a new instinct by which they see and hear only that which can create a sensation, and accordingly their report becomes not only a careless one, but hopelessly distorted.
>
> —HUGO MUNSTERBERG, "THE CASE OF THE REPORTER," *McCLURE'S*, 1911

THE WORLD IS BORING, BUT THE NEWS IS EXCITING. IT'S a paradox of modern life. Journalists and bloggers are not magicians, but if you consider the material they've got to work with and the final product they crank out day in and day out, you must give them some credit. Shit becomes sugar.

If there is one special skill that journalists can claim, it is the ability to find the angle on any story. That the news is ever chosen over entertainment in the fight for attention is testament to their skill. High-profile bloggers rightly take great pride in this ability. This pride and this pressure is what we media manipulators use against them. Pride goeth before the fall.

No matter how dull, mundane, or complex a topic may be, a good reporter must find the angle. Bloggers, descended from these journalists, have to take it to an entirely new level. They need to find not only the angle but the click-driving headline, an eye-catching image; generate comments and links; and in some cases, squeeze in some snark. And they have to do it up to a dozen times a day without the help of an editor. They can smell the angle of a story like a shark smells blood in the water. Because the better the angle, the more the blogger gets paid.

As Drew Curtis of Fark.com says, "Problems occur when the journalist has to find an angle on a story that doesn't have one." It's not a new criticism, as the *Washington Post* wrote in 1899:

> The New York Times *has such abnormal keenness of vision that it is occasionally able to see that which does not exist. The ardency of its desire sometimes overcomes the coolness of its reasons, so that the thing it wants to see shows up just where it wants it to be, but in so intangible a form that no other eye is able to detect, no other mind finds ground to suspect its presence.*[1]

The difference between the *New York Times* and blogs a century later is that the *New York Times* was dealing with at least somewhat worthy material. Bloggers latch onto the most tenuous wisps of news on places like Facebook or Twitter and then apply their "abnormal keenness" to seeing what is not there. A writer for the *Mediabistro* blog *10,000 Words* once advised new bloggers that they could find good material by scanning community bulletin boards on craigslist for "what people are complaining about these days."[2] I'm not a sociologist, but I'm pretty sure that doesn't qualify as representative news. Considering that anyone can post anything on craigslist, this gives me a pretty good idea of how to create some fake local news. If they don't mind seeing what isn't there, I'm happy to help.

Angle-hunters sometimes come up empty. In a perfect world, writers should be able to explore a story lead, find it leads nowhere, and abandon it. But that luxury is not available online. As the veteran bloggers John Biggs and Charlie White put it in their book *Blogger Boot Camp*, there is "no topic too mundane that you can't pull a post out of it."

This is their logic. As a marketer, it's easy to fall in love with it.

Blogs will publish anything if you manufacture urgency around it. Give a blogger an illusionary twenty-minute head start over other media sources, and they'll write whatever you want, however you want it. Publicists love to promise blogs the exclusive on an announcement. The plural there is not an accident. You can give the same made-up exclusive to multiple blogs, and they'll all fall over themselves to publish first. Throw in an arbitrary deadline, like "We're going live with this on our website first thing in the morning," and even the biggest blogs will forget fact-checking and make bold pronouncements on your behalf.

Since bloggers *must* find an angle, they *always* do. Small news is made to look like big news. Nonexistent news is puffed up and made into news. The result is stories that look just like their legitimate counterparts, only their premise is wrong and says nothing. Such stories hook onto false pretenses, analyze a false subject, and inform falsely.

When I say it's okay for you to make stuff up because everybody else is doing it, I'm not kidding. MG Siegler is, and he's one of the dominant voices in tech blogging (*TechCrunch, PandoDaily*). According to him, most of what he and his competitors write is bullshit. "I won't try to put

115

some arbitrary label on it, like 80%," he once admitted, "but it's a lot. There's more bullshit than there is 100% pure, legitimate information."[3] I'd commend him for coming clean, but this uncharacteristic moment of self-awareness in 2012 hasn't seemed to have changed his blogging habits.

Shamelessness is a virtue in Siegler's world. It helps create nothing from something. It helps people at the *Huffington Post* stomach creating stories like: "Amy Winehouse's Untimely Death Is a Wake Up Call for Small Business Owners." The same holds true for reputable outlets too. They need only the slightest push to abandon all discretion, like the *Daily Mail* in the UK did when I had some deliberately provocative ads posted on the American Apparel website and pretended they were part of a new campaign. "Has American Apparel Gone too Far with 'Creepy' Controversial New Campaign?" the *Mail*'s headline read. According to *whom* had it gone too far? The article quotes "Some Tweeters."[4]

Thanks for the free publicity, guys! God knows what it would have cost to *pay* to run those full page ads in their paper.

Whatever will be more exciting, get more pageviews, *that* is what blogs will say happened. Like when *Gawker* bought a scoop from man who had pictures of a wild Halloween night with politician Christine O'Donnell. According to editor Remy Stern, the skeevy man's one concern was "that a tabloid would imply that they had sex, which they did not." The headline of the *Gawker* article was . . . drumroll . . . "I Had a One-Night Stand With Christine O'Donnell."[5]

ALWAYS WRONG, NEVER IN DOUBT

At American Apparel I had to deal with a pesky blog called *BNET* on which a "reporter" named Jim Edwards would troll through the company's financial disclosures and come up with some of the most fantastical misinterpretations I could imagine. We invited this on ourselves. Having made the company and its advertising such a juicy subject for gossip and entertainment blogs, it was natural that other pageview-hungry writers would try to get in on the game. Still, even as I knowingly fed that monster, I did not expect what happened with Edwards.

The man once asked critically—in a blog post, not a request for comment—why the company did not roll a last-minute necessary-to-make-payroll personal loan from Dov Charney at 6 percent interest into the larger loan from investors at 15 percent interest? (I assume the answer is so obvious to normal people like you that I do not need to explain how 6 percent is *less than* 15 percent.) Edwards posed this question not once but several times, in several posts, each with a more aggressive headline (e.g., "How American Apparel's CEO Turned a Crisis Into a Pay Raise").

From our conversation after he published his post:

> Me: "I don't know if you recall, but we discussed your asser-
> tion about the 6% interest rate. . . . You issued a correction
> on this story in 2009."
> Jim Edwards: "I do recall. But I'm quoting the status of Char-
> ney's loans directly from the proxy. Is the proxy wrong?"
> Me: YOUR BASIC UNDERSTANDING OF MATH IS
> WRONG!

He made bold speculations, like, "Why American Apparel CEO Must Resign" and "Is American Apparel's CEO Facing the Endgame?" In retrospect he seems even more foolish, since not a single one of his predictions turned out to be right. Or he'd concoct ridiculous conspiracy theories, including one that accused the company of timing controversial ads with SEC-mandated announcements to distract the public from corrupt dealings inside the company—and as proof would use the *very nonexistent loan scandal* he'd uncovered. (Not to mention that the ads weren't new, and some weren't even actual ads—just fake ones I'd leaked online.)

One kook is hardly a problem. But the obliviousness and earnest conviction a kook maintains in their own twisted logic makes for great material for other sites to disingenuously use by reporting on what the kook reported. As part of the CBS Interactive Business Network, Edwards's blog on *BNET* featured the CBS logo at the top. Since he looked like he had some official industry status, his questions became fodder for fashion websites at the national level.

Fictive interpolation on one site becomes the source for fictive interpolation on another, and again in turn for another, until the origins are eventually forgotten. To paraphrase Charles Horton Cooley, the products of our imagination become the solid facts of society. It's a process that happens not horizontally but vertically, moving each time to a more reputable site and seeming more real at each level. And so, in Edwards's case, American Apparel was forced to deal with a constant stream of controversy borne of one man's uncanny ability to create an angle where there wasn't one. (He was rewarded soon after with a new gig at . . . *Business Insider!*)

Imagine if an enemy had decided to use him as a cat's paw, as I have done with other such bloggers. The damage could have been even worse. As I wrote to a company attorney at the time, who mistakenly believed we could "reason" with the blogger:

> Basically, these blogs have a hustle going where one moves the ball as far as they can up the field, and then the next one takes it and in doing so reifies whatever baseless speculation was included in the first report. *Jezebel* needs Jim Edwards' "reporting" to snark on, Jim Edwards needs *Jezebel*'s "controversy" to justify his analysis, and all this feeds into the fashion news websites who pass the articles along to their readers. Posting a comment on his blog doesn't interrupt this cycle.

Neither would the lawsuit the lawyer was considering. It would just give Edwards more to talk about. In this situation I was tasked with defending a company against exactly the type of subtle mischaracterizations and misleading information that I use on behalf of other clients. The insanity of that fact is not lost on me. What makes it all the more scary in this case is that there wasn't someone like me behind the scenes, exerting influence over the information the public saw. The system was manipulating itself—and I was called in to mitigate that manipulation—with more manipulation.

What else could I expect? Early on I worked tirelessly to encourage bloggers to find nonexistent angles on stories *I* hoped they would promote. I made it worth their while—dangling pageviews, traffic, access, and occasionally advertising checks to get it going. After a point they no longer needed me to get those things. They got traffic and links by writing anything extreme about my clients, and if I wouldn't be their source, they could make one up or get someone to lie. Other advertisers were happy to profit from stories at our expense. The *Jezebel*/Edwards cycle wasn't some conspiracy; it was partly my creation.

It should be obvious that companies must be on guard against the immense pressures that bloggers face to churn out exciting news to their advantage. Do something perfectly innocent—prepare to have it wrenched out of context into a blog post. Do something complicated—expect to have it simplified until it's unrecognizable. It goes in both directions. Do nothing—you can still turn it into something. Do something wrong, don't despair; you can spin it beyond comprehension. If you play in this world as a manipulator, prepare for faux outrage (which becomes real outrage) when you don't deserve it, and expect actual violators to get off without a peep. Those are the economics in the angle-hungry world of Jim Edwards.

It's why I can safely say that all the infamous American Apparel controversies were made up. Either I made them up or bloggers did. To the public, this process was all invisible. Only as an insider was I able to know that bloggers were seeing that which was not there. They had been so trained to find "big stories" that they hardly knew the difference between real and made up.

It's even hard for me to avoid falling for the occasional confabulations myself—there are too many, and they are often too pervasive to completely resist. For that reason, even some employees at American Apparel succumbed to the persistent accusations of people like Edwards and began to believe them. The accumulation of "reporting" trumped their own personal experience. There are thousands of these unnamed and unknown victims out there, collateral damage in a system where bloggers and marketers can just make stuff up.

BOOK TWO

THE MONSTER ATTACKS

WHAT BLOGS MEAN

XIII

IRIN CARMON, *THE DAILY SHOW*, AND ME

THE PERFECT STORM OF HOW TOXIC BLOGGING CAN BE

> Most crucially, that machine, whether it churns through social media or television appearances, doesn't reward bipartisanship or deal making; it rewards the easily retweetable or sound bite–ready statement, the more outrageous the better.
>
> —IRIN CARMON, *JEZEBEL*

IN THE FIRST HALF OF THIS BOOK YOU SAW THE INSIDE
on how to manipulate blogs. There are fatal flaws in the blogging medium
that create opportunities for influence over the media—and, ultimately,
culture itself. If I were writing this book two or three years ago, it would
have ended there.

I did not fully understand the dangers of that world. The costs of the
cheap power I had in it were hidden, but once revealed, I could not shake
them. I had used my tactics to sell T-shirts and books, but others, I found,
used them more expertly and to more ominous ends. They sold everything from presidential candidates to distractions they hoped would pla-
cate the public—and made (or destroyed) millions in the process.

Realizing all this changed me. It made it impossible for me to continue
down the path that I was on. The second half of this book explains why. It
is an investigation not in how the dark arts of media manipulation work
but of their consequences.

HOW BLOGS CREATE THEIR OWN
NARRATIVES FOR FUN AND PROFIT

In 2010, I oversaw the launch of a new line of a Made in USA, environmentally friendly nail polish for American Apparel. Although American Apparel typically manufactures all of its products at its vertically
integrated factory in L.A., for this product we'd collaborated with an
old-fashioned family-owned factory in Long Island, where even their
ninety-year-old grandmother still worked on the factory floor. Shortly
after shipping the polish to rave reviews, we noticed that several bottles had cracked or burst underneath the bright halogen lights in our
stores.

It didn't pose a risk to our customers, but to be safe rather than sorry, we informed the factory that we'd be pulling the polish from store shelves and expected immediate replacements. We'd discussed the plan in-depth on a weekly conference call with our relevant employees. A confidential e-mail was sent to store managers informing them of the changes and asking them to place the bottles in a cool, dry place in the store until instructions for proper disposal were given. The last thing we wanted, even with environmentally friendly nail polish, was to throw fifty thousand bottles of it in trashcans in twenty countries.

A *Jezebel* blogger named Irin Carmon somehow received this innocent internal communication and e-mailed me at 6:25 A.M. West Coast time (*Gawker* is in Manhattan) to ask about it. Well, she pretended to ask me about it, since she signed her e-mail with the following:

> Our post with the initial information is going up shortly, but I
> would be more than happy to update or post a follow-up. Thanks
> so much. Irin

By the time I rubbed the sleep from my eyes, the post was already live. When I saw it, all I could feel was a pit in my stomach—and, frankly, that surprised me. I knew how blogs worked, was plenty cynical, but even then I sensed that this would be awful.

The headline of *Jezebel*'s piece: "Does American Apparel's New Nail Polish Contain Hazardous Material?"

To settle *Jezebel*'s reckless conjecture: The answer is no, it doesn't. Unequivocally no. For starters, the leaked e-mail specifically says the problem was with the glassware and mentions nothing about the polish. But Carmon wasn't actually interested in any of that and she definitely wasn't interested in writing an article that addressed the issue fairly. Why would she want an actual answer to her incredibly disingenuous question? The post was already written. Hell, it was already published.

As I had not intended to discuss the nail polish bottles publicly yet, it took about an hour for me to get a statement approved by the company lawyers. During that time dozens of other blogs were already parroting her claims. Major blogs, many of which had posted positive reviews of the nail polish on their sites, followed her bogus lead. The story was so compelling (American Apparel! Toxic polish! Exploding glass!) they *had* to run with it, true or not.

Within about an hour I e-mailed the following statement to Carmon, thinking I was taking her up on the offer for a follow-up to her first post:

> After receiving a few reports of bottles breaking, we made the internal decision to do a voluntary recall of the bottles on both a retail and public level.
>
> We chose this small US manufacturer to produce our nail polish because we support their business model and have a fondness for [the] family who runs it. However, one of the realities of all manufacturing is first-run glitches. We worked all last week with the manufacturer to make the improvements necessary for the second run. Another reason we sought out a US-based company is so we would be able make changes, and now we can investigate what went wrong as quickly as possible. We still believe in the factory we're working with and the new polish will be in stores within the next two weeks.
>
> We will offer an exchange of two new bottles or a $10 gift card for anyone who brings in a unit from the original run or a receipt.
>
> On another note, one thing we're taking very seriously is the disposal of the bottles we had in the stores. Even though our polish was DBP-, toluene-, and formaldehyde-free, we don't want our stores just tossing it in the trash. We're using our internal shipping and distribution line to arrange a pickup and removal of the polish to make sure it gets done right.

I felt this was a great—and ethical—response. But it was too late. Carmon copied and pasted my statement to the bottom of the article and left the headline exactly as it was, adding only "Updated" to the end of it. Even though the statement disproved the premise of her article, Carmon's implication was that she was mostly right and was just adding a few new details. She wasn't—she'd been totally wrong, but it didn't matter, because the opportunity to change the readers' minds had passed. The facts had been established.

To make matters worse, Carmon replied to my last e-mail with a question about *another* trumped-up story she planned to write about the company. She ended again with:

> By the way, just FYI—I'd love to be able to include your responses in my initial post, but unfortunately I won't be able to wait for them, so if this is something you can immediately react to, that would be great.

The controversy eventually meant the undoing of the nail polish company we'd worked so hard to support. Had these blogs not rushed to print a bogus story, the problem could have been handled privately. The massive outcry that followed Carmon's post necessitated an immediate and large-scale response that the cosmetic company could not handle. No question, they'd made mistakes, but nothing remotely close to what was reported. Overwhelmed by the controversy and the pressure from the misplaced anger of the blogger horde, the small manufacturer fell behind on their orders. Their operations fell into disarray, and the company was later sued by American Apparel for $5 million in damages to recover various losses. As the lawyers would say, while the nail polish company is responsible for their manufacturing errors, if not for Carmon's needless attack and rush to judgment—the proximate cause—it all could have been worked out.

Carmon is a media manipulator—she just doesn't know it. She may think she is a writer, but everything about her job makes her a media manipulator. She and I are in the same racket. From the twisting of the facts, the creation of a nonexistent story, the merciless use of attention for profit—she does what I do. The system I abused was now abusing me and the people I cared about. And nobody had any idea.

A PATTERN OF MANIPULATION

Did you know that *The Daily Show with Jon Stewart* hates women? And that they have a long history of discriminating against and firing women?

Sure, one of its cocreators is female, and one of its best-known and longest-running correspondents is a woman, and there really isn't any evidence to prove what I just claimed, but I assure you, I'd never lie.

This was the manufactured scandal that *Jezebel* slammed into *The Daily Show* in June 2010. Irin Carmon's piece blindsided them just as her *Jezebel* nail polish story had blindsided us. It began when Carmon posted an article titled, "*The Daily Show*'s Woman Problem."[2] Relying on some juicy quotes from people no longer with the show, Carmon claimed that the show had a poor record of finding and developing female comedic talent. She was also determined to make a name for herself. In order to accomplish this, she didn't actually speak to anyone who still worked for *The Daily Show*. It was much easier to use a collection of anonymous and off-the-record sources—like an ex-employee who hadn't worked there for eight years. As you should expect by now, the article was a sensation.

The cluster of stories that followed were read more than five hundred thousand times. The story was picked up by ABC News, the *Huffington Post*, the *Wall Street Journal*, E!, *Salon*, and others. In a memo to his staff, Carmon's boss and the publisher of *Gawker*, Nick Denton, commended the story for getting the kind of publicity that can't be bought. Denton wrote, "It was widely circulated within the media, spawned several more discussions, and affirmed our status as both an influencer and a muckraker." Jon Stewart was even forced to respond to the story on air. The *New York Times* rewarded Carmon and the website with a glowing profile: "A Web Site That's Not Afraid to Pick a Fight."[2]

For a writer like Carmon, whose pay is determined by the number of pageviews her posts receive, this was a home run. And for a publisher like Denton, the buzz the story generated made his company more attractive to advertisers and increased the valuation of his brand.

That her story was a lie didn't matter. That it was part of a pattern of manipulation didn't matter.

The women of *The Daily Show* published an open letter on the show's website a few days after the story hit.[3] Women accounted for some 40 percent of the staff, the letter read, from writers and producers to correspondents and interns, and had over a hundred years' experience on the show among them. The letter was remarkable in its clarity and understanding of what the blogger was doing. They addressed it, "Dear People

Who Don't Work Here" and called Carmon's piece an "inadequately researched blog post" that clung "to a predetermined narrative about sexism at *The Daily Show*."

If I hadn't experienced the exact situation myself, the letter would have made me hopeful that the truth would win out. But that's not how it works online. The next day the *New York Times* ran an article about their response. " 'The Daily Show' Women Say the Staff Isn't Sexist" the headline blared.[4]

Think about how bullshit that is: Because the *Jezebel* piece came first, the letter from *The Daily Show* women is shown merely as a response instead of the refutation that it actually was. No matter how convincing, it only reasserts, in America's biggest newspaper, Carmon's faulty claim of sexism on the show. They could never undo what they'd be accused of—no matter how spurious the accusation—they could only deny it. And denials don't mean anything online.

Kahane Cooperman, a female co–executive producer at the show, told the *New York Times*: "No one called us, no one talked to us. We felt like, we work here, we should take control of the narrative." She didn't know how it works. *Jezebel* controls the narrative. Carmon made it up; no one else had a right to it.

The day after the story ran, but before the women of *The Daily Show* could respond, Carmon got another post out of the subject: "5 Unconvincing Excuses for *Daily Show* Sexism," as she titled it—dismissing in advance the criticism leveled by some concerned and skeptical commenters. It was a preemptive strike to marginalize anyone who doubted her shaky accusations and to solidify her pageview-hungry version of reality.[5]

In the titles of her first and second articles, you can see what she is doing. *The Daily Show*'s "Woman Problem" from her first post became their "Sexism" in her second. One headline bootstraps the next; the what-ifs of the first piece became the basis for the second. Her story proves itself.

When the *New York Times* asked Carmon to respond to the women of *The Daily Show*'s claim that they were not interviewed or contacted for the story (which restated the allegations), she "refused to comment further." Yet when *The Daily Show* supposedly invoked this right by not speaking to Carmon it was evidence that they were hiding something. A double standard? I wouldn't expect anything different.

129

Did Carmon update her piece to reflect the dozens of comments released by *Daily Show* women? Or at least give their response a fair shake? No, of course not. In a forty-word post (forty words!) she linked their statement with the tag "open letter" and whined that she just wished they spoken up when she was writing the story. She didn't acknowledge the letter's claim that they actually *had* tried to speak with her and neglected to mention that it's *her job* to get their side of the story before publishing, even if that's difficult or time-consuming.[6]

How many *Jezebel* readers do you think threw out their original impression for a new one? Or even saw the update? The post making the accusation did 333,000 views. Her post showing the *Daily Show* women's response did 10,000 views—3 percent of the impressions of the first shot.

Did Carmon really send repeated requests for comment to *The Daily Show*? A major television show like that would get hundreds of requests a week. Who did she contact? Did she provide time for them to respond? Or is it much more likely that she gave the show a cursory heads-up minutes before publication? In my experience, the answers to these questions are appalling. No wonder she wouldn't explain her methods to the *Times*. All I have to go on is my personal history with Carmon, and it tells me that at every juncture she does whatever will benefit her most. I've seen the value she places on the truth—particularly if it gets in the way of a big story.

There is something deeply twisted about an arrangement like this one. Carmon's accusation received five times as many views as the post about *The Daily Show* women's response, even though the latter undermines much of the former. There is something wrong with the way the writer is compensated for both pieces—as well as the third, fourth, or fifth she managed to squeeze out of the topic (again, more than five hundred thousand pageviews combined). Finally, there is something wrong with the fact that Denton's sites benefit merely by going toe-to-toe with a cultural icon like Jon Stewart—even if their reports are later discredited. They know this; it's why they do it.

This is how it works online. A writer finds a narrative to advance that is profitable to them, or perhaps that they are personally or ideologically motivated to advance, and are able to thrust it into the national consciousness before anyone has a chance to bother checking if it's true or not.

Emily Gould, one of the original editors of *Gawker*, later wrote a piece for Slate.com entitled "How Feminist Blogs Like *Jezebel* Gin Up Page Views by Exploiting Women's Worst Tendencies" in which she explained the motivations behind such a story:

> *It's a prime example of the feminist blogosphere's tendency to tap into the market force of what I've come to think of as "outrage world"—the regularly occurring firestorms stirred up on mainstream, for-profit, woman-targeted blogs like* Jezebel *and also, to a lesser degree,* Slate's *own* XX Factor *and* Salon's Broadsheet. *They're ignited by writers who are pushing readers to feel what the writers claim is righteously indignant rage but which is actually just petty jealousy, cleverly marketed as feminism. These firestorms are great for page-view-pimping bloggy business.*[7]

Let me go a step further. Writers like Irin Carmon are driven more by shrewd self-interest and disdain for the consequences than they are by jealousy. It's a pattern for Carmon, as we've seen. She's not stopping, either.

Just a few months later, needing to reproduce her previous success, she saw an opportunity for a similar story, about producer and director Judd Apatow. After spotting him at a party, she tried to recapture the same outrage that had propelled her *Daily Show* piece into the public consciousness by again accusing a well-liked public figure of something impossible to deny.

The actual events of the evening: Director Judd Apatow attended a party hosted by a friend. Carmon attempted to corner and embarrass him for story she wanted to write but failed. Yet in the world of blogging, this becomes the headline: "Judd Apatow Defends His Record on Female Characters." It did about thirty-five thousand views and a hundred comments.[8]

Carmon tried to "get" him, and did. I guess I have to give her credit, because this time she actually talked to the person she hoped to make her scapegoat. But still, you can actually see, as it happens, her effort to trap

Apatow with the same insinuations and controversy that she did with Stewart. In the interview, Carmon repeatedly presented criticism of Apatow's movies as generally accepted fact that she was merely the conduit for, referring to his "critics" as though she wasn't speaking for herself.

From the interview:

> Q: So you think that's unfair that you've gotten that criticism?
> A: Oh, I definitely think that it's unfair. . . . But that's okay.
> Q: I wonder if you could elaborate on your defense a little bit.
> A: I'm not defensive about it.
> Q: Do the conversation and the criticism change the way you work?
> A: I don't hear any of the criticism when I test the movies and talk to thousands of people. I think the people who talk about these things on the Internet are looking to stir things up to make for interesting reading, but when you make movies, thousands of people fill out cards telling you their intimate feelings about the movies, and those criticisms never came up, ever, on any of the movies.

In other words, there is nothing to any of her claims. But the post went up anyway. And she got paid just the same. Notoriety from events of 2010 and 2011 worked very nicely for Carmon—in the form of a staff position at Salon.com and a spot on the *Forbes* "30 Under 30" list.

Honestly, her tactics may have once impressed me. I have no problem when people get their piece of the profits—particularly when the whole scene is such a farce. The problem is when they get too greedy. The problem is when they stop being able to see anything *but* the need for their own gain.

Today, I'm not impressed anymore. I am depressed. Because the corrupt system I helped build is no longer in anyone's control. The manipulators are indistinguishable from the publishers and bloggers—the people we were supposed to be manipulating. Everyone is now a victim, including me and the companies I work for. And the costs are incredibly high.

XIV

THERE ARE OTHERS

THE MANIPULATOR HALL OF FAME

The problem is that you get up in the morning and you realize you're twenty minutes late so you have to write a couple things fast before you have coffee and who's not going to suffer from that?

—CHOIRE SICHA, FORMER MANAGING EDITOR OF *GAWKER* AND FOUNDER OF *THE AWL*

SOMETIMES ONLY A MANIPULATOR CAN SPOT ANOTHER manipulator's work. In figuring out how to exploit the incentives of blogs, I discovered something pretty stunning: I wasn't the only one. But where I felt I worked for companies doing good things (selling great books, selling clothes made in America), others wielded influence and power over national debates. They changed politics and upended people's lives.

By now most everyone has heard the saga of Shirley Sherrod, the black woman who lost her job as a rural director for the U.S. Department of Agriculture after a video of her purportedly making a racist speech surfaced online. Behind it was a manipulator just like me.

This video caused a national shitstorm. Within hours it had gone from one blog to dozens of blogs to cable news websites, and then to the newspapers and back again.* Sherrod was forced to resign shortly after. The man who posted that video was the late Andrew Brietbart.

Of course we now know Sherrod is not a racist. In fact, the speech she was giving was about how *not* to be racist. But the bloggers and reporters who repeated the story were writing about it iteratively, using only the limited material they had been given by Breitbart. And each report became more extreme and confident than the last—despite the lack of any new evidence to support their stories.

It was an embarrassing moment in modern politics (which says a lot). The fiasco ended with President Obama denouncing his own administration's premature rush to judgment and apologizing personally to Sherrod. He lamented to *Good Morning America*: "We now live in this media cul-

---

*According to Media Matters for America, FoxNews.com and the blog *Gateway Pundit* picked the story up first, followed within minutes by *Hot Air* and dozens of other blogs (most of which embedded the YouTube video and repeated the "racist" claim). The first television station to repeat the story, later that day, was a CBS affiliate in New York City. Next came the *Drudge Report*, followed by lead stories on nearly every nighttime cable news show and then morning show in the country. You could say it traded up the chain perfectly.

ture where something goes up on YouTube or a blog and everybody scrambles."

Breitbart (now deceased) was the master of making people scramble. Whenever I need to understand the mind of blogging, I try to picture Andrew Brietbart sitting down at his computer to edit and publish that video. Because he was not a racist either. Nor was he the partisan kook the Left mistook him for. He was a media manipulator just like me. He understood and embodied the economics of the web better than anyone. And in some ways I envy him, because he was able to do it without the guilt that drove me to write this book.

Breitbart was the first employee of the *Drudge Report and* a founding employee of the *Huffington Post*. He helped build the dominant conservative and liberal blogs. He's wasn't an ideologue; he was an expert on what spreads—a provocateur.

From his perspective, the wide discrediting of his Sherrod video was not a failure. Not even close. The Sherrod story put him and his blog on the lips—in anger and in awe—of nearly every media outlet in the country. Sherrod was just collateral damage. The political machine was a plaything for Breitbart, and he made it do just what he wanted (dance and give him attention). He'd never confess as much, so I'll do it for him.

Breitbart teed up the story perfectly. By splitting the edited Sherrod clip into two pieces (two minutes, thirty seconds, and one minute, six seconds, respectively), he made it quick to consume and easy for bloggers to watch and republish. Since the unedited clip is forty-three minutes long, it was doubtful anyone would sit through the whole thing to rain on his parade. The post was titled "Video Proof: The NAACP Awards Racism," and he spent most of his thirteen hundred words fighting the imaginary foil of efforts to suppress the Tea Party, instead of explaining where the video came from.

For all the complaints from blogs, cable channels, and newspapers about being misled, Breitbart had actually given them a highly profitable gift. In getting to report on his accusations, and then the reversal, and then the discussion "about the Breitbart/Sherrod controversy," news outlets actually got three major stories instead of one. Most stories last only a few minutes, but the Sherrod controversy lasted nearly a week. It's still good for follow-ups today. Better than anyone Breitbart understood that the media doesn't mind being played, because they get something out of it—namely, pageviews, ratings, and readers.

Breitbart, who died suddenly of heart failure in early 2012, might not be with us any longer, but it hardly matters. As he once said, "Feeding the media is like training a dog. You can't throw an entire steak at a dog to train it to sit. You have to give it little bits of steak over and over again until it learns." Breitbart did plenty of training in his short time on the scene. Today, one of the dog's masters is gone, sure, but the dog still responds to the same commands.

THE MASTER AND THE STUDENT

More important, the legacy of Brietbart lives on in James O'Keefe. The young O'Keefe, mentored and funded by Breitbart, also knows what spreads, and he uses that knowledge for evil ends. O'Keefe is responsible for stories nearly as big as the Sherrod piece. He posed as a pimp in a set of undercover videos that supposedly show the now defunct community activist group ACORN giving advice to a pimp on how to avoid paying taxes. He recorded NPR seemingly showing its willingness to conceal the source of a large donation from a Muslim group. Once he even planned a bizarre attempt to seduce an attractive CNN correspondent on camera in order to embarrass the station.

Like Breitbart's clips, O'Keefe's work is heavily and disingenuously edited—far beyond what the context and actual events would support. His clips spread quickly because they are perfectly designed to suit a specific and vocal group: angry Republicans. By prefitting the narrative to appeal to conservative bloggers, his sensational stories quickly overwhelm the atrophied verification and accountability muscles of the rest of the media and become real stories. And even when they don't, as was the case with the CNN story, it's still enough to get their names in the news.

O'Keefe learned from Brietbart that in the blogging market there is a profound shortage of investigative material or original reporting. It's just too expensive to produce. So rather than bear those costs, O'Keefe's stories are hollow shells—an edited clip, a faux investigation—that blogs can use as a substitute for the real thing. Then he watches as the media falls over itself to propagate it as quickly as possible. Short, shocking narratives with a reusable sound bite are all it takes.

Because they assume the cloak of the persecuted underdog, the inevitable backlash helps O'Keefe and Brietbart rather than hurting them. Nearly all of O'Keefe's stories have been exposed as doctored to some extent. When forced to reveal the unedited footage of the NPR and ACORN stunts, most of the main accusations were found to have been amplified or manipulated. But by that point the victims had already lost their jobs or been publicly branded.

For instance, the ACORN clip shows O'Keefe wearing a comical pimp hat, a fur coat, and a cane to the meetings, when in reality he wore a suit and tie. He'd edited in frames with the other costume after the fact. By the time this was exposed six months later, the pimp image was indelibly stuck in people's minds, and the only effect of the discovery was to put O'Keefe's name back in the news. Being caught as a manipulator can only help make you more famous.

LEARNING FROM BOTH

Andrew Breitbart did eventually issue a correction for the widely disproved Sherrod story. At the top of the article:

Correction: While Ms. Sherrod made the remarks captured in the first video featured in this post while she held a federally appointed position, the story she tells refers to actions she took before she held that federal position.

A bullshit correction, to say the least.

Sherrod's attempt to clear her name and later to sue Breitbart for libel and slander were just other chances for him to bluster. The press release Breitbart issued was an exercise in defiant misdirection: "Andrew Brietbart on Pigford Lawsuit: 'Bring It On.'" It's exactly what I would have advised him to do if he'd asked me—in fact, I've basically done the exact same thing, only I was a bit more vulgar. Remember, I'm the guy who put out a press release with the headline: "Tucker Max Responds to CTA De-cision: 'Blow Me.'"

I did that because the best way to make your critics work for you is to make them irrationally angry. Blinded with rage or indignation, they spread your message to every ear and media outlet they can find. Breitbart telling his haters to bring it on certainly accomplished this, as did completely side-stepping the Sherrod issue and pretending this was some giant political conspiracy about reparations for slavery. In refusing to acknowledge, even in the slightest, that she may have been innocent of everything he accused her of, Breitbart played it like an old pro.

If you can put aside the unfortunate fate that befell Sherrod, you can see what masterful music Breitbart and O'Keefe are able to play on the instruments of online media. When they sit down to publish on their blogs, they are not simply political extremists but ruthless seekers of attention. From this attention comes fame and profit—a platform for best-selling books, lucrative speaking and consulting gigs, donations, and millions of dollars in online advertising revenue.

Some of you may be able to ignore the morality of it. I wasn't. Not anymore. I can't forget that Sherrod, as a randomly selected target, suffered deeply. And that well-meaning employees at various nonprofits lost their jobs after being framed by O'Keefe. I can't *not* focus on that.

Those people are the casualties of a media system defined by what spreads—wholly at the mercy of fraud, exaggeration, stunts, and a thousand subtle felonies against the truth.

XV

CUTE BUT EVIL

ONLINE ENTERTAINMENT TACTICS THAT DRUG YOU AND ME

{ There is no more Big Lie, only Big Lulz, and getting gamed is no shame. It's the seal on the social contract, a mark of our participation in this new covenant of cozening.

—WIRED }

YOU SIT DOWN TO YOUR COMPUTER TO WORK. FIVE minutes later you're on your fifth YouTube video of talking babies. What happened? Do you just not have any self-control? Sorry, but self-control has got nothing to do with it. Not when the clip was deliberately made more attractive by subliminally embedded images guaranteed to catch your attention. Not when the length of the video was calibrated to be precisely as long as average viewers are statistically most likely to watch.

Would you also be surprised to hear that the content of the video was designed around popular search terms? And that the title went through multiple iterations to see which got the most clicks? And what if the video you watch after this one (and the one after that and after that) had been recommended and optimized by YouTube with the deliberate intention of making online video take up as much time in your life as television does?[1]

No wonder you can't get any work done. They won't let you.

The key, as megawatt liberal blogger Matt Yglesias advised when interviewed for the book *Making It in the Political Blogosphere*, is to keep readers addicted: "The idea is to discourage people from drifting away. If you give them a break, they might find that there's something else that's just as good, and they might go away."

We once naively believed that blogs would be a boon to democracy. Unlike TV, the web wasn't about passive consumption. Blogs were about engagement and citizen activism. Blogs looked like they would free us from a crummy media world of bias, conflict, manipulation, and sensationalism. But as James Fennimore Cooper presciently observed in the nineteenth century, "If newspapers are useful in overthrowing tyrants, it is only to establish a tyranny of their own."

Tyranny is an understatement for the media today. Those between the ages of eight and eighteen are online roughly eight hours a day, a figure that does not include texting or television. America spends more than fifty billion minutes a day on Facebook, and nearly a quarter of all Internet browsing time is spent on social media sites and blogs. In a given month, blogs stream something like 150 million video streams to their users. So of course there is mass submission and apathy—everyone is distracted, deliberately so.[2]

The idea that the web is empowering is just a bunch of rattling, chattering talk. Everything you consume online has been "optimized" to make you dependent on it. Content is engineered to be clicked, glanced at, or found—like a trap designed to bait, distract, and capture you. Blogs are out to game you—to steal your time from you and sell it to advertisers—and they do this every day.

THE ART OF THUMBNAIL CHEATING

You see a link to a video in a YouTube search that makes it look like a hot girl is in it, so you click. You watch, but she's nowhere to be found. Welcome to the art of "thumbnail cheating." It's a common tactic YouTube publishers use to make their videos more tantalizing than the competition.

The most common play is to use a girl, preferably one who looks like she might get naked, but it can be anything from a kitten to a photo of someone famous. Anything to give the clip an edge. Some of the biggest accounts on YouTube were built this way. The technique can drive thousands or even tens of thousands of views to a video, helping it chart on most viewed lists and allowing it to spread and be recommended.

Online video publishers do this with YouTube's consent. Originally, YouTube chose a video thumbnail from the ½, ¼, or ¾ points of the video. So smart manipulators simply inserted a single frame of a sexy image at exactly one of those points in order to draw clicks. Members of the YouTube Partner Program—the people who get paid for their contributions to YouTube through ad revenue and make millions for the company—are allowed to use *any* image they choose as their thumbnail, even images that don't ever appear in the video. Sure, YouTube asks that the image be "representative" but if they were actually serious about quashing profitable trickery, why allow the practice at all?

GENETICALLY MODIFIED ENTERTAINMENT

LOLcats, the cute captioned kitty photos, are a viral mainstay that started as good-time fun but are much more than that now. It's not enough that some may make you chuckle while others may not. A hit or a miss is a risk that must be avoided.

In May 2011, the Cheezburger Network—now also the powerhouse purveyor of fail photos, funny infographics, and daily links, with nearly a half-billion pageviews a month—hired a prominent data scientist. His job: to build a team to monitor every pageview and metric the sites get in order to shape the content around that information. That is, in his words, to engineer "more smiles for people per day." A media empire paid by the smile can't afford anything less.

I mean no disrespect. After all, I sold an Internet meme site I owned called FailDogs.com to the Cheezburger network. I knew I was never going to be as good as they were. I was just one person, and I couldn't turn the fifteen minutes of fame from the site into a business. But Cheezburger could, by rendering users powerless to resist the urge to click. And they could do it with an irresistible veneer of cuteness masking their tactics.

Entire companies are now built on this model, exploiting the intersection between entertainment, impulse, and the profit margins of low-quality content. What they produce is not so much information but genetically modified information—pumped with steroids and hormones.

Demand Media, owner of eHow, Lance Armstrong's Livestrong.com, Cracked.com, Answerbag.com, and others, specializes in this type of algorithmically created media. Relying heavily on computer algorithms and massive data dumps, they craft online perfection in the form of low-cost, click-heavy content that advertisers love. Like successive sieves, each refines the contents of the one that came before it; Demand's automated editing systems pump out up to thirty thousand video clips and articles about trivial topics like baking cookies or "best of" lists. It generates millions of pageviews a day, and all of it sucks.

Their process is simple. First, Demand's algorithm trolls the web for lucrative search terms. It dreams up a piece of media, such as a video tutorial or a brief article, that combines as many popular terms as possible and estimates a lifetime value (LTV) of its financial worth. A second algorithm examines this concept again, creating options for the most search-friendly and provocative title. These options are fed to a human editor trained in the same art, who selects the best one. Then another editor reviews the previous editor's choice and optimizes it further, before settling on the final pitch for what should be created.

It is here, after being processed through secret computer algorithms and surgically modified by data analysts instead of editors, that the product is finally ready for writers. These writers are paid to follow the exacting prescriptions of more data-driven instructions. By the time the content is ready to be published, advertisements will have already been sold against it. These advertisers are Demand's real audience.[3]

When these content rules are not explicitly mandated by data specialists and analysts, they are implicit; bloggers know to default to what will spread and please the advertisers. People taught the logic of machines are Demand's final sieve. As one Demand Media editor e-mailed to a new contributor whose first article was rejected for not following their surefire format for going viral: "The mistakes you've made indicate you're new to Demand. This will become second nature as you learn the formats and the site requirements."[4] It's a second nature known well by YouTubers, LOL makers, podcasters, bloggers, and tweeters.

DRUGGED AND DELUSIONAL: THE RESULT

I remember seeing Jeff Jarvis, the blogger best known for his condescending (and unsolicited) advice to the newspaper industry, at a tech conference once. He sat down next to me, ostensibly to watch and listen to the talk. Not once did he look up from his laptop. He tapped away the entire time, first on Twitter, then on Facebook, then moderating comments on his blog, and on and on, completely oblivious to the world. It struck me then that whatever I decided to do with the rest of my life, I did not want to end up like him. Because at the end of the talk, Jarvis got up and spoke during the panel's Q&A, addressing the speakers as well as the audience.

In the world of the web, why should not paying attention preclude you from getting your say?

That's what web culture does to you. Psychologists call this the "narcotizing dysfunction," when people come to mistake the busyness of the media with real knowledge, and confuse spending time consuming that with doing something. In 1948, long before the louder, faster, and busier world of Twitter and social media, Paul Lazarsfeld and Robert Merton wrote:

> *The interested and informed citizen can congratulate himself on his lofty state of interest and information and neglect to see that he has abstained from decision and action. In short, he takes his secondary contact with the world of political reality, his reading and listening and thinking, as a vicarious performance. . . . He is concerned. He is informed. And he has all sorts of ideas as to what should be done. But, after he has gotten through his dinner and after he has listened to his favored radio programs and after he has read his second newspaper of the day, it is really time for bed.*[5]

This is the exact reaction that web content is designed to produce. To keep you so caught up and consumed with the bubble that you don't even realize you're in one. The more time kids spend online, studies show, the worse their grades are. According to Nielson, active social networkers are 26 percent *more* likely to give their opinion on politics and current events off-line, even though they are exactly the people whose opinions should matter the least.

"Talkativeness is afraid of the silence which reveals its emptiness," Kierkegaard once said. Now you know why sharing, commenting, clicking, and participating are pushed so strongly by blogs and entertainment sites. They don't want silence. No wonder blogs auto refresh with new material every thirty seconds. Of course they want to send updates to your mobile phone and include you on e-mail alerts. If the users stops for even a second, they may see what is really going on. And then the business model would fall apart.

XVI

THE LINK ECONOMY

THE LEVERAGED ILLUSION OF SOURCING

Our readers collectively know far more than we will ever know, and by responding to our posts, they quickly make our coverage more nuanced and accurate.

—HENRY BLODGET, EDITOR AND CEO OF *BUSINESS INSIDER*

Truths are more likely to have been discovered by one man than by a nation.

—DESCARTES

IN 2010, AFTER MANY YEARS OF SUCCESSFULLY TRAD-ing bogus stories up the chain, I was in the ironic position of desperately trying to stop it from happening—at the highest of levels: CNN. It was more than just karma. When you feed the monster as I had, it will eventually come back and attack you.

This was the situation: A disgruntled store manager sent e-mails to *Gawker* "exposing" what he or she claimed were discriminatory hiring practices at American Apparel. Why *Gawker*? Because he or she knew that *Gawker* loved to write about the company—snarky blog coverage I had encouraged both directly and covertly in the past. The manager alleged that the company refused to hire "ugly people," and supposedly enforced this policy via photographs sent to corporate headquarters. *Gawker* ate it up.

The manager's anonymous e-mails, along with a handful of "leaked documents" about American Apparel's dress code, were published on the site as proof that the accusations were true. There was only one problem. Not only were the practices *not* discriminatory—legally or morally—but they were not even new. The same dress code had been written about nearly a year earlier by other blogs.

More important, asking for a photograph of a retail applicants' personal style was far from invasive surveillance. American Apparel isn't Panopticon. The company was simply looking to make sure that managers hired the kind of real people who shopped in our stores—expressly reducing the pressure for cosmetic alterations like breast augmentation, heavy makeup, tattoos, piercing, plucking, hair dying, and straightening that most retailers actually do select for. We were specifically trying to *reduce* discrimination. Not that the leaked documents were some smoking gun, anyway. What *Gawker* had was a hodge-podge of unsanctioned and unverified notes from low-level employees, style advice from the creative department, and little else.

The controversy was a farce. The only source was the anonymously complaining ex-employee, and even then their claims were significantly exaggerated by the sites that wrote about them. I watched as this initial report from *Gawker* spread from sites across the news spectrum, getting bigger and more outrageous with each new mention. Fashion blogs turned the accusations into proven fact; the anonymous words of the ex-employee became "officially stated policy" on others. Stock blogs "analyzed" the effect the policy would have on the stock price. Other news blogs rolled up other allegations to take the story to new levels—like remarks supposedly overheard by chattering retail employees that they represented as company statements.

It came to a head when a reporter at CNN—the top of the news chain—contacted me, because they had watched the story develop and wanted to report on it.

This was our e-mail exchange (edited only for formatting and length):

> To: Ryan Holiday
> From: CNN
>
> CNN is covering the story about you and your possible hiring practices reported by gawker.com. Would you be able to answer the accusations on CNN this Saturday evening either in the 5pm or 7pm hour?

The key bullshit word here is "possible" placed right before "hiring practices." Obviously the reporter believed these were the actual hiring practices or they wouldn't be doing a story. But since CNN couldn't report on just rumors, they wanted to make it a story by getting me to deny it. I knew this was an attempt to pretend there were two sides to the issue. But there weren't two sides; there was simply the truth and an untruth.

To appeal to the reporter's sanity and expose how this story had been traded up the chain, I responded with the following e-mail, after passing along the company's official statement:

> To: CNN
> From: Ryan Holiday
>
> Hopefully you can tell from our statement that the Gawker report is probably misconstrued at best, possibly inaccurate in other areas. It's important to point out that the verification and anonymous sourcing politics for blogs and the one that you surely have at CNN are very different and can't be conflated.
>
> It's unfair and inaccurate to hold this up as being something the company engaged in primarily based on the fact that another less rigorous outlet mentioned it first. What we attempted to say in the statement was that as a company who has always challenged beauty and diversity norms in the fashion industry— not quietly but as the central part of our creativity—accusations like that are not only unfounded but are contrary to what we're committed to. What I was attempting to convey in my original emails is that in the past outlets have used the vehicle of "reporting on what _____ is reporting" to include information they likely wouldn't have included through their own editorial standards. Hopefully CNN does not do that.

After a long pause, the reply:

> To: Ryan Holiday
> From: CNN
> Subject: CNN no longer doing Gawker story segment
>
> After a lot of consideration we decided to no longer do the segment.

Though I narrowly dodged a bullet with CNN, it was during this incident that I began to understand the web's sourcing problems from a new perspective. A dubious accusation on a gossip blog nearly became a frighteningly *nongossip* story from the "most trusted name in news." There had been no overt manipulation, yet something completely untrue had spread from one site to another as though some invisible hand had guided it along. Thankfully, it did not make it to air on CNN, but it could have had I not stepped in.

Henry Blodget, in a revealing onstage interview with reporter Andrew Sorkin, explained the increasingly common cycle like this: "There are stories that will appear on Gawker Media—huge conversations in the blogosphere—everything else. It's passed all over. Everyone knows about it. Everybody's clicking on it. Then, finally, an approved source speaks to the *New York Times* or somebody else, and the *New York Times* will suddenly say, 'Okay now we can report that.'"

This is exactly what happened with the near CNN and *Gawker* debacle. A story that originated on *Gawker* as a controversy was the center of an enormous amount of buzz online. It then grew and grew as it spread from site to site, until the buzz was noticed by CNN, which tried to get me to discuss the story with them on air. CNN, of course, would never have been able to break the story themselves, nor would they have been interested in bothering with something so small as a manager's anonymous e-mail. But if someone else made it a hot topic first, they were happy to do their own piece on it. It's the same tactic I abuse when I turn nothing into something. Get a small blog to pick a story up and pass it upward to bigger and more credible outlets, which simply link to the previous report and don't bother to verify it.

Both the blogs and the mainstream media are shirking their duty—and that makes them ripe for exploitation (or in the case of American Apparel and CNN, a missile that can strike your company at any time). And yet most of the social media elite want this for our future.

THE DELEGATION OF TRUST

This cycle has roots in two journalistic habits—one from the new media world and one from the old. When combined, they become a major danger.

Reporters can hardly be everywhere at once. For most of recent history, media outlets all used the same self-imposed editorial guidelines, so relying on one another's work was natural. When a fact appeared in the *Chi-*

cago Tribune, it is pretty safe for the *San Francisco Chronicle* to repeat that same fact, since both publications have high verification standards.

These were the old rules:

1. If the outlet is legitimate, the stories it breaks are.
2. If the story is legitimate, the facts inside it are.
3. It can be assumed that if the subject of the story is legitimate, then what people are saying about it probably is too.

These rules allow one journalist to use the facts brought forth by another, hopefully with attribution. This assumption makes researching much easier for reporters, since they can build on the work of those who came before them, instead of starting from the beginning of a story. It's a process known as the "delegation of trust."[1]

The web has its own innovation on the delegation of trust, known as "link economy." Basically it refers to the exchange of traffic and information between blogs and websites. Say the *Los Angeles Times* reports that Brad Pitt and Angelina Jolie are splitting up. Perez Hilton would link to this report on his blog and add his own thoughts. Then other blogs would link to Perez's account and maybe the original *Times* source as well. This is an outgrowth from the early days of blogging, when blogs lacked the resources to do much original reporting. They relied on other outlets to break stories, which they then linked to and provided commentary on. From this came what is called the link economy, one that encouraged sites to regularly and consistently link to each other. I send you a link now, you send me a link later—we trade off doing the job of reporting.

The phrase "link economy" was popularized by Jeff Jarvis, who you met here earlier. His credentials as a blogger, journalism professor at the City University of New York's Graduate School of Journalism, and author of books such as *What Would Google Do?* have made him incredibly influential. Unfortunately, he's also an idiot, and the link economy he advocates is a breeding ground for manipulation.

The link economy encourages blogs to point their readers to other bloggers who are saying crazy things, to borrow from each other without verification, and to take more or less completed stories from other sites, add a layer of commentary, and turn it into something they call their own.

To borrow a term from computer science, the link economy is recursive—blogs pull from the blogs that came before them to create new content. Think of how a mash-up video relies on other clips to make something new, or how Twitter users retweet messages from other members and add to them.

But as the trading up the chain scam makes it clear, the media is no longer governed by a set of universal editorial and ethics standards. Even within publications, the burden of proof for the print version of a newspaper might differ drastically from what reporters need to go live with a blog post. As media outlets grapple with tighter deadlines and smaller staffs, many of the old standards for verification, confirmation, and fact-checking are becoming impossible to maintain. Every blog has its own editorial policy, but few disclose it to readers. The material one site pulls from another can hardly be trusted when it's just as likely to have been written with low standards as with high ones.

The conditions on which the delegation of trust and the link economy need to operate properly no longer exist. But the habits remain and have been mixed into a potent combination. The result is often embarrassing and contagious misinformation.

Like the time when *Crain's New York* e-mailed me to ask if American Apparel would be closing any of its stores in Manhattan because of the financial crisis. No, I replied emphatically. *No.* So they found a real estate agent who didn't work for American Apparel to say we might. Headline: "American Apparel likely to shed some NY stores" (even though my quote in the article said we wouldn't). The *Crain's* story was linked to and used as a source by *Jezebel,* and then by *New York* magazine's *The Cut* blog, then by *Racked NY*. AOL's *Daily Finance* blog turned it into a slideshow: "10 Leading Businesses Shuttering Stores Because of Downturn." None of those sites needed to ask me any questions, since *Crain's* had asked and answered for them—they could just link.* A week later, for unknown reasons, *Crain's* republished the article under a new headline ("Unraveling American Apparel Could Put NYC Stores on the Block"), which, after showing up on Google Finance, started the same chain over again.[2]

*One blogger from AnnArbor.com did e-mail me. He asked, "Since AA was closing stores in NYC, would we be closing in Ann Arbor too?" No. *No!* It didn't stop him, either.

More than a year later every one of those stores is still open. The links still point to the same bad story.

A few years back a young Irish student posted a fake quotation on the Wikipedia page of composer Maurice Jarre shortly after the man died. (The obituary-friendly quote said in part, "When I die there will be a final waltz playing in my head that only I can hear.") At the time, I'm not sure the student understood the convergence of the link economy and the delegation of trust. That changed in an instant, when his fabricated quote began to appear in obituaries for the composer around the world.

It's difficult to pinpoint where it started, but at some point, a reporter or a blogger saw that quotation and used it in an article. Eventually the quote found its way to *The Guardian*, and from there it may as well have been real. The quote so perfectly expressed what writers wished to say about Jarre, and the fact that it was in *The Guardian*, a reputable and prominent newspaper, made it the source of many links. And so it went along the chain, its origins obscured, and the more times it was repeated, the more real it felt.

This is where the link economy fails in practice. Wikipedia editors may have caught and quickly removed the student's edit, but that didn't automatically update the obituaries that had incorporated it. Wikipedia administrators are not able to edit stories on other people's websites so the quote remained in *The Guardian* until they caught and corrected it too. The link economy is designed to confirm and support, not to question or correct. In fact, the stunt was only discovered after the student admitted what he'd done.

"I am 100 percent convinced that if I hadn't come forward, that quote would have gone down in history as something Maurice Jarre said, instead of something I made up," he said. "It would have become another example where, once anything is printed enough times in the media without challenge, it becomes fact."[3]

The proponents of the link economy brush aside these examples. The posts can be updated, they say; that's the beauty of the Internet. But as far as I know there is no technology that issues alerts to each trackback or every reader who has read a corrupted article, and there never will be. The evolution of a news story is a lot like biological evolution. It jumps around, cross contaminates, and occasionally develops at the same time in multiple places. It's impossible to track or correct.

Senator Eugene McCarthy once compared the journalists covering his 1968 presidential campaign to birds on a telephone wire. When one got up to fly to a different wire, they'd all follow. When another flew back, the rest would too. Today this metaphor needs an update. The birds still follow one another's leads just as eagerly—but the wire need not always exist. They can be and often are perched on illusions, just as blogs were when they repeated Maurice Jarre's manufactured remarks.

THE LINK ILLUSION

In the link economy, the blue stamp of an html link *seems* like it will support weight. (As had the links to *The Guardian* story containing the false quote.) If I write on my blog that "Thomas Jefferson, by his own remarks, admitted to committing acts considered felonious in the State of Virginia," you'd want to see some evidence before you were convinced. Now imagine that I added a link to the words "acts considered felonious." This link could go to anything—it could go to a dictionary definition of "felonious acts" or it could go to a pdf of the entire penal code for the state of Virginia. Either way, I have vaguely complied with the standards of the link economy. I have rested my authority on a source and linked to it, and now the burden is on the reader to disprove the validity of that link. Bloggers know this and abuse it.

Blogs have long borrowed on the principle that links imply credibility. Even Google exploits this perception. The search engine, founded by Larry Page and Sergey Brin when they were Stanford students, copies a standard practice from academia in which the number of citations a scientific paper gets is an indicator of how influential or important it is. But academic papers are reviewed by peers and editorial boards—shaky citations are hard to get away with.

Online links look like citations but rarely are. Through flimsy attribution blogs are able to assert wildly fantastic claims that will spread well and drive comments. Some might be afraid to make something up outright, so the justification of "I wasn't the first person to say this" is very appealing. It's a way of putting the burden all on the other guy, or on the reader.

People consume content online by scanning and skimming. To use the bird metaphor again, they are what William Zinsser called "impatient bird[s], perched on the thin edge of distraction." Only 44 percent of users on Google News click through to real the actual article. Meaning: *Nobody clicks links*, even interesting ones. Or if they do they're not exactly rigorous in pouring over it to make sure it proves the point in the *last* article they read.

If readers give sites just seconds for their headlines, how much effort will they expend weighing whether a blog meets the burden of proof? The number of posts we read conscientiously, like some amateur copy editor and fact-checker rolled into one, are far outpaced by the number of articles we just assume are reliable. And the material from one site quickly makes its way to others. Scandalous statements get traction wider and faster—and their dubious nature is more likely to be obscured by the link economy when it's moving at viral speed. Who knows how many times you and I have passed over spurious assertions made to look legitimate through a bright little link?

A BROKEN PHILOSOPHY

May becomes *is* becomes *has*, I tell my clients. That is, on the first site the fact that someone "may" be doing something becomes the fact that they "are" doing something by the time it has made the rounds. The next time they mention your name, they look back and add the past tense to their last assertion, whether or not it actually happened. This is recursion at work, officially sanctioned and very possible under the rules of the link economy.

Under these circumstances it is far too easy for mistakes to pile on top of mistakes or for real reporting to be built on lies and manipulations— for analysis to be built on a foundation of weak support. It becomes so easy, as one reporter has put it, for things to become an amalgam of an amalgam.

The link economy encourages bloggers to repeat what "other people are saying" and link to it instead of doing their own reporting and standing behind it. This changes the news from what has happened into what someone said the news is. Needless to say, these are not close to the same things.

One of my favorite books is Kathryn Schulz's *Being Wrong: Adventures in the Margin of Error*. Though media mistakes are not the subject of the book, Schulz does do a good job of explaining why the media so regularly gets it wrong. Scientists, she says, replicate each other's experiments in order to prove or disprove their findings. Conversely, journalists replicate one another's conclusions and build on top of them—often when they are not correct.

The news has always been riddled with errors, because it is self-referential instead of self-critical. Mistakes don't occur as isolated incidents but ripple through the news, sometimes with painful consequences. Because blogs and the media have become so interdependent and linked, a lapse of judgment or poor analysis in one place affects many places.

Science essentially pits the scientists against each other, each looking to disprove the work of others. This process strips out falsehoods, mistakes, and errors. Journalism has no such culture. Reporters look to one-up each other on the same subjects, often adding new scoops to existing stories. Meanwhile, people like Jeff Jarvis explicitly advise online newspapers and aspiring blogs not to waste their time trying "to replicate the work of other reporters." In the age of the link, he says, "this is clearly inefficient and unnecessary." Don't waste "now-precious resources matching competitors stories" or checking and verifying them like a scientist would. Instead, pick up where they left off and see where the story takes you. Don't be a perfectionist, he's saying; join the link economy and delegate trust.

When I hear people preach about interconnectedness and interdependence—like one reporter who suggested he and his colleagues begin using the tag NR (neutral retweet) to preface the retweets on Twitter that they were posting but not endorsing—I can't help but think of the subprime mortgage crisis. I think about one bank that hands off subprime loans to another, which in turn packages them and hands them to another still. *Why are you retweeting things you don't believe in?!* I think about the rating agencies whose job was to monitor the subprime transactions but were simply too busy, too overwhelmed, and too conflicted to bother doing it. I think of falling dominoes. I wonder why we would do that to ourselves again—multiplied many times over in digital.

Of course replication is expensive. But it is a known cost, one that should be paid up front by the people who intend to profit from the news. It is a protection and a deterrent all at once. The unknown cost comes from failure—of banks or of trust or of sources—and it is borne by everyone, not just the businesses themselves.

When Jarvis and others breathlessly advocate for new concepts they do not understand, it is both comical and dangerous. The web gurus try to tell us that this distributed, crowd-sourced version of fact-checking and research is more accurate, because it involves more people. But I side with Descartes and have more faith in a scientific approach, in which every man is responsible for his own work—in which everyone is questioning the work of everyone else, and this motivates them to be extra careful and honest.

The old media system was a long way from perfect, but their costly business model, so derided by these web gurus, pushed for at least a semblance of scientific replication. It found independent confirmation wherever possible. It advocated editorial independence instead of risky interdependence. It is expensive, sure, and definitely unsexy, but it is a step above the pseudo-science of the link economy. It was certainly better than what we have online, where blogs do nothing but report what "[some other blog] is reporting . . ." where blogs pass along unverified information using the excuse, "but I linked to where I stole it from."

To simply know where something came from, or just the fact that it came from somewhere else, does not alleviate the problems of the delegation of trust. In fact, this is the insidious part of the link economy. It creates the appearance of a solution without solving anything. Some other blog talked to a source (don't believe them; here's the link) *so now they don't have to.* That isn't enough for me. We deserve better.

I happened to get lucky that CNN decided not to run their poorly sourced story. I appealed to their reason and humanity and it worked. Nearly two years have passed since then. To this day I consider the incident a fluke, and I assume I will never be so lucky again. And neither will anyone else.

XVII

EXTORTION VIA THE WEB

FACING THE ONLINE SHAKEDOWN

Companies should expect a full-scale, organized attack from critics. One that will simultaneously overrun blog comments, Facebook fan pages, and an onslaught of blogs, resulting in mainstream press appeal. Start by developing a social media crises plan and developing internal fire drills to anticipate what would happen.

JEREMIAH OWYANG, ALTIMETER GROUP, WEB-STRATEGIST.COM

IN BYGONE DAYS A COMPANY MIGHT HIRE A PR MAN TO make sure people talked about their company. Today, even a company with little interest in self-promotion must hire one, simply to make sure people *don't* say untrue things about their company. If it was once about spreading the word, now it's as much about stopping the spread of inaccurate and damaging words.

When the entire system is designed to quickly repeat and sensationalize whatever random information it can find, it makes sense that companies would need someone on call 24/7 to put out fires before they start. That person is often someone like me.

One of my first big contracts was a ten-thousand-dollar gig to handle a group of trolls who had been vandalizing a company's Wikipedia page and filling it with lies and rumors. These "facts" were then showing up in major newspapers and on blogs that were eager for any gossip they could find about the company. How do we just make it stop?, the company pleaded. We just want to be left alone.*

It's the same predicament Google found itself in when Facebook hired a high-profile PR agency to execute an anonymous whisper campaign against them through manufactured warnings about privacy. Bloggers of all stripes had been pitched, with the idea of building enough buzz for the grand finale: editorials in the *Washington Post, Politico, USA Today,* and the *Huffington Post.* Like my client, Google was stunned senseless by the plot. Imagine a $200 billion company saying, Make it stop. We just want to be left alone. But they were effectively reduced to that. "We're not going to comment further," Google told reporters during the firestorm of controversy. "Our focus is delighting people with great products."

---

*I heard an even more anguished version of this cry from the family of a celebrity who contacted me after their son's death. They wanted help with Wikipedia users who were inserting speculative and untrue information about his tragic accident.

Sure, go ahead and focus on that Google, but it doesn't matter. Once this arms race has begun, things can't just go back to normal. It escalates: A company sees how easy it is to plant stories online and hires a firm to attack its competitor. Blindsided by the bad publicity, the rival hires a firm to protect itself—and then to strike back. Thus begins an endless loop of online manipulation that can cost hundreds of thousands of dollars. And that's the easiest of the PR battles a company may have to face.

Consider what happened to the French yogurt giant Danone, which was approached by Fernando Motolese, a video producer in Brazil, with two hypothetical videos.

One, he said, was a fun spoof of their yogurt, which was designed to improve digestive health and, um, other bodily functions. The other, he said, was a disgusting version of the first video, with all the indelible scatological images implied by such a spoof. He might be more inclined to release the first version, he said, if Danone was willing to pay him a fee each time it was seen.

"It felt sort of like blackmail," said Renato Fischer, the Danone representative who fielded the inquiry, to MIT's *Technology Review*.[1] Well, that's because it *was* blackmail. It was extortion via viral video.

THE IMPLICIT SHAKEDOWN

Molotese's hustle is one of many styles of a shakedown that happen across the web countless times a day. Its only distinguishing feature was its brazenness. It's usually couched in slightly more opaque terms.

Take Michael Arrington's *TechCrunch* post entitled "Why We Often Blindside Companies." What begins as an apparent discussion of the site's news policy I see as a veiled threat to the Silicon Valley tech scene. After a start-up founder had, for the "second time," publicly announced news about her own life before Arrington's site had a chance to write about it (*TechCrunch* told her they were writing a story about her, so she broke the news herself), Arrington decided to make an example out of her. First he told his readers that he had nasty personal information on the founder that he had been reluctant to publish. This was a not so subtle reminder that he had dirt on everyone and that his personal whim decided whether it got out or not. Then Arrington took his stand, saying the founder would no longer be "getting any calls from [him] in the future to give her a heads up that [*TechCrunch* is] breaking news about her start up." As though the journalist's job to speak to sources they are writing about was a courtesy. He concluded on a friendlier note: "Treat us with respect and you'll get it back. That's all we ask."* He may have ended his post nicely, but his message sounds no less extortionary to me than Molotese's.[2]

Many other blogs do the same thing through a combination of a sense of entitlement and laziness. A group of hotel chains is currently litigating a lawsuit against TripAdvisor and other travel sites over defamatory reviews that the sites won't remove. A mostly positive 2010 *Financial Times* article about the rising influence of blogs covering the luxury watch market featured a small complaint from a watch manufacturer about a blogger who often got important details and product specifications wrong, in addition to having typos and bad grammar. In response, the editor of another watch-industry blog, *TheWatchLounge*, leaped to the site's defense: "What is the luxury watch industry doing to help him become a better writer?" he demanded to know. "And for that matter what is the industry doing to help any of these bloggers become better writers?"[3]

I would ask the same question of him that I once posed to a blogger who kept getting a story about American Apparel wrong. "When you find a mistake," he'd said, "e-mail me and point it out." I had to ask: Hey man, why is *my* job to do *your* job?

A while back, a plane of a major airline experienced potentially catastrophic trouble in the air. Despite a flaming engine and poor odds, the pilot managed to land it safely, saving the lives of four-hundred-plus passengers. Yet, as events transpired, Twitter users went berserk and reported that the plane had tragically crashed. In reality, the plane had not only landed safely, but the pilot acted like a gentleman from another generation, offering the passengers his personal telephone number if they had more questions or wanted someone to talk to. He exuded humble and quiet heroism that should have been recognized.

---

*Before he ran for president, then senator Barack Obama advised his fellow politicians about the burgeoning political blogosphere: "If you take these blogs seriously, they'll take you seriously." As long as we can all admit that we have to assuage bloggers' egos in order to be treated fairly. . . .

Only nobody knew about it, because the story online was so different. The *Harvard Business Review* criticized the airline for not responding quickly enough with marketing spin and for not magically stopping the rampant online speculation. They wrote: "What a pity that social media users, in their well-known enthusiasm for being first to share breaking news to their followers, would unwittingly *conspire* to obscure the big story of a pilot's life-saving landing" [emphasis mine].

Yes, *a pity*. A word a neighborhood thug might use in the hypothetical, "It'd be *a pity* if something ever happened to this nice little shop of yours," and then try to collect monthly protection. These *are* the economics of extortion. The threat is less overt than "pay us or else," but it's a demand nonetheless. You must provide more fuel to the story and get out in front of it (even when there are more important things going on, like, you know, not letting the jet crash), or your reputation will be ruined. To not do this is to risk a vivid misperception that is impossible to correct with the truth, or anything else.

A CULTURE OF FEAR

Most social media experts have accepted this paradigm and teach it to their clients without questioning it: Give blogs special treatment or they'll attack you. At any time, a hole could be dug by blogs, Twitter, or YouTube that the company must pay to fill in. And depending on the intentions of the person who dug it, they may also ask to be paid to not dig them anymore.

Being right is more important to the person being written about than the person writing. So who do you think blinks first? Who has to spend thousands of dollars advertising online to counteract undeserved bad press? Who ultimately hires a spinmaster like me to start filling the discussions with good things just to drown out the bullshit?

Today there are dozens of firms that offer reputation-management services to companies and individuals. Though they dress up their offerings with jargon about performance metrics and customer feedback, their real service is to handle the disturbing, nasty, and corrupt dealings I've talked about in this book, so you don't have to. In a way, that's what I do too. I figure out how to stretch Arrington's definition of what the rules are as much as possible.

Navigating this terrain has become a critical part of brand management. The constant threat of being blindsided by a false controversy, or crucified unfairly for some misconstrued remark, hovers over everyone in the public sphere. Employees, good, bad, or disgruntled and desperate for money, know that they have the means to massively embarrass their employers with well-placed accusations of mistreatment or harassment. People know that going to a blog like *Consumerist* is the fastest way to get revenge for any perceived customer-service slight.

That there are a million eyes watching, each incentivized to demagogue their way to a traffic payday, dominates discussions in corporate boardrooms, design departments, and political strategy sessions. What effect does it have? Aside from making them rightly cynical, it forces them to act in two ways—deliberately provocative or conservatively fake. In a word: unreal.

Blogs criticize companies, politicians, and personalities for being artificial but mock them ruthlessly for engaging in media stunts, and blame them for even the slightest mistake. Nuance is a weakness. As a result, politicians must stick even more closely to their prepared remarks. Companies bury their essence in even more convoluted marketing-speak. Public figures cannot answer a question with anything but: "No comment." Everyone limits their exposure to risk by being fake.

It's now common for indie bands to avoid or turn down as much online press as possible, with some even going as far as obscuring their likenesses or withholding their names. Why? They are petrified of the backlash that has sunk so many promising "blog-buzz" bands that came before them. With the hype comes the threat of hate, and I don't think this is limited to music blogs.

Overstock.com was compelled to address this unpredictable and aggressive web culture in a recent 10-K filing with the SEC. It is a precautionary measure many companies will have to take in the future—to let investors know how blogs could impact their financials with little warning and little recourse. Designating it as one of three major risk factors to the company, Overstock.com wrote, "Use of social media may adversely impact our reputation."

162

There has been a marked increase in use of social media platforms and similar devices, including weblogs (blogs), social media websites, and other forms of Internet-based communications which allow individuals access to a broad audience of consumers and other interested persons. Consumers value readily available information concerning retailers, manufacturers, and their goods and services and often act on such information without further investigation, authentication and without regard to its accuracy. The availability of information on social media platforms and devices is virtually immediate as is its impact. Social media platforms and devices immediately publish the content their subscribers and participants post, often without filters or checks on accuracy of the content posted. The opportunity for [the] dissemination of information, including inaccurate information, is seemingly limitless and readily available. Information concerning the Company may be posted on such platforms and devices at any time. Information posted may be adverse to our interests, it may be inaccurate, and may harm our performance, prospects or business. The harm may be immediate, without affording us an opportunity for redress or correction. Such platforms also could be used for dissemination of trade secret information, compromise of valuable company assets all of which could harm our business, prospects, financial condition and [the] results of operations.

Alarmist? Maybe. But I have seen hundreds of millions of dollars of market cap evaporate on the news of some bogus blog post. When the blog *Engadget* posted a fake e-mail announcing a supposed delay in the release of a new iPhone and Apple operating system, it knocked more than *$4 billion off* Apple's stock price. The 2008 election was nearly derailed when the same "citizen reporter," on separate occasions, tricked both Obama and a campaigning Bill Clinton into saying something vulnerable and honest by misrepresenting herself. The sixty-one-year-old woman later admitted that the two figures had "had no idea [she] was a journalist," nor that she was recording them with a hidden device. Then, angered by the lack of compensation from the *Huffington Post* for her "scoops," she resigned by publishing private e-mails between herself and Arianna Huffington—just to get one last blast of attention at someone else's expense.

I've even done this myself, by advising a friend who needed to strike back at a very famous talent agent (with a legendary bad temper and a reputation for screwing people over) how to have a lawyer draft a letter announcing his intention to file an embarrassing lawsuit, which he could then leak to gossip blogs. Not a real lawsuit, mind you, but the *illusion* of one through an intention letter. The threat made it on *TMZ, ESPN*, and a host of other blogs.

I ran into the friend recently and learned the outcome of the tactic: They paid him five hundred thousand dollars to go away. I think about this often. They may have stolen from my friend, but I still shook someone down. What strikes me is not that it was some elaborate, orchestrated con—I don't feel like I discovered some criminal instinct inside myself either—it's that the tools were so accessible and easy to use, it was almost difficult not to do so. In fact, it came so effortlessly that I didn't even remember doing it until he reminded me.

The way someone can be exploited through both the legal system (anyone can be sued for anything) and the media, when they cover it (libel of public figures generally requires malicious intent or reckless disregard of the truth), reminds me of the gruesome accident in *Meet Joe Black* in which Brad Pitt's character is hit by a car, tossed up in the air, and hit by another car going in the other direction.

To not be petrified of a shakedown, a malicious lie, or an unscrupulous rival planting stories is to be unimportant. You only have nothing to fear if you're a nobody. And even then, well, who knows?

XVIII

THE ITERATIVE HUSTLE

ONLINE JOURNALISM'S BOGUS PHILOSOPHY

> With social media, there are no editors. There is no waiting for confirmation. When you tweet or retweet, you are not checking the facts or even so much concerned if you are spreading a lie. . . . But this is how process journalism now works. It's journalism as beta.
>
> —JON ORLIN, *TECHCRUNCH*

> Nick [Denton] is very much of the mind that you do it now. And the emphasis is to get it out there and be as correct as you can, but don't let that stand in the way of getting the story out there.
>
> —JESSICA COEN, EDITOR, *JEZEBEL*

> There is nothing more shocking than to see assertion and approval dashing ahead of cognition and perception.
>
> —CICERO

IN THIS BOOK I HAVE WRITTEN A LOT ABOUT THE ECO-
nomics of blogs. I've done my best to point my finger at the forces behind the
medium rather than at bloggers themselves. It's how I have always tried to
look at this problem, even while I was besieged by unfair controversies or
stabbed in the back in public. But that attitude breaks down and becomes
impossible when it comes to a certain style of blogging: Iterative Journalism.

Not satisfied merely to have their naked greed accepted as a motivation, publishers and media gurus had to invent a pseudo-philosophy. And
after hearing them blather on about it long enough, I have to expose it for
the scam that it is.

Iterative journalism, process journalism, beta journalism—whatever
name you use, it's stupid and dangerous. It calls for bloggers to publish
first and then verify what they wrote *after* they've posted it. Publishers
actually believe that their writers need to do every part of the news-
making process, from discovery to fact-checking to writing and editing
in *real time*. It should be obvious to anyone who thinks about it for two
seconds why that is a bad thing—but they buy the lie that iterative journalism improves the news.

Having observed this process in action many times, I know that this
isn't true. It's the reason I now spend my time playing defense instead of
offense. I end up stuck putting out fires that never needed to start in the
first place. It's why I get e-mails at 6:00 A.M. from writers like Irin Carmon
asking for a comment on a story of the most dubious origins that they
already had decided to "break."

Why would bloggers do anything else? Erik Wemple, a blogger for the
Washington Post, writes: "The imperative is to pounce on news when it
happens and, in this case, before it happens. To wait for another source is
to set the table for someone who's going to steal your search traffic." So by
the time I've woken up in the morning too much misinformation has

been spread around the web to possibly be cleaned up. The "incentives are lined up this way," Tommy Craggs of *Deadspin* tells us, so we better get used to it.[1]

WHAT IS ITERATIVE JOURNALISM?

First, let's start with what iterative journalism is *not*. It is not saying, "This is what we don't know or need to know for this story to be important." It is not saying: "Everybody stop! I am going to get to the bottom of this for you." Instead, iterative journalists throw up their hands, claim to be knowledge-less, and report whatever they've heard as the news.

Seeking Alpha practiced it perfectly on one recent story: "If the newspaper is correct, and I have no way of verifying it, then this stock is in big trouble." Really? *No way at all?* At its best, iterative journalism is what *TechCrunch* does: rile up the crowd by repeating sensational allegations and then pretend that they are waiting for the facts to come in. They see no contradiction between publishing a post with the headline "Paypal Shreds Ostensibly Rare Violin Because It Cares" and then writing, "Now a lot of this story isn't out yet and I have a line in to Paypal about this, so before we get out the pitchforks lets discuss what happened."[2]

Iterative journalists follow blindly wherever the wisps of the speculation may take them, do the absolute minimum amount of research or corroboration, and then post this suspect information immediately, as it is known, in a continuous stream. As Jeff Jarvis put it: "Online, we often publish first and edit later. Newspaper people see their articles as finished products of their work. Bloggers see their posts as part of the process of learning."

This "learning process" is not some epistemological quest. Dropping the ruse, Michael Arrington of *TechCrunch* put it more bluntly: "Getting it right is expensive, getting it first is cheap." And by extension, since it doesn't cost him anything to be wrong, he presumably doesn't bother trying to avoid it. It's not just less costly; it makes more money, because every time a blog has to correct itself, it gets another post out of it—more pageviews.*

---

*From an *SB Nation* sports post about the NFL lockout: "There are 382 more updates to this story. Read most recent updates."

The iterative approach sells itself as flexible and informative, but much more realistically, it manifests in the forms of rumors, half-truths, shoddy reporting, overwhelming amounts of needless information, and endless predictions and projections. Instead of using slow-to-respond official sources or documents, it leans on rumors, buzz, and questions. Events are "liveblogged" instead of filtered. Bloggers post constantly, depending on others to point out errors or send in updates, or for sources to contact them.

Iterative journalism is defined by its jumpiness. It is as jumpy as reporters can get without outright making things up. Only the slightest twitch is needed for a journalist to get a story live. As a result, stories claiming massive implications, like takeover talks, lawsuits, potential legislation, pending announcements, and criminal allegations, are often posted despite having minuscule origins. A tweet, a comment on a blog, or an e-mail tip might be enough to do the trick. Bloggers don't fabricate news, but they do suspend their disbelief, common sense, and responsibility in order to get to big stories first. The pressure to "get something up" is inherently at odds with the desire to "get things right."

A blog practicing iterative journalism would report they are hearing that Google is planning to buy Twitter or Yelp, or break the news of reports that the president has been assassinated (all falsely reported online many times now). The blog would publish the story as it investigates these facts—that is, publish the rumor first while they see if there is anything more to the story. Hypothetically, a media manipulator for Yelp would be behind the leak, knowing that getting the rumors of the acquisition out there could help them jack up the price in negotiations. I personally wouldn't kick off reports about the president's death, because I wouldn't get anything from it, but plenty of pranksters would.

If a blog is lucky, the gamble it took on a sketchy iterative tip will be confirmed later by events. If they are unlucky, and this is the real insidious part of it, the site simply continues to report on the *reaction* to the news, as though they had nothing to do with creating it. This is what happened to *Business Insider* when they wrongly made the shocking claim that New York governor David Paterson would resign. The end of the headline was simply updated from "NYT's Big David Paterson Bombshell Will Break Monday, Governor's Resignation To Follow" to "NYT's Big

David Paterson Bombshell Will Break Monday, *Governor's Office Denies Resignation In Works*"[3] [emphasis mine].

They should have learned their lesson months earlier, after falling for a similar hoax. A prankster posted on CNN's online iReport platform that a "source" had told them that Steve Jobs had had a severe heart attack.* It was the user's first and only post. It was posted at 4:00 A.M. It was obviously a hoax. Even the site MacRumors.com, which *writes about nothing but rumors*, knew this post was bogus and didn't write about it. Nonetheless, following its iterative instincts, *Business Insider's* sister blog, *Silicon Alley Insider*, rushed to advance the story as a full-fledged post. Apple's stock price plummeted. Twenty-five minutes later, the story in tatters—the fake tip deleted by iReport; the rumor denied by Apple—*Business Insider* rewrites the lead with a new angle: " 'Citizen journalism' . . . just failed its first significant test."[4] Yeah, that's who failed here. You know who didn't? Those who were shorting Apple stock.

Ultimately, that is why iterative journalism is so attractive for publishers. It eliminates costs such as fact-checkers or staff time to build relationships with sources. It is profitable, because it allows writers to return to the same story multiple times and drives more comments, links, and excitement than normal, non-"breaking" news. To call it a learning experience or a process, or anything but a way to make more money, is a lie.

COVERING THEIR ASSES

Iterative journalists claim they welcome corrections as a way of justifying the risks they take when they break news. But then again, I also recall hearing Nick Denton complain to a packed house at SXSW 2012 that American Apparel and Dov Charney "waste a lot of editorial time" when we call his writers to complain about inaccurate stories. If only there was some way to avoid that. . . .

---

*I imagine these repeated and exhausting rumors of Jobs's death made it all the more painful for his family when they were eventually placed in the position, three years later, of announcing that he had actually passed away. No family should have to worry: Are people going to believe us? Or, Will he get less than his proper due because the public's patience has been wasted through so many premature reports?

Even so, no blog wants to be embarrassingly wrong, so instead of standing behind embarrassing stories resulting from their silly approach to journalism, blogs duck behind qualifiers: "We're hearing . . ."; "I wonder . . ."; "Possibly . . ."; "Lots of buzz that . . ."; "Sites are reporting . . ."; "Could . . . , Would . . . , Should . . ."; and so on. In other words, they toss the news narrative into the stream without taking full ownership and pretend to be an impartial observer of a process they began.

For example, these are the first two sentences of *New York* magazine's *Daily Intel* blog post about the David Paterson story I mentioned earlier:

> *After weeks of* **escalating buzz** *about a New York Times piece that* **would** *reveal a "bombshell" scandal about New York Governor David Paterson, Business Insider* **is reporting** *that the story will* **likely** *come out tomorrow and will be followed by the governor's resignation (!!). Though the nature of the revelation is* **still a mystery, reports are** *that this story is "much worse" than Paterson's publicly acknowledged affair with a state employee [emphases mine].*[5]

Welcome to Covering Your Ass 101. Nearly every claim is tempered by what *might* happen or attributed to someone else. It says all it can and nothing at the same time. It is the perfect disingenuous hedge. Which worked out great for *Daily Intel*, since the story turned out to be totally wrong. Not that anyone learned from mistake—the posts were just updated with more speculation and guessing. One mistake is replaced by more mistakes.

Another common iterative tactic is to write about the rumors "that other people are writing about." This lets them blog about an undeveloped story without having to take ownership of it. The *Daily Beast* chose this path when they wrote a story about "still-below-the-radar-but-getting-tough-to-ignore buzz" that a female politician's husband was a closeted homosexual. Such rumors, of course, were spread by the politician's political enemies and enjoyed by her opposition. The writer even admitted that the claims were nothing more than "uncorroborated speculation" in the first sentence. But that doesn't matter. We no longer discuss if rumors are true, only that they being talked about *right now*.

This is justified by the self-serving distinction between reporting the rumors and reporting *about* the rumors. In reality there is no difference whatsoever. The public's time is wasted with manipulative information because of the flawed contention that speculation about the implications of speculation gets us closer to the truth—instead of muddying the waters further.

A TEST CASE

There are certainly some advantages to iterative journalism—it's cheap, it's fast, it gets people's attention. Take its most compelling performance: reporting the death of Osama bin Laden.

At 10:25 P.M., a user named Keith Urbahn broke the big news on Twitter. "So I'm told by a reputable person they have killed Osama Bin Laden. Hot damn." Urbahn was first. He passed along the info as he heard it, and it worked. Word spread rapidly on Twitter and quickly onto blogs before the mainstream media even knew what happened. "Long before the news media and as President Obama was learning about the details of the events in Pakistan," wrote social media guru Brian Solis, "individuals following @ReallyVirtual, @mpoppel, and @keithurbahn witnessed firsthand as the operation developed and the real news emerged."

His first source (a television news producer, of all people) turned out to be correct, and therefore Urbahn was correct before anyone else. Blogs dominated the story with their iterative approach and got the news to the public accurately and quickly. They wrote history before the mainstream media had a chance to get their expert pundits in the makeup chair, before even the official confirmation by the United States government. It wasn't until twenty minutes after Urbahn tweeted the story that the news was confirmed and reported by the first news station.*

Another way to look at it, though, is that the greatest success of iterative journalism gave us a story twenty minutes earlier than it would have

---

*Urbahn got more than that one message out before the president's announcement; he got several. He wrote, of his own breaking news: "Don't know if it's true, but let's pray it is" and "Ladies, gents, let's wait to see what the President says. Could be misinformation or pure rumor."

come otherwise. Bravo. A whole twenty fucking minutes. The world is forever in your debt.

To think it matters whether it came twenty minutes sooner or later basically misses the entire point of the news. What matters is that *the man was dead*. To correct the well-meaning Brian Solis, it's pretty ridiculous to think that social media heard about the raid on bin Laden's compound before the president who ordered it.

Why is that a goal anyway? The twenty minutes is a vapid victory. And yet it is all that iterative journalism brings us when it works *well*. This was the instance—the exception—in which the person passing along earth-shattering news that he's only partially confident about, that he himself says "could be misinformation or pure rumor," is a hero instead of a fool.

But let's look at another test case. What do we get when iterative journalism fails?

The answer is: a lot of pain and suffering for innocent people. Like when the blog *Eater LA* published a report from an anonymous reader stating that a popular Los Angeles wine bar not only had egregious health code violations, but also was advertising gourmet items on its menu while really serving generic substitutes. It was the kind of tip iterative publisher's love to see, and *Eater* immediately put the story out there—before verifying it or contacting the restaurant:

> **Besides not adhering to simple food saftey [sic] standards, such as soap, sanitizing, and throwing out chicken salad that's 2 weeks old, 90% of all "fresh" menu items are cooked days beforehand and sit in the fridge. [emphasis theirs]**

Like so many iterative reports, it turned out to be wrong. *Completely wrong.* So *Eater* added an update that said the proprietors disputed the story. Yet the post—the disgusting hygiene allegations and the headline—remained the same. The post stayed up for people to read and comment on. Only after a second update—prompted by the threat of a lawsuit—did *Eater* begin to admit any wrongdoing. It said, in part:

> *We ran this tip without contacting the owners of the restaurant, who have since refuted the tip in its entirety. We apologize to the owners*

of the restaurant, and our readers, for not investigating our source's claims before airing them on the site. The resulting post didn't rise to our standards, and we shouldn't have published it.

Yet, adhering to the rules of iterative journalism, the original post remains up some two years later. The updates are at the bottom of the post and are still seen *after* the now repudiated anonymous allegations. Only with the direct threat of legal action were the restaurant owners able to reply to a story that the blog admitted shouldn't have been published. It was not, however, enough to make them take the post down. Or reveal the identity of the malicious tipster.

This is only one example of the myth of iteration having real consequences.* Imagine if the restaurant had been a larger, publicly traded company. Stocks move on news—any news—and rumors passed on by high-profile blogs are no exception. It does not matter if they are updated or corrected or part of a learning curve; blogs are read by real people who make opinions and decisions as they read.

Process journalism, fed by controversy, rumors, and titillating scandals, is a beast that gives no quarter. Those who have never been on the other side of this equation don't realize that it is precisely in situations like a scandal, an IPO, a lawsuit, or a tragic event that the subjects of the story are least able to communicate with the press. Legal reasons may preclude commenting publicly; SEC rules occasionally forbid speaking with the press; personal shame or simply the overwhelming nature of dealing with the event may make it impossible to response to every single media inquiry immediately. It is with the stories upon which we most need to tread lightly, to speak carefully on behalf of those who cannot speak, that bloggers are unwilling to do so, because it is not in their interest.

Forcing someone to dispute a preposterously untrue allegation is just as much slander as making the accusation. The types of stories that scream out to be written and broken before they are fully written are precisely the types of stories that cannot be taken back. The scandals, the controversies, and the shocking announcements—the ones I have shown

---

*See Evgeny Morozov's *The Net Delusion* for a discussion of blogs' premature and overblown coverage of the 2009–2010 Iranian revolution and the subsequent crackdown on activists and social media in Iran.

in this book to be so easy to fabricate or manipulate—cannot be unwritten or walked back. They spread too quickly. They stick too easily.

And when they inevitably turn out to be wrong (or have less than the whole story), the subjects find themselves asking the same question that wrongly disgraced former United States secretary of labor Ray Donovan asked the court when he was acquitted of false charges that ruined his career: "Which office do I go to to get my reputation back?"

SLAVES TO THE ITERATIVE GRIND

Bill Simmons, a sportswriter who famously set off an iterative journalism frenzy when he accidentally published a private message confirming rumors of the trade of Randy Moss to the Vikings in 2010, wrote: "Twitter, which exacerbates the demands of immediacy, blurs the line between reporting and postulating, and forces writers to chase too many bum steers." The allure of the scoop in the iterative world, he said, "entices reporters to become *enslaved* to certain sources, push transparent agendas, and 'break' news before there's anything to officially break" [emphasis mine].

Yet despite this, the best and brightest (and richest) online publishers push iterative reporting as the de facto model. The danger of real-time journalism hides in plain sight: Its jumpiness can easily be exploited by interested parties—people like me. Leaking or sharing information with the right blog introduces a narrative that can immediately and overwhelmingly take hold. By the time the proper facts have been established, it is too late to dislodge a now commonly held perception. In this model, the audience is viewed as nothing more than a dumb mob to be manipulated and used to create pageviews.

It's a vicious cycle. The lead bum steer of an iterative story starts a stampede. And after so many of these stampedes, the audience is conditioned to expect an endless parade of bigger and bigger scoops that no reporter could ever deliver. What spread yesterday—drove tweets of "Holy shit, did you hear?"—is hardly enough to spread the same way today. So it must be newer, faster, crazier. Now they must maintain it constantly by reporting on even more tenuous material and making crazier conclusions from it. And why shouldn't they? They can just apologize later.

Our friends Jeff Jarvis and Michael Arrington like to use the metaphor of beta to explain this new form of journalism—like how Google rolls out their new services with software bugs still in it. *It's just like that*, they say. They forget we're not dealing with software or ones and zeros; we're dealing with the news and information, and those things affect people's lives. Or more likely, Jarvis and Arrington know this and don't care, content to advocate a concept with painful consequences for everyone but them. It's made them wealthy and influential; what does it matter if the metaphor is wrong?

What Google says when they release a product in beta is that the fundamentals are strong but the superficialities are a work in progress—aesthetics, feature additions, nagging issues. The iterative journalism reporting model suggests the opposite—the structure, the headline, the links, and the picture slideshows are there, but the *facts* are suspect. What kind of process is that?

If there is a coding mistake, I won't get an incorrect view of the market or an industry. I won't begin to wrongly think that So-and-So is a racist or some restaurant is filled with cockroaches when it actually isn't. Software as beta means the risk of small glitches; the news as beta means the risk of a false reality.

The poet Hesiod once wrote that rumor and gossip are a "light weight to lift up, but heavy to carry and hard to put down." Iterative journalism is much the same. Its practices come easily, almost naturally, given the way blogs are designed and the way the web operates. It *seems* cheaper, but it's not. The costs have just been externalized, to the readers and the subjects of the stories, who write down millions each year in falsely damaged reputations and perceptions. Iterative journalism makes the news cheap to produce but expensive to read.

XIX

THE MYTH OF CORRECTIONS

Our web folks will ask, "Can't we post it and say we're checking it?" The feeling nowadays is, "We don't make mistakes, we just make updates."

—ROXANNE ROBERTS, *WASHINGTON POST* RELIABLE SOURCES COLUMNIST

We certainly helped to spread it (and debunk it) faster than it would have on its own. But did *TechCrunch* and all the other media who published the fake story suffer a loss of credibility? You tell us. But my sense is, not really. We helped move the story towards the truth.

—JON ORLIN, *TECHCRUNCH*

Is it not obvious that society cannot continue indefinitely to get its news by this wasteful method? One large section of the community organized to circulate lies, and another large section of the community organized to refute the lies! We might as well send a million men out into the desert to dig holes, and then send another million to fill up the holes.

—UPTON SINCLAIR, *THE BRASS CHECK*

ITERATIVE JOURNALISM IS POSSIBLE BECAUSE OF A belief in the web's ability to make corrections and updates to news stories. Fans of iterative journalism acknowledge that while increased speed may lead to mistakes, it's okay because the errors can be fixed easily. They say that iterative journalism is individually weak but collectively strong, since the bloggers and readers are working together to improve each story—iteratively.

As someone who has been both written about as a developing story and worked with people who are written about this way all the time, I can assure you that this is bullshit. *Corrections online are a joke.* All of the justifications for iterative journalism are not only false—they are literally the opposite of how it works in practice.

Bloggers are no more eager to seek out feedback that shows they were wrong than anyone else is. And they are understandably reluctant to admit their mistakes publicly, as bloggers must do. The bigger the fuckup, the less likely people want to cop to it. It's called "cognitive dissonance." We've known about it for a while.

Seeing something you know to be untrue presented in the news as true is exasperating. I don't know what it feels like to be a public figure (I realize it's hard to be sympathetic to their feelings), but I have had untruths spread about me online, and I know that it sucks. I know that as a press agent, having seen that many of these mistakes bloggers make are easily preventable, it is extra infuriating. And they feel absolutely no guilt about making them.

If you want to get a blogger to correct something—which sensitive clients painfully insist upon—be prepared to have to be an obsequious douche. You've got to flatter bloggers into thinking that somehow the mistake wasn't their fault. Or be prepared to be an asshole. Sometimes the resistance is so strong, and the entitlement so baked in, that you have to risk your friendly to each other's face relationship by calling the blogger out to their publisher boss.

Sometimes it has to get even more serious than that. One of my favorite all-time blogger corrections stories involves Matt Drudge, the political blogger sainted in the history of blogging for breaking the Monica Lewinsky story. But few people remember the big political "scandal" Drudge broke before that one. Based on an unnamed source, Drudge accused prominent journalist and Clinton adviser Sidney Blumenthal of a shocking history of spousal abuse—and one covered up by the White House, no less.

Except none of it was true. Turns out there was no evidence that Blumenthal had ever struck his wife, nor was there a White House cover-up. The story quickly fell apart after it became clear an anonymous Republican source had whispered into Drudge's ear to settle a political score against Blumenthal. Drudge eventually admitted it to the *Washington Post*: "[S]omeone was using me to try to go after [him]. . . . I think I've been had."

Yet Drudge's posted correction on the story said only, "I am issuing a retraction of my information regarding Sidney Blumenthal that appeared in the *Drudge Report* on August 11, 1997." He refused to apologize for the pain caused by his recklessness, even in the face of a $30 million libel suit. And four years later, when the ordeal finally ended, Drudge *still* defended iterative journalism: "The great thing about this medium I'm working in is that you can fix things fast."[1]

There's only one word for someone like that: dickhead.

I deal with people like him every day. Why do they get to be this way? They're the ones who were wrong—and it was their job to be right, wasn't it? Nope. Not according to their philosophy. Remember, the onus for pointing out inaccuracy falls on basically everybody but the person who gets paid to report facts for a living.

CORRECTING PEOPLE WHO ARE WRONG FOR A LIVING

I once gave the show *The Price is Right* a five-hundred-dollar American Apparel gift card to use as a prize. We thought it'd be funny, since the show is television's longest-running guilty pleasure. (Honestly, I was just excited as a fan.) The episode aired in September and was quickly posted by one of my employees on the company's YouTube account. Everyone loved it and got the irony—a cool brand slumming it on a show only old people care about. Well, everyone got it except the popular advertising blog *Brand Channel*, which posted a nonironic piece titled "American Apparel Taps Drew Carey for Image Turnaround."[2] With excruciating obliviousness they proceeded to discuss the merits of my "surprising choice" to film a "back-to-school commercial, featuring a mock version of classic US game show *The Price is Right* hosted by an all-American TV personality Drew Carey."

How does one begin to correct that? Where would you even start? We're not dealing with the same reality. If I had even known how to communicate to that idiot that Drew Carey was, in fact, the actual host of *The Price Is Right*, and that the video the blogger watched was a clip from an actual episode and not a commercial, I still would have to convince the writer to retract the *entire thing*, because an update couldn't have fixed how wrong it was. Since I no longer foolishly hope for miracles, I didn't even try to correct it, even as other blogs repeated the claims. I just had to sit there and watch as people believed something so stupid was true; the writer was wrong to the point of it actually working to their advantage.

If I'd wanted to try to get a correction, however, it would not have made much of a difference. Getting a correction posted takes time, often hours or days, occasionally weeks, because bloggers deliberately drag their feet. Posts do most of their traffic shortly after going live and being linked to. By the time your correction or update happens, there is hardly much of an audience. I recall sending e-mails to *Gawker* and *Jezebel* on several occasions over matters of factual errors and not receiving a response. Only after e-mailing again (from the same device) was I told, "Oh, I never got your e-mail." Sure, guys, whatever you say. My anonymous tips seem to arrive in their inboxes just fine—it's the signed corrections that run into issues.

My experience is not uncommon. A friend, a car blogger earnestly passionate about his job, once e-mailed the writer of a less than reputable car site after they published a rumor that turned out to be false.

> Him: Why keep the headline up, since we now know it's not true?
> Blogger: You guys are so funny.

Bloggers often stick their updates way down at the bottom, because they are vain, just like the rest of us—they'd rather not shout their mistakes loudly for all to hear, or have them be the first thing the reader sees. In other cases blogs will just paste your e-mail at the bottom of the post, as though it's "your opinion" that they're wrong. Of course it isn't just an opinion or they wouldn't have been forced to post it. But they get to keep the article up by framing it as a two-sided issue. The last thing they want to do is rewrite or get rid of their post and throw away the few minutes of work they put into it.

BEING WRONG

Factual errors are only one type of error—perhaps the least important kind. A story is made of facts, and it is the concrescence of those facts that creates a news story. Corrections remove those facts from the story—but the story and the thrust remain. Even writers averse to acknowledging errors who have done so will only under the rarest of circumstances follow the logic fully: The challenged fact requires a reexamination of the premises built on top of it. In other words: We don't need an update; we need a *rewrite*.

Like when *Business Insider* editor Henry Blodget reported "unconfirmed rumors" that three prominent journalists had been hired away from their old media jobs for blogging gigs with salaries of close to half a million dollars a year. He reported this despite the fact—as he admits, and as he quoted in the article—that a source told him the numbers were "laughable." The next day, in a post titled "DAILY BEAST: We're Not Paying Howard Kurtz $600,000 a Year!" he acknowledged that in response to his story another source had shot down his speculation, calling it "wildly inflated figures of hyper-active imaginations." Not to be discouraged, Blodget finished this update with some "new information": another set of rumors about what other journalists were being paid. All the same, he concluded—despite having the reasons for the conclusion demolished— "it looks like a new golden age for those in the news business."

The real golden age for journalists is the one when a guy like Blodget not only gets traffic by posting jaw-dropping rumors, but then also gets traffic the next day by shooting down the same rumors he created. And then he has the balls to start the cycle all over again with his very next breath. That he was wrong doesn't even begin to cover it: The man has an aversion to the truth and not the slightest bit of guilt about it.

He's not alone. I once heard Megan McCarthy (*Gawker, TechMeme,* CNET) speak at a SXSW panel about how false stories, such as a fake celebrity death, spread online. During the Q&A I got up and asked, "This is all well and good, but what about mistakes of a less black-and-white variety? You know, something a little more complex than whether someone is actually dead or not. What about subtle untruths or slight mischaracterizations? How does one go about getting those corrected?" She laughed: "I love *your* idea that there can be nuance on the Internet."

THE PSYCHOLOGY OF ERROR

If it were simply a matter of breaking through the endemic arrogance of bloggers and publishers, iterative journalism might be fixable. But the reality is that learning iteratively doesn't work for readers either—not even a little.

Think of Wikipedia, which provides a good example of the iterative process. By 2010 the article on the Iraq War had accumulated more than twelve thousand edits. Enough to fill twelve volumes and seven thousand printed pages (someone actually did the math on this for an artistic book project). Impressive, no doubt. But that number obscures the fact that though the twelve thousand changes collectively result in a coherent, mostly accurate depiction, it is not what most people who looked at the Wikipedia entry in the last half decade saw. Most of them did not consume it as a final product. No, it was read, and relied upon, in piecemeal—while it was under construction. Thousands of other Wikipedia pages link to it; thousands more blogs used it as a reference; hundreds of thousands of people read these links and formed opinions accordingly. Each corrected mistake, each change or addition, in this light is not a triumph but a failure. Because for a time it was wrongly presented as being correct or complete—even though it was in a constant state of flux.

The reality is that while the Internet allows content to be written iteratively, the audience does not read or consume it iteratively. Each member usually sees what he or she sees a single time—a snapshot of the process—and makes his or her conclusions from that.

An iterative approach fails because, as a form of knowledge, the news exists in what psychologists refer to as the "specious present." As sociologist Robert E. Park wrote, "News remains news only until it has reached the persons for whom it has 'news interest.' Once published and its significance recognized, what was news becomes history." Journalism can never truly be iterative, because as soon as it is read it becomes fact—in this case, poor and often inaccurate fact.

Iterative journalism advocates try to extend the expiration date of the news's specious present by asking readers to withhold judgment, check back for updates, and be responsible for their own fact-checking.* Bloggers ask for this suspended state of incredulity from readers while the news is being hashed out in front of them. But like a student taking a test and trying to slow down time so they can get to the last few questions, it's just not possible.

Suppressing one's instinct to interpret and speculate, until the totality of evidence arrives, is a skill that detectives and doctors train for years to develop. This is not something us regular humans are good at; in fact, we're wired to do the opposite. The human mind "first believes, then evaluates," as one psychologist put it. To that I'd add, "as long as it doesn't get distracted first." How can we expect people to transcend their biology while they read celebrity gossip and news about sports?

The science shows that we are not only bad at remaining skeptical, we're bad at correcting our beliefs when they're proven wrong. In a University of Michigan study called "When Corrections Fail," political scholars Brendan Nyhan and Jason Reifler coined a phrase for it: the "backfire effect."[3] After showing subjects a fake news article, half of the participants were provided with a correction at the bottom discrediting a central claim in the article—just like one you might see at the bottom of a blog post. All of the subjects were then asked to rate their beliefs about the claims in the article.

183

---

*Conveniently, this would be a reading style that would generate the most pageviews for the blog.

Those who saw the correction were, in fact, *more likely* to believe the initial claim than those who did not. And they held this belief *more confidently* than their peers. In other words, corrections not only don't fix the error—they backfire and make misperception worse.

What happens is that the correction actually reintroduces the claim into the reader's mind and forces them to run it back through their mental processes. Instead of prompting them to discard the old thought, as intended, corrections appear to tighten their mind's grip on the now disputed fact.

In this light, I have always found it ironic that the name for the *Wall Street Journal* corrections section is "Corrections & Amplifications."* If only they knew that corrections actually are amplifications. But seriously, there can't really be that many cases where a newspaper would ever need "amplify" one of its initial claims, could there? What are they going to do? Issue an update saying that they didn't sound haughty and pretentious enough the first go-round?

Bloggers brandish the correction as though it is some magical balm that heals all wounds. Here's the reality: Making a point is exciting; correcting one is not. An accusation is much likelier to spread quicker than a quiet admission of error days or months later. Upton Sinclair used the metaphor of water—the sensational stuff flows rapidly through an open channel, while the administrative details like corrections hit the concrete wall of a closed dam.

Once the mind has accepted a plausible explanation for something, it becomes a framework for all the information that is perceived after it. We're drawn, subconsciously, to fit and contort all the subsequent knowledge we receive into our framework, whether it fits or not. Psychologists call this cognitive rigidity. The facts that built an original premise are gone, but the conclusion remains—the general feeling of our opinion floats over the collapsed foundation that established it.

Information overload, "busyness," speed, and emotion all exacerbate this phenomenon. They make it even harder to update our beliefs or remain open-minded. When readers repeat, comment on, react to, and hear

*Comparatively, the wire service Reuters puts their updates and new facts at the tops of their articles and often reissues them over the wire to replace the older one.

rumors—all actions blogs are designed to provoke—it becomes harder for them to see real truth when it is finally presented or corrected.

In another study researchers examined the effect of exposure to wholly fictional, unbelievable news headlines. Rather than cultivate detached skepticism, as proponents of iterative journalism would like, it turns out that the more unbelievable headlines and articles readers are exposed to, the more it warps their compass—making the real seem fake and the fake seem real. The more extreme a headline, the longer participants spend processing it, and the more likely they are to believe it. The more times an unbelievable claim is seen, the more likely they are to believe it.[4]

It is true that the iterative model can eventually get the story right, just like in theory Wikipedia perpetually moves toward higher quality pages. The distributed efforts of hundreds or thousands of blogs can aggregate a final product that may even be superior to what one dedicated newsroom could ever make. When they do, I'll gladly congratulate them—they can throw themselves a tweeter-tape parade for all I care—but I'll have to remind them when it's all over that it didn't make a difference. More people were misled than helped.

The ceaseless, instant world of iterative journalism is antithetical to how the human brain works. Studies have shown that the brain experiences reading and listening in profoundly different ways; they activate different hemispheres for the exact same content. We place an inordinate amount of trust in things that have been written down. This comes from centuries of knowing that writing was expensive—that it was safe to assume that someone would rarely waste the resources to commit to paper something untrue. The written word and the use of it conjures up deep associations with authority and credence that are thousands of years old.

Iterative journalism puts companies and people in an impossible position: Speaking out only validates the original story—however incorrect it is—while staying silent and leaving the story as it was written means that the news isn't actually iterative. But acknowledging this paradox would undermine the premise of this very profitable and gratifying practice. I can't decide if it is more ironic or sad that the justification for iterative journalism needs its own correction. If only Jeff Jarvis would post on his blog: "Oops, turns out errors are a lot more difficult to correct that we thought . . . and trying to do so only makes things worse. I guess we shouldn't have pushed this whole ridiculous enterprise on everyone so hard."

That would be the day.

Instead, the philosophy behind iterative journalism is like a lot of the examples of bad stories I have mentioned. The facts supporting the conclusions collapse under scrutiny, and only the hubris of a faulty conclusion remains.

CHEERING ON OUR OWN DECEPTION

> Our illusions are the house in which we live; they are our news, our heroes, our adventure, our forms of art, our very experience.
>
> —DANIEL BOORSTIN, *THE IMAGE*

I WAS ONCE INVITED TO A LUNCH AT SPAGO WITH THE
CEO of the *Huffington Post*, Eric Hippeau. Some of the site's editors attended for a bit of a roundtable discussion about the media during lunch.
It was 2010, and the Internet and national media were in a frenzy over
reports of unintended accelerations in Toyota cars. While we were eating
Eric asked the group a question: How could Toyota have better responded
to the wildly out of control PR crisis?

Being that this was a room full of Internet folks, as soon as the answers
started, the pontification became overwhelming: "I think transparency is
critical." "These companies need to be proactive." "They needed to get out
in front of this thing." "The key is reaching out to bloggers." Blah blah
blah.

It was a conversation I'd heard a thousand times and seen online almost every day. But to hear Eric Hippeau do it in person, to my face, was
unbearable.

Finally I interrupted. "None of you know what you're talking about," I
said. "None of you have been in a PR crisis. You've never seen how quickly
they get out of hand. None of you have come to terms with the fact that
sites like yours, the *Huffington Post*, pass along rumors as fact and rehash
posts from other blogs without checking them. It's impossible to fight
back against that. The Internet is the problem here, not the solution."

The room was mostly silent after that. When I left I was thanked for my
thoughts, but I knew I'd never be invited back, despite spending more
than six figures with them that year. I was rude, no question, but I couldn't
get over how inappropriate it was for a news organization to sit down and
evaluate someone else's PR performance instead of evaluating the veracity
and quality of its own coverage.

In subsequent months I would be vindicated more than I could have
anticipated at the time. First, the *Huffington Post* was hit with a PR crisis

and failed miserably at responding by the standards they laid out at lunch. When sued by a cadre of former and current writers for their unpaid contributions, the *Huffington Post* was anything but "transparent." They clammed up, likely on the advice of their lawyers, and didn't cover the lawsuit on their own site. It was not until a few days later that Arianna Huffington posted her first—and the only—statement about it on the *Huffington Post*. Hardly "being proactive" or "getting out in front of it." The lawsuit was clearly a money grab, but the *Huffington Post* had to mostly stand there and take a public beating, watching powerlessly as other blogs gleefully dissected and discussed the lawsuit without a shred of empathy. Just as *Huffington Post* had done to Toyota and other companies during our lunch and countless times on their site.

Second, and most important, Toyota was largely exonerated after a full investigation by NASA, no less. Many of the cases of computer issues supposedly causing unintended acceleration were dismissed entirely, and most were found to be caused by driver error. Drivers had been hammering the accelerator instead of the brakes! And then blamed the car! In other words, the scandal that Toyota was so heavily criticized for not handling right had been baseless. Toyota hadn't been reckless, the media had. It was the sites like *Huffington Post*, so quick to judge, that had disregarded their duties to their customers and to the truth. As journalist Ed Wallace wrote for *BusinessWeek* in an apology to Toyota, "[A]ll the reasons why the public doesn't trust the media crystallized in the Toyota fiasco."

Though I'm proud of what I said in that room, and was ultimately proven right, if I had a chance to do it again I would probably say something different. I would say: "What the fuck are you guys talking about this for?"

Are we seriously discussing how Toyota—a multibillion-dollar corporation, that like all others sells us things we can't afford and don't need—should have done a better job marketing to us? Toyota is either making faulty cars or it's not; the response is meaningless public relations bullshit. Are we actually putting our heads together to come up with advice on how to bait the hook so we're more likely to bite?

Why are we cheering on our own deception?

Because that's exactly what we are doing when we have conversations about how marketers and PR specialists could do their job better. Like one blogger who complained that Tiger Woods's press conference apology had "too many cliches" in it. You're missing the forest for the trees. The whole thing is a cliché. Yeah, it was fake. So are celebrities. At least we can plainly recognize the press conference as a staged event when we see it.

Users on *BuzzFeed* can actually play a game in which they try to guess if stories will go viral or not, and winners get ranked on a list of "Top Viral Predictors." Talk about staged—they're producing content around whether other pieces of content might be read by a lot of other people on the Internet. Nobody online wants to point out how fake and insidious that is because it's too lucrative.* It's easier to co-opt readers with marketing bullshit than it is to protect their interests or provide worthwhile material.

Online publishers *need* to fill space. Companies *need* coverage of their products. Together blogs, marketers, and publicists cannot help but conspire to meet one anothers' needs and dress up the artificial and unreal as important. Why? Because that's how they get paid.

I never got over the shock of discovering that it was basically impossible to burn a blog. No matter how many times I've been caught leaking bad info, spinning, spamming, manufacturing news—it never changed anything. The same bloggers continued to cover my stories and bite when I created the news. They don't mind being deceived, not at all. In fact, it often makes for a bonus "story behind how we got the story wrong" post.

Public relations and marketing are something companies do to move product. It is not meaningful, it is not cool. Yet because it is cheap, easy, and lucrative to cover, blogs want to convince you that it is. And we've mostly accepted that, consuming such schlock like it's news.

ADVERTISING AS CONTENT

Mashable, the influential tech blog, actually keeps a *Billboard* magazine-style chart called "Top 20 Viral Ads" for each month. Read that again

---

*Especially for *BuzzFeed*, which uses this information in collaboration with paying brands to make their "advertorial" content more viral.

slowly: It's a chart of popular video advertisements. You know, videos designed to sell viewers more crap.

As the CEO of a viral video agency that did $25 million in billing last year advised me: "Get out there and make your own noise. Advertise the advertising." The attraction to turning advertisements into content was something I often exploited with American Apparel. Blogs so desperately need material that I would send them screenshots of ads and say, "Here is an exclusive leak of our new controversial ad." The next day: "Exclusive! American Apparel's Controversial New Ad." The chatter about these advertisements always perplexed me: Don't they know that generally companies have to pay to generate this kind of attention?

It's the same logic behind the old trick of getting a music video or a commercial banned in order to make it a news story. As in MTV.com reporting "Rihanna's 'S&M' Video Restricted By YouTube, Banned In 11 Countries." MTV doesn't play music videos anymore, but they're still getting attention by writing about the stunts pulled by people who do! Do you think PETA is upset when their proposed Super Bowl commercial is rejected every year? No, that's the entire point. They get the attention— and they don't have to pay for the ad space.

But at least the Super Bowl is a big deal. Here's a tweet from Staci Kramer, editor of *paidContent*: "Lisa Gurry, @bing director, tells @darrenrovell1 search engine will have 2 mins of ad time in LeBron 'Decision' on ESPN. #pcbuzz."[1] Let me translate that gibberish for you: Staci heard a paid representative of one company tell a different reporter that they planned to *run a television commercial* during a press conference at which an overpaid athlete would announce the team he would play for. Staci felt that was newsworthy buzz and shared it with the world.

I don't think it's buzzworthy; I think it is pathetic worship of our own deception.

BLOGGER-SPONSORED CONFERENCES

I love when blogs cover their own conferences as though there was no conflict of interest in hosting an event and loudly proclaiming its newsworthiness to your readers. Blogs often liveblog their own conferences, getting literally dozens of posts out of covering the words that came out of the mouths of the people the site paid to speak. In addition to driving millions of pageviews (and videos and tweets), the real goal of this coverage is to make the conference seem newsworthy enough that people pay to attend next year. The reader who is just browsing headlines sees how many are dedicated to this one event and all the "news" it generates and thinks, "Hey, am I missing something?" No, it's just an ordinary pseudo-event, with the same hustlers saying things to get attention, only in this case the publisher paid to make it all happen.

Some examples:

TechCrunch hosts TechCrunch Disrupt

AllThingsDigital hosts D: All Things Digital Conference

PSFK hosts PSFK Salons

Mashable hosts the Mashable Connect Conference

GigaOm hosts six different conferences

COVERAGE ABOUT COVERAGE

Within hours of the death of Osama bin Laden, before the body was even cold, blogs were already writing the story of how the story broke. From FastCompany.com ("Osama Bin Laden Dead, The Story Twitter Broke") to the *New York Times*'s *Media Decoder* blog ("How the Bin Laden Announcement Leaked Out"), dozens of blogs quickly moved from reporting the news to reporting news about the news.

Coverage about coverage is *not* more coverage, though it may feel like it. One is information we can make use of—for example, it's important to know that a killer like bin Laden is no longer a threat to our physical safety. The other is worthless filler—news that tells us how we were told about the news. Yet blogs write these stories because they are easy, because they are self-promotional and glorifying, and because they make them seem relevant by their association with actually important news.

There is a subset of this coverage that is all the more preposterous. Every few months blogs trot out the tired old story of how to pitch coverage to them. They advise publicists to do a better job e-mailing the blogger and assuaging their ego if they want the blogger to write about their clients. From a reader's perspective this is all rather strange. Why is the blog revealing how it can be manipulated? In turn, why do we not head for the hills when it is clear that blogs pass this manipulation on to us?

Some favorite headlines:

Rules of Thumb for Pitching Silly Claims to TechCrunch (*TechCrunch*)

How Not to Pitch a Blogger, #648 (*ReadWriteWeb*)

DEAR PR FOLKS: Please Stop Sending Us "Experts" and "Story Ideas"—Here's What to Send Us Instead (*Business Insider*)

A private note to PR people (Scobleizer.com)

How to Pitch a Blogger (as in, *Brazen Careerist*, the blogger writing it)

The Do's and Don'ts of Online Publicity, for Some Reason (Lindsay Robertson, *Jezebel*, *NYMag*, *Huffington Post*)

The unintended consequence of that kind of coverage is that it is essentially a manual with step-by-step instructions on how to infiltrate and deceive that blogger with marketing. I used to be thankful when I'd see that; now I just wonder: Why are you doing this to yourselves?

TOO LOW-HANGING FRUIT

Nothing tires me more than the convergence of moronic marketers and bloggers with little regard for the truth.

At least my plays involved some level of elaborate strategy. I'll grant that what I do can be difficult to defend against. It's one thing when it is possible to plant a story; it's another entirely when blogs write stories about how people plant stories on their site. It's another still when the readers are tricked into speculating about how companies can do a better job covering up disasters or blunders.

Only when you see this type of coverage for what it is—lazy, cheap, and self-interested—does it lose its allure; only then can you stop watching your own manipulation as entertainment.

The media and the public are supposed to be on the same side. The media, when it's functioning properly, protects the public against marketers and their ceaseless attempts to trick people into buying things. I've come to realize that that is not how it is today. Marketers and the media—me and the bloggers—we're on the same team, and way too often you are played into watching with rapt attention as we deceive you. And you don't even know that's going on because the content you get has been dressed up and fed to you as news.

THE DARK SIDE
OF SNARK

WHEN INTERNET HUMOR ATTACKS

{
We grow tired of everything but turning others into ridicule, and congratulating ourselves on their defects.

—WILLIAM HAZLITT, *ON THE PLEASURE OF HATING* (1826)
}

ONCE, KNOWING A CLIENT WAS ABOUT TO BE HIT WITH a questionable lawsuit (a shakedown via the media), I suggested we respond by embracing the absurdity rather than fighting against it. The first thing we did was file a countersuit that included all sorts of completely trivial but hilarious details about the plaintiff, along with other juicy bits of gossip. Then I sent both our lawsuit and the original to bloggers—and instead of denouncing or denying anything—I made some jokes in my e-mail. It was all to hint: Make fun of the lawsuit instead of taking it seriously.

Humor is an incredibly effective vehicle for getting pageviews and spreading narratives. So I made the easiest story for blogs to write the one in which they made snarky fun of the entire mess. To me that was better than having a serious discussion about a seriously *untrue* claim against my client. Plus, after the first blog gave the plaintiff (instead of the defendant, my client) the rougher treatment, all the other blogs outdid themselves to give it worse. They made the other party the fool instead of us and ignored any of the potentially negative accusations in the lawsuit.

In this case I felt the end justified the means, since the original lawsuit was dubious. It saved us from being unfairly criticized. Yet it struck me how easy it was to use snark to distract the media and shift the nature of their coverage. I saw that encouraging snark worked just as well for untrue facts as it does for true ones. And that it was impossible to truly control.

Though it worked to my advantage this one time, I've seen this impulse to mock and snark exact incredible costs on clients. I'm sure that sounds weird, because humor seems like such an innocent thing. It seems that way until you watch a client say something that a blogger misconstrues in order to make fun of them. Or you see some site air a suspect accusation against someone—say, that a politician had an affair—and then other blogs, readers, and comedians use that as material to make snarky jokes. The way they see it, it's not their job to prove whether the accusation is true. They're entertainers. The whole subject's sketchy or inaccurate origins get lost once the jokes pile up. All that matters is that people are talking about it. And once blogs do this, they will not relent. Not until the subject is reduced to a permanent caricature.

DEFINING SNARK

New Yorker critic David Denby came closest to properly defining snark in his book *Snark: It's Mean, It's Personal, and It's Ruining Our Conversation*. He didn't succeed entirely, but "[s]nark attempts to steal someone's mojo, erase her cool, annihilate her effectiveness [with] the nasty, insidious, rug-pulling, teasing insult, which makes reference to some generally understood shared prejudice or distaste" will do.

My definition is a little simpler: You know you're dealing with snark when you attempt to respond to a comment and realize that there is nothing you can say. The remark doesn't mean anything—though it still hurts—and the person saying it doesn't care enough about what they said, or anything else for that matter, that would allow you to criticize them back. If I call you a douche, how would you defend yourself without making it worse? You couldn't.

Yet a snark victim's first instinct is to appeal to reason—to tell the crowd, Hey, that's not true! They're making this up! Or appeal to the humanity of the writer by contacting them personally to ask, Why are you doing this to me? I try to stop these clients. I tell them, I know this must hurt, but there's nothing you can do. It's like jujitsu: The energy you'd exert in your defense will be used against you to make the embarrassment worse.

I'm not always successful. Once, in the middle of some ridiculous controversy, Dov put out a statement that said that anyone who actually believed any of it could call his personal cell phone to talk about it. All this did was create something else for blogs to make fun of—the CEO posting his cell phone number online!—and generate about a thousand prank phone calls.

Snark is profitable and easy for blogs. It's the perfect device for people with nothing to say but who *have* to talk (blog) for a living. Snark is the grease of the wheels of the web. Discussing issues fairly would take time and cognitive bandwidth that blogs just don't have. It's the style of choice because it's click-friendly, cheap, and fast.

Bloggers love to hide snark in adjectives, to cut an entire person down with just a few words. You find it in nonsensical mock superlatives: Obama is the "compromiser in chief." Jennifer Lopez is Hennifa Yopez. Dov Charney is pervy and lives in a "masturbatorium." Jennifer Love Hewitt gains a few pounds and becomes Jennifer Love Chewitt. Tucker Max is rapey. What do these words mean? Why do bloggers use them? Lines such as these are intended not so much to wound as to prick. Not to humiliate but to befuddle. Not to make people laugh but to make them smirk or chuckle. To annihilate without effort.

SNARK IN ACTION: A MOST EFFECTIVE WEAPON

You can see snark (and its problems) embodied in Nikki Finke, the notorious Hollywood blogger, and her annual tradition of "live snarking" Hollywood award shows on the blog *DeadlineHollywood*. One year, Finke's live snarking of the Academy Awards was filled with constant criticism that the show was "gay," because it had too much singing and dancing. Funny, right? The height of incisive comedy, to be sure. After repeatedly calling it the "GAYEST OSCARS EVER," Finke turned around and railed against the academy's choice to recognize comedian Jerry Lewis with a humanitarian award because of "antigay slurs"—jokes he'd told during his telethon that raised *more than $60 million* for muscular dystrophy. "Humanitarian my ass," she wrote. Good one, Nikki.

This is snark in its purest form: aggressively, self-righteously full of shit. Finke had made her own gay jokes just minutes before, but somehow she's not only *not* a hypocrite, she's superior to Lewis, even though he actually got off his ass and helped people. Snark is magical that way. You can see why bloggers love to use it.

Denby said that snark is an attempt to "annihilate someone's effectiveness." Well, that's exactly what happened to Scott Adams, the famed creator of *Dilbert*. In addition to the massive audience he had through his comic, Adams became popular online as a blogger, due to his controversial opinions. By all accounts he relished this ascendancy—going so far, I think, as to deliberately stir people up through politically incorrect posts. He loved the attention and traffic that blogs gave him.

Then, in 2011 Adams published a series of posts on his blogs about supposedly unfair restrictions society puts on men regarding sex and gender roles. Although his post was poorly thought out, it was by no means a new topic. Many people—from evolutionary biologists to feminists to comedians—have attributed social problems like infidelity and violence to repressed male emotions and genetics. But the blog cycle lined up so that Adams was wrong for touching the subject. He had set himself up to be snarked.

By that I mean he became a victim of relentless, vitriolic attacks. According to *Jezebel*, Adams's post could best be paraphrased as: "Now I am going to reveal my deeply-held douchebag beliefs." (*Bitch* magazine snarkily reduced it further: "Scott Adams, Douchetoonist.") Or as another blog began, "Let's check in with our old pal Scott Adams—Dilbert creator, former Seattleite, and raving lunatic who spends his days being his own best friend. What's that crazy kook talking about now? Rape? Dick Tweets? This should be good."

Adams said some dumb things, but he had not said any of that. He was accused of advocating rape. Though he'd actually said nothing close, he was misquoted and mischaracterized, first humorously and then in serious outrage. A petition titled "Tell Scott Adams that raping a woman is not a natural instinct" was started and got more than two thousand online signatures.

The response utterly disoriented and overwhelmed Adams. First he tried to delete his post, but that just brought more attention to it. Then he repeatedly tried to defend himself and clarify what he'd really meant. As I tell my clients, that's the equivalent of a squeaky cry of, *"Why is everyone making fun of me?!"* on the playground. Whether it happens in front of snarky blogs or a real-life bully, the result is the same: Everyone makes fun of you even more.

So it went for Scott Adams, no longer best known online as a famous, generation-defining cartoonist but a cross between a buffoon and a misogynistic rape apologist. Everything he does is now a convenient chance for blogs to link readers to their hilarious past coverage, to rehash the same jokes, and to repeat the same accusations. It's a hole Adams simply cannot dig himself out of.

If I had been advising Adams, I would have told him that you lived by the sword of online attention, and now you may have to die by it. In other words, I would tell him to bend over and take it. And then I'd apologize. I'd tell him the whole system is broken and evil, and I'm sorry it's attacking him. But there's nothing that can be done.

SNARK IS HOLLOW AND EMPTY

Unsurprisingly, many bloggers defend snark. According to Adam Sternbergh in *New York* magazine, the standard criticism of snark is wrong, because snark is actually a good thing. "When no one—from politicians to pundits—says what he actually means," he wrote, "irony becomes a logical self-inoculation. Similarly, snark, irony's brat, flourishes in an age of doublespeak and idiocy that's too rarely called out elsewhere. Snark is not a honk of blasé detachment; it's a clarion call of frustrated outrage."

To call this "snark is actually good" interpretation generous would be an understatement. Of course the snarky are dissatisfied and disillusioned—who isn't? The mistake is to assume blogs are crying for change or proposing a solution. There is no admirable "call of frustrated outrage"; it is just shouting for the sake of getting clicks and raising their profile. It's a cheap way to write without thinking while still sounding clever. The contention is ridiculous, that the real reason bloggers make fun of everything is because they hope it will change things.

Snark is intrinsically destructive. It breaks things; it does not build. No politician has ever responded to a joke about his inconsistent policy positions or demagoguery—and certainly not one about his weight or receding hairline—by saying, "You know what? *They're right!* I'm going to be different now!"

If snark was really about change, then bloggers would need to actually believe in what they were saying beneath the humor. It wouldn't change from day to day—we would expect to find consistency in their criticisms, like we do with brilliant satirists like Jon Stewart. But we don't.

An example from my personal experience: After years of joking that Dov Charney was a rapist, a failed businessman, an idiot, a monster, a stock manipulator, and a million other things, *Gawker* nevertheless invited him and American Apparel to their first annual Fleshbot Awards to be given the honor of Sexiest Advertiser. Tucker Max, who *Gawker* had accused of equally defamatory things, was invited too. Why would they invite and reward the people they regularly mock so much? I think part of it is that *Gawker* believes we're all so addicted to feeding the monster that we'll endure any awkward indignity just to get a little more attention. Tucker told them to go fuck themselves, which made me proud.

I did attend to accept the award on Dov's behalf (purely for reconnaissance purposes). I was shocked to find out how smart and friendly in person the bloggers who had said these horrible things were. Then it hit me: They hadn't meant anything they wrote. It had all been a game. If Dov hadn't been a convenient target, they'd have just said the same stuff about someone else. *Gawker* even e-mailed me afterward to ask if we'd sponsor next year's show, as if to say, "We're happy to pick on someone else if you'll be our friend."

WHAT'S THE POINT?

The argument breaks down anyway, even if it wasn't hypocritical. The proper response to fakeness is not to ineffectually lob rocks at palace windows but to coherently and ceaselessly articulate the problems with the dominant institutions. To stand *for* and not simply *against*. But bloggers of this generation, of my generation, are not those types of people. They are not leaders. They lack the strength and energy to *do* anything about "the age of doublespeak and idiocy." All that is left is derision.

Snark offers an outlet for their frustration. Instead of channeling their energy toward productive means, snark dissipates it by throwing itself against anything powerful or successful. If you are big enough to absorb the blows, they think, you deserve them.

For the outsiders without access, snark is their only refuge. And bloggers are outsiders by choice. (Part of *Deadspin*'s tagline is actually, "Sports News without Access. . . .") They can only mock, scorn, lie, and disrupt.

They cannot serve their readers, expose corruption, or support causes. Bloggers are disaffected and angry, and their medium enables it.

As an astute college journalist at Columbia University, who saw through the faux bravery of blogging and the supposed boldness and social value in jabbing from the sidelines, observed:

> Snark is not the response of "the masses" to the inane doublespeak of politicians. It's a defense mechanism for writers who, having nothing to say, are absolutely terrified of being criticized or derided. Snarky writing reflects a primal fear—the fear of being laughed at. Snarky writers don't want to be mocked, so they strike first by mocking everyone in sight.[1]

There is a reason that the weak are drawn to snark while the strong simply say what they mean. Snark makes the speaker feel a strength they know deep down they do not possess. It shields their insecurity and makes the writer feel like they are in control. Snark is the ideal intellectual position. It can criticize, but it cannot be criticized.

Consider Nikki Finke again, who by all accounts is an incredibly vain and perpetually sensitive person. She demands studio heads pay her the proper respect (under the implied threat of bad coverage), and she's filed numerous civil lawsuits for the most trivial of offenses (E*TRADE for $7.5 million for recording a phone call without the "This call may be recorded" warning; a car dealership over the terms of her extended warranty; the *Hollywood Reporter* for supposedly stealing her story ideas; and according to her rival and colleague Sharon Waxman, a hotel for giving her food poisoning). She rarely leaves her home and abstains from essentially all public appearances. She deliberately made sure that there is only one photo of her available online—and it's very old. It is clear that Finke is a deeply insecure and miserable person.

When we give her a podium, this is the baggage that comes along with it. And every so often it falls on an unsuspecting person or group like the pile of self-loathing and jealous bricks that it is. Could one of the producers of the "gayest Oscars ever" respond by saying that Finke's attack clearly came from such a place? No, because then they would be "whiny," "humorless," or "old." God forbid they make a typo in their reply—because then it is all over.

In my experience, it doesn't end with Nikki Finke. Sports bloggers are clearly jealous of the athletic abilities and fame of the professionals they cover; *Pitchfork* album reviews are a sad attempt by the writers to show how many big words they know; *Gawker* writers bitterly lament that some people get to be socialites and celebrities while they have to work for a living. None of this can be used as a response by people like me, of course—"Hey! This guy is a human too, he messes up, he's a hypocrite!" "They're just jealous" is too trite to work as an explanation (even when it's true), and so the snark stands. To respond is merely to expose the jugular once more—to show that you're human and vulnerable and easily rattled.

This is why blogs love to call people douchebags*:

Your Daily Douchebag: John Mayer Edition (PerezHilton.com)

Meanwhile . . . McCain Locks Up the Notorious Douchebag Demographic (*Huffington Post*)

Are MGMT Douchebags? Does it Matter? (*Huffington Post*)

Bud Selig Is Bad for Baseball, a Douchebag (*SB Nation*)

Internet "douchebag" Allthis responds to controversy (*VentureBeat*)

Andrew Breitbart: Death of a Douche (*Rolling Stone* blog)

---

*Gawker held a user poll (see: pseudo-events) for the Douche of the Decade in 2010. It turned out that I had worked for or advised *three* of the ten finalists. Apparently I have a thing for douchebags and didn't even know it.

To be called a douche is to be branded with all the characteristics of what society deigns to hate but can't define. It's a way to dismiss someone entirely without doing any of the work or providing any of the reasons. It says, You are a fool, and everyone thinks it. It is the ultimate insult, because it deprives the recipient of the credentials of being taken seriously.

Roger Ebert calls snarking "cultural vandalism." He's right. Snark makes culture impossible, or rather, it makes the conditions that make culture possible impossible. Earnestness, honesty, vulnerability: These are the targets of snark. "Snark functions as a device to punish human spontaneity, eccentricity, nonconformity, and simple error. Everyone is being snarked into line," he wrote. Yet even Ebert couldn't resist the temptation to snark over the tragic death of *Jackass* star Ryan Dunn. On Twitter, which cries out for snide one-liners, Ebert wrote: "Friends don't let jackasses drink and drive." He apologized shortly afterward, but I doubt that make Dunn's family or friends feel any better.

His remark illustrates the cycle beautifully. For his snarky joke, Ebert was gleefully punished by the angry online horde, who rushed to hurt his feelings in return. (They ignored that Ebert was a recovering alcoholic and may have gotten carried away.) Hackers had his Facebook fan page temporarily deleted, and the second comment atop the apology he was essentially extorted to give still says, "Glad your Facebook page is gone! . . . just like your career." And the snarker is snarked.

As Scott Adams said later in an interview: "Ideas are society's fuel. I drill a lot of wells; most of them are dry. Sometimes they produce. Sometimes the well catches on fire." What *Jezebel* did with their fury and snark was eliminate the freedom of that process. They didn't simply attack Adams by demanding that papers stop publishing his comics but pulled the ultimate grim trigger: They turned him into a laughingstock.

If controversial ideas are the victims of snark, who benefits from it? Who doesn't mind snark? Who likes it? The answer is obvious: People with nothing to lose. People who need to be talked about, like attention-hungry reality stars. There is nothing that you could say that would hurt the cast of *Jersey Shore*. They need you to talk about them, to insult them, and to make fun of them is to do that. They have no reputation to ruin, only notoriety to gain.

So the people who thrive under snark are exactly those who we wish would go away, and the people we value most as cultural contributors lurk in the back of the room, hoping not to get noticed and hurt. Everything in-between may as well not exist. Snark encourages the fakeness and stupidity it is supposedly trying to rail against.

I once saw snark as an opportunity to advance narratives in the media cheaply. But I have been burned by it enough, seen enough of its victims' shell-shocked faces, to know that it is not worth it.

XXII

THE 21st-CENTURY DEGRADATION CEREMONY

BLOGS AS MACHINES OF HATRED AND PUNISHMENT

> It is taking one's conjectures rather seriously to roast someone alive for them.
>
> —MONTAIGNE

SOCIOLOGIST GERALD CROMER ONCE NOTED THAT the decline of public executions coincided almost exactly with the rise of the mass newspaper. Oscar Wilde said it better: "In the old days men had the rack. Now they have the Press."

If only they knew what was coming next:

Online lynch mobs. Attack blogs. Smear campaigns. Snark. Cyber-bullying. Distributed denial of service attempts. Internet meltdowns. Anonymous tipsters. Blog wars. Trolls. Trial by comment section.

It is clear to me that the online media cycle is not a process for developing truth but for performing a kind of cultural catharsis. Blogs, I understood from Wilde and Cromer, served the hidden function of dispensing public punishments. Think of the Salem witch trials: They weren't court proceedings but ceremonies. In that light, the events three hundred years ago suddenly feel very real and current: Oh, they were doing with trumped-up evidence and the gallows what we do with speculation and sensationalism. Ours is just a more civilized way to tear someone to pieces.

My experience with digital lynch mobs is unique. I get frantic calls from sensitive millionaires and billionaires who want me to fend one off. Occasionally they ask that I discreetly direct this mob toward one of their enemies. I am not afraid to say I have done both. I feel I can honestly look myself in the mirror and say the people I protected deserved my efforts—and so did the people I set my sights on. But it is a power I don't relish using, because once I start, I don't stop.

Ask the blogger we went after during Tucker's movie campaign. The ad I ran, which the blog *MediaElites* later called "one of the most despicable personal attacks" they'd ever seen, read in part: "Tucker Max Facts #47: Domestic violence is not funny. Unless *Gawker* editor Richard Blakeley gets arrested for it."* The *New York Post* once caught wind of a campaign of mine against an enemy after my e-mail account was hacked. They were so appalled that they ran a full-page article about it in their Sunday addition: "Charney [really, me] Wages Bizarre Cyber Battle." This article, along with the press I'd bagged to embarrass our target, hangs on my wall like a hunting trophy.

THE DEGRADATION CEREMONY

These acts of ritualized destruction are known by anthropologists as "degradation ceremonies." Their purpose is to allow the public to single out and denounce one of its members. To lower their status or expel them from the group. To collectively take out our anger at them by stripping them of their dignity. It is a we-versus-you scenario with deep biological roots. By the end of it the disgraced person's status is cemented as "not one of us." Everything about them is torn down and rewritten.

The burning passion behind such ceremonies, William Hazlitt wrote in his classic essay "On the Pleasure of Hating," "carries us back to the feuds, the heart-burnings, the havoc, the dismay, the wrongs, and the revenge of a barbarous age and people." You nudge blogs toward those dangerous instincts. They love the excitement of hunting and the rush of the kill without any of the danger. In the throes of such hatred, he writes, "the wild beast resumes its sway within us."

Ask controversial WikiLeaks founder Julian Assange what it feels like to be the sacrificial victim. In less than a year he went from intriguing web hero to ominous pariah, from a revolutionary to a fool. Assange did not suddenly become an awful, evil, and flawed person overnight. He had not changed. But tempers had. Times had. So when a set of very suspect allegations of sexual misconduct came to light, it was the perfect opportunity for a little of that ol' time ritualized destruction.

Over a span of just two weeks, *Gawker*'s headlines on Assange went

---

*Blakeley *had* been arrested recently for a domestic dispute, and the story had been covered up. I wanted people to know. He later pled guilty but only to harassment.

from cute—"What Happened to WikiLeaks Founder Julian Assange's Weird Hair?"—to cutthroat—"Are WikiLeaks Activists Finally Realizing Their Founder Is a Megalomaniac?" Shortly thereafter they launched WikileakiLeaks.org, a semiserious site that asked anonymous users to send in embarrassing information about Assange and the inner workings of the WikiLeaks organization. The only reason: "WikiLeaks Founder Julian Assange Accused then Immediately Un-Accused of Rape." (Note: "Un-Accused." Or don't. Blogs sure didn't.)

Before *Gawker* decided to go the negative route with the Assange story, they tested another direction. Writing the day after the allegations surfaced: "Is WikiLeaks' Julian Assange a Nerdy Sex God?" In other words, it wasn't the allegations that suddenly marked a point of no return; they were just a convenient cover. Blogs needed an exciting new angle about someone they'd already covered a lot. In *Gawker*'s process you can see what happened writ large across popular culture—a brief consideration of the possible narratives before settling on one of complete destruction: Nothing personal, Julian, but you fit the bill.*

I have no idea whether Assange is guilty or not. But neither do the people who decided to roast him alive for it. I do think there were plenty of reasons to have proceeded cautiously with the story. There's a long history of government agencies using scandals to discredit enemies, and we do know that Assange had angered nearly every powerful government in the world (some government officials talked of assassination and/or trying him for treason). Having been behind one or two of these kinds of attacks myself, my instinct is to suspect that there may be someone like me out there working the mob. In fact, many blogs initially suspected the same thing. But that didn't stop them once the ceremony started.

Most important, almost all the "evidence" blogs used in interpretations of Assange's character to convince themselves of his guilt was available and known before the charges came to light. What were labeled as quirks and endearing, rebellious qualities just weeks before suddenly became "creepy." His celebrated need for secrecy was now "disingenuous" and "paranoid." His noble mission for transparency was no longer about freedom but about his own "enormous ego."

Again, Assange hadn't changed. Someone had just reframed him. The role blogs needed him to play had shifted. So Assange became a different person, according to the coverage. He was turned into a caricature of himself. As a result, any redeeming value of his work was utterly irrelevant. That is, the very same work that supposedly made him worth talking about in the first place.

At the risk of sounding like a public service announcement: This can happen to you too. After building Assange up, blogs destroyed him, not because he did anything wrong (although he very well may have; let me stress again that this has nothing to do with his guilt or innocence), but because his ascendancy made them feel angry and small, and now they had ammunition to act on those feelings. Assange learned what it feels like when anyone can leak heinous allegations that the media propagates before verifying. He got to experience personally what he had, through WikiLeaks, helped do to many others.

THE COSTS OF SCANDAL HYSTERIA

A few years ago I was part of a high-profile multimillion-dollar lawsuit involving Dov Charney and Woody Allen. After being wrongfully accused in a series of sensationalized (and later disproved) sexual harassment lawsuits, Dov and American Apparel ran two large billboards in New York City and Los Angeles featuring a satirical image of Woody Allen dressed as a Hasidic Jew with the words "The Highest Rabbi" in Yiddish. Allen sued the company for $10 million for wrongfully using his likeness.

You may remember hearing about it. But you probably didn't know that the billboards—which ran for only a few weeks—were intended to be a statement against the kind of hysterical media-driven destruction talked about here. They were designed to reference the public crucifixion Allen endured during a personal scandal years earlier. Ironically, this was totally because blogs and newspapers were too focused on the lawsuit's big-name celebrity drama to discuss the intended message.

In response, I helped Dov write a long statement that was eventually turned into an editorial in *The Guardian*. It said, in part:

> *My intention was to call upon people to see beyond media and lawsuit-inspired scandal, and to consider people for their true value and for their contribution to society.*
>
> *I feel that the comments of a former friend of Woody Allen, Harvard professor and famous civil rights lawyer Allan Dershowitz, apply to this particular phenomenon: "Well, let's remember, we have had presidents . . . from Jefferson, to Roosevelt, to Kennedy, to Clinton, who have been great presidents. . . . I think we risk losing some of the best people who can run for public office by our obsessive focus on the private lives of public figures."*
>
> *I agree that the increasingly obsessive scrutinization of people's personal lives and their perceived social improprieties has tragically overshadowed the great work of too many artists, scientists, entertainers, entrepreneurs, athletes, and politicians, including Woody Allen.[1]*

Today blogs are our representatives in these degradation ceremonies. They level the accusations on the behalf of the "outraged public." How dare you hold yourself up in front of us as a human being instead of as a caricature, they seem to say. If you don't feel shame, then we will make you feel shame. The onlookers delight in the destruction and pain. Blogs lock onto targets for whatever frivolous reason, which makes sense, since they often played a role in creating the victim's celebrity in the first place, usually under equally frivolous pretenses.

You used to have to be a national hero before you got the privilege of the media and the public turning on you. You had to be a president or a millionaire or an artist. Now we tear people down just as we've begun to build them up. We do this to our fameballs. Our viral video stars. Our favorite new companies. Even random citizens who pop into the news because they did something interesting, unusual, or stupid. First we celebrate them, then we turn to snark, and then, finally, to merciless decimation. No wonder only morons and narcissists enter the public sphere.

It feels good to be a part of something—to tear down and berate. It's not surprising to me that the media would want to assume this role. Consider how the ceaseless, staged, and artificial online news chase makes today's generation of reporters feel. They attended an expensive grad school and live in New York City or San Francisco or Washington, D.C. The wondrous $200,000 a year journalism job is not some myth to them; it was an opportunity dangled in front of them—just as the first generation of reporters after it went extinct. Their life is nothing like that myth. Bloggers must write and film and publish an insurmountable amount of material per day, and only if they're lucky will any of it be rewarded with a bonus or health insurance. Yet the people they cover are often rich and successful or worse, like idiotic and talentless reality television stars. It's enough to make anyone bitter and angry. And indeed they are. They grind with the "rage of the creative underclass," as *New York* magazine called it.

Philosopher Alain de Botton once pointed out that Greek tragedies, though popular entertainment in their day, had a purpose. Despite being gossipy, sometimes salacious, and often violent, they taught the audience to think about how easily an unfortunate situation could befall them, and to be humbled by the flaws of another person. Tragedies could be learned from. But the news of the twenty-first century, he writes, "with its lexicon of perverts and weirdos, failures and losers, lies at one end of the spectrum," and "tragedy lies at the other."

There is nothing to be learned from the tragic rise and fall of public men that we see on blogs. That is not their function. Their degradation is mere spectacle that blogs use to sublimate the general anxieties of their readers. To make us feel better by hurting others. To stress that the people we're reading about are freaks, while we are normal.

And if we're not getting anything out of it, and nobody learns anything from it, then I don't see how you can call blogs anything other than a digital blood sport.

213

XXIII

WELCOME TO
UNREALITY

The quack, the charlatan, the jingo, and the terrorist can flourish only where the public is deprived of independent access to information. But where all news comes at second-hand, where all testimony is uncertain, men cease to respond to truths and respond simply to opinions. The environment in which they act is not realities themselves but the pseudo-environment of reports, rumors, and guesses. The whole reference of thought comes to be what somebody asserts and not what actually is.

—WALTER LIPPMAN,
LIBERTY AND THE NEWS

IN THIS BOOK I HAVE ILLUSTRATED THE WAYS IN WHICH bloggers, as they sit down at their computers, are prompted to speculate, rush, exaggerate, distort, and mislead—and how people like me encourage these impulses

Blogs are assailed on all sides, by the crushing economics of their business, dishonest sources, inhuman deadlines, pageview quotas, inaccurate information, greedy publishers, poor training, the demands of the audience, and so much more. These incentives are *real,* whether you're the *Huffington Post* or some tiny blog. Taken individually, the resulting output is obvious: bad stories, incomplete stories, wrong stories, unimportant stories.

To me, the individual bad stories coughed up by blogging culture looked like success. Their failings were my opportunities. But when I started to see what this process amounted to *collectively*—the cumulative effect of tens of thousands of such posts, written and uploaded day in and day out—my pride turned to fear.

What happens when this material becomes the basis for tomorrow's material—when CNN uses *Gawker* for story ideas? What is the result of millions of blogs fighting to be heard over millions of other blogs—each hoping for a share of an increasingly shrinking attention span? What happens when the incentives rippled through every part of the media system?

These results are unreality. A netherworld between the fake and the real where each builds on the other and they cannot be told apart. This is what happens when the dominant cultural medium—the medium that feeds our other mediums—is so easily corrupted by people like me.

When the news is decided not by what is important but by what readers are clicking; when the cycle is so fast that the news cannot be anything else but consistently and regularly incomplete; when dubious scandals pressure politicians to resign and scuttle election bids or knock millions from the market caps of publicly traded companies; when the news frequently covers itself in stories about "how the story unfolded"—unreality is the only word for it. It is, as Daniel Boorstin, author of 1962's *The Image: A Guide to Pseudo-Events in America*, put it, a "thicket . . . which stands between us and the facts of life."

A SLOW CREEP

Let's start a basic principle: Only the unexpected makes the news. This insight comes from Robert E. Park, the first sociologist to ever study newspapers. "For the news is always finally," he wrote "what Charles A. Dana described it to be, 'something that will make people talk.'" Nick Denton told his writers the same thing nearly one hundred years later: "The job of journalism is to provide surprise."* News is only *news* if it departs from the routine of daily life.

But what if most of what happens is expected? Most things do not depart from the routine. Most things are not worth talking about. But the news *must* be. And so the normal parts of life are omitted from the news by virtue of being normal. I don't mean to say that the constant search for newness or the unexpected is what distorts the news. That would be unfair, because *almost everything* blogs do distorts the news. But this one basic need—fundamental to the very business of blogging—inherently puts our newsmakers at odds with reality. It can only show us a version of reality that serves their needs.

What's known as news is not a summary of everything that has happened recently. It's not even a summary of the most important things that have happened recently. The news, whether it's found online or in print, is just the content that successfully navigated the media's filters. Possibly with my help. Since the news informs our understanding of what is occurring around us, these filters create a constructed reality.

Picture a funnel. At the top we have everything that happens, then everything that happens that comes to be known by the media, then

---

*Remember Bennett as well, trying "not to instruct, but to startle."

everything that is considered newsworthy, then what they ultimately decide to publish, and finally what spreads and is seen by the public.

The news funnel:

ALL THAT HAPPENS

ALL THAT'S KNOWN BY THE MEDIA

ALL THAT IS NEWSWORTHY

ALL THAT IS PUBLISHED AS NEWS

ALL THAT SPREADS

In other words, the media is a mechanism for systematically limiting the information seen by the public.

But we seem to think that the news is informing us! The Internet is what technologists call an "experience technology." The more it is used, the more trust users have in it. The longer a user engages with it, the more comfortable they get and the more they believe in the world it creates.

As we become immersed in blogs our trust in the information we get from them increases. I saw an example of this very clearly in my own education: I watched "Internet sources" go from strictly forbidden in school research to the status quo, and the citing of Wikipedia articles in papers from unacceptable to "okay, but only for really general background information." Internet culture has done one thing with this trust: utterly abused it.

EMBRACING THE FAKE

In April 2011, *Business Insider* editor Henry Blodget put out an advisory to the PR world. He was drowning in elaborate story pitches and information about new services. He just couldn't read them all, let alone write about them. So he proposed a solution: The publicists could write about the product launches of their own clients, and Blodget's site would edit and publish them. "In short," he concluded, "please stop sending us e-mails with story ideas and *just contribute directly to Business Insider*. You'll get a lot more ink for yourself and your clients and you'll save yourself a lot of wasted work" [emphasis mine].[1] His post was seen more than ten thousand times, and each and every view, I can only assume, was followed by a marketer cumming all over their pants.

In Blodget's overzealous drive to create traffic for his site, he didn't mind misinforming. He didn't care who wrote it, so long as it got page-views. He was willing to let PR and marketing professionals and people like me write about their own clients—which he would then pass off as real news and commentary to his readers.

Consider the pseudo-event that is critical to the concept of unreality. As Daniel Boorstin defined them—way back in the 1960s—pseudo-events are anything planned deliberately to attract the attention of the media. A quick run down the list of pseudo-events shows their indispensability to the news business: press releases, award ceremonies, red-carpet events, premieres, product launches, anniversaries, grand openings, "leaks," the contrite celebrity interview after a scandal, the sex tape, the tell-all, the public statement, controversial advertisements, marches on Washington, press junkets, and on and on. While these events do occur, they are not by any stretch of the imagination *real*, since they have been meticulously staged and serve no purpose other than to generate press. The event is not intended to accomplish anything itself but instead to introduce certain narratives into the media.

Apple orchestrates its famous product releases and press conferences at great expense because the publicity helps sell iPhones and iPads. Naturally, that's what a company that wants to increase sales would do: Stage an event, bait the media, profit. Very simple and, honestly, pretty expected. But Blodget, with his "Dear PR Folks" advisory, wasn't falling for a pseudo-event. He was the perpetrator. By inviting publicists to collaborate with him to create fake news he became the purveyor of unreality and its publisher.

Blog economics both depend on and indulge in pseudo-events even more than old media—they thrive on the artificiality. By the nature of being planned, staged, and designed for coverage, pseudo-news is a kind of news subsidy. It is handed to blogs like a glass of water to a thirsty man. As deadlines get tighter and news staffs get smaller, fake events are exactly what bloggers need. More important, because they are clean, clear, and not constrained by the limits of what happens naturally, pseudo-events are typically much more interesting to publishers than real events.

FROM THE FAKE, THE REAL

It's at these vulnerable points that manipulation becomes more powerful than reality. The process is simple: Create a pseudo-event, trade it up the chain, elicit real responses and action, and you have altered reality itself. I may understand the consequences of it now, but that doesn't stop a part of me, even as I write this, from seeing this thirst as an opportunity to insert messages into the discussion online. You can't count on people to restrain themselves from taking advantage of an absurd system—not with millions of dollars at stake. Not when the last line of defense—the fourth estate, known as the media—is involved in the cash grab too.

From here we get the defining feature of our world today: a blurred line between what is real and what is fake; what actually happens and what is staged; and, finally, between the important and the trivial.* There is no doubt in my mind that blogs and blogging culture were responsible for this final break. When blogs can openly proclaim that getting it first is better than getting it right; when a deliberately edited (fake) video can reach, and within hours require action by, the president of the United States; when the perception of a major city can be shaped by what photo-

---

*An actual *TechCrunch* headline: "Rumors of Apple Rumors Now Leading to Rumors of Counter-Rumors."

graphs spread best in an online slideshow; and when someone like me can generate actual outrage over advertisements that don't actually exist—the unreal becomes impossible to separate from the real.

If fake news simply deceived, that would be one thing. The problem with unreality and pseudo-events is not simply that they are unreal; it is that they don't *stay* unreal. While they may themselves exist in some netherworld between real and fake, the domain in which they are consumed and acted on is undoubtedly real. In being reported, these counterfeit events are laundered and passed to the public as clean bills—to buy real things.

As Walter Lippmann wrote, the news constitutes a sort of pseudo-environment, but our responses to that environment is not pseudo but *actual* behavior. In 1922, Lippmann warned us "about the worldwide spectacle of men"—government officials, bankers, executives, artists, ordinary people, and even other reporters—"acting upon their environment moved by stimuli from their pseudo-environment."

That world is exactly what we have now. It's a world where, in 2002, Vice President Dick Cheney leaked bogus information to an attention-hungry reporter for the *New York Times,* and then mentioned his own leak on *Meet the Press* to help convince us to invade Iraq.[2] "There's a story in the *New York Times* this morning, and I want to attribute the *Times,*" Cheney said, citing himself, using something he had planted in the press as proof that untrue information was now "public" and accepted fact. He used his own pseudo-event to create pseudo-news.

I use unreality to get free publicity. Cheney used his media manipulations to drive the public toward war. And no one knew until it was way too late. By the time they did the facts had been established, the fake made real by media chatter, and a real war had been waged. From the pseudo-environment came actual behavior.

Welcome to unreality, my friends. It's fucking scary.

XXIV

HOW TO READ
A BLOG

AN UPDATE ON ACCOUNT
OF ALL THE LIES

{
Truth is like a lizard; it leaves its tail in your fingers
and runs away knowing full well that it will grow a
new one in a twinkling.

—IVAN TURGENEV TO LEO TOLSTOY
}

WHEN YOU SEE A BLOG BEGIN WITH "ACCORDING TO A tipster . . ." know that the tipster was someone like me tricking the blogger into writing what I wanted.

When you see "We're hearing reports" know that reports could mean anything from random mentions on Twitter to message board posts, or worse.

When you see "leaked" or "official documents" know that the leak really meant someone just e-mailed a blogger, and that the documents are almost certainly not official and are usually fake or fabricated for the purpose of making desired information public.

When you see "BREAKING" or "We'll have more details as the story develops" know that what you're reading reached you too soon. There was no wait and see, no attempt at confirmation, no internal debate over whether the importance of the story necessitated abandoning caution. The protocol is going to press early, publishing before the basics facts are confirmed, and not caring whether it causes problem for people.

When you see "Updated" on a story or article know that no one actually bothered to rework the story in light of the new facts—they just copied and pasted some shit at the bottom of the article.

When you see "Sources tell us . . ." know that these sources are not vetted, they are rarely corroborated, and they are desperate for attention.

When you see a story tagged with "EXCLUSIVE" know that it means the blog and the source worked out an arrangement that included favorable coverage. Know that in many cases the source gave this exclusive to multiple sites at the same time or that the site is just taking ownership of a story they stole from a lesser-known site.

When you see "said in a press release" know that it probably wasn't even actually a release the company paid to officially put out over the wire. They just spammed a bunch of blogs and journalists via e-mail.

When you see "According to a report by" know that the writer summarizing this report from another outlet has but the basest abilities in reading comprehension, little time to spend doing it, and every incentive to simplify and exaggerate.

When you see "We've reached out to So-and-So for comment" know that they sent an e-mail two minutes before hitting "publish" at 4:00 A.M., long after they'd written the story and closed their mind, making absolutely no effort to get to the truth before passing it off to you as the news.

When you see an attributed quote or a "said So-and-So" know that the blogger didn't actually talk to that person but probably just stole the quote from somewhere else, and per the rules of the link economy, they can claim it as their own so long as there is a tiny link to the original buried in the post somewhere.

When you see "which means" or "meaning that" or "will result in" or any other kind of interpretation or analysis know that the blogger who did it likely has absolutely zero training or expertise in the field they are opining about. Nor did they have the time or motivation to learn. Nor do they mind being wildly, wildly off the mark, because there aren't any consequences.

When you hear a friend say in conversation "I was reading that . . ." know that today the sad fact is that they probably just glanced at something on a blog.

RELYING ON ABANDONED SHELLS

The process for finding, creating, and consuming information has fundamentally changed with the advent of the web and the rise of blogging. However, the standards for what constitutes news are different, the vigor with which such information is vetted is different, the tone with which this news is conveyed is different, and the longevity of its value is different. Yet, almost without exception, the words we use to describe the news and the importance readers place on them remains the same.

In a world of no context and no standard, the connotations of the past retain their power, even if those things are fractions of what they once were. Blogs, to paraphrase Kierkegaard, left everything standing but cunningly emptied them of significance.

Words like developing, exclusive, and sources are incongruent with our long-held assumptions about what they mean or what's behind them. Bloggers use these "substance words" (like Wikipedia's weasel words) to give status to their flimsy stories. They use the language of Woodward and Bernstein but apply it to a media world that would make even Hearst queasy. They us what George W. S. Trow called "abandoned shells."

Why does this matter? We've been taught to believe what we read. That where there is smoke there must be fire, and that if someone takes the time to write down and publish something, they believe in what they are saying. The wisdom behind those beliefs is no longer true, yet the public marches on, armed with rules of thumb that make them targets for manipulation rather than protection.

I have taken advantage of that naïveté. And I'm not even the worst of the bunch. I'm no different than everyone else; I too am constantly tricked—by bloggers, by publishers, by politicians, and by marketers. I'm even tricked by my own monstrous creations.

THE AGE OF NO AUTHORITIES

And so fictions pass as realities. Everyone is selling and conning, and we hardly even know it. Our emotions are being triggered by simulations—

unintentional or deliberate misrepresentations—of cues we've been taught were important. We read some story and it feels important, believing that the news is real and the principles of reporting took place, but it's not.

Picture a movie poster for an independent film that wants to be received as artistic and deep. It probably features the laurel leaves icon—for awards like "Best Picture," "Critic's Choice," or "Official Selection." These markers originally symbolized a handful of important film festivals. Then it became important for every city, even neighborhoods inside cities, to have their own film festival. There also the significant differences in the "winners" and the few dozen or even hundreds of "selections." The use of the festival laurels is to conjure up the implicit value associated with scarcity for the viewer despite the enormous gap between the connotation and the reality.

The laurel leaf illusion is a metaphor for the web. It underpins everything from the link economy—a link looks like a citation, yet it is not—to headlines that bait our clicks. It's why trading up the chain works and it's the reason why you could get your name in the press tomorrow through HARO.

What these people are trying to do is to find some, any, stamp of approval or signal of credibility. Blogs have a few minutes to write their posts, few resources, and little support, but because of the One-Off Problem they need to be heard over thousands of other sites. They desperately need something that says "this is not like those other things" even though it is. So they make up differentiators and misuse old ones.

"In the age of no-authority" wrote Trow, "these are the authorities."

We live in a media world that desperately needs context and authority but can't find any because we destroyed the old markers and haven't created reliable new ones. As a result, we couch new things in old terms that are really just husks of what they once were. Skepticism will never be enough to combat this. Not even enough to be a starting point.

It is now almost cliché for people to say, "if the news is important, it will find me." This belief itself relies on abandoned shells. It depends on the assumption that the important news will break through the noise while the trivial will be lost. It could not be more wrong. As I discovered in my media manipulations, the information that finds us online—what spreads—is the worst kind. It raised itself above the din not through its value, importance, or accuracy but through the opposite, through slickness, titillation, and polarity.

I made a lot of money and had a great time playing with the words that make up the news. I exploited the laziness behind the news and people's reading habits. But from the abuse of abandoned shells came another one.

Our knowledge and understanding is the final empty, hollow shell. What we think we *know* turns out to be based on nothing, or worse than nothing—misdirection and embellishment. Our facts aren't fact, they are opinions dressed up like facts. Our opinions aren't opinions; they are emotions that feel like opinions. Our information isn't information; it's just hastily assembled symbols.

There is no way that is a good thing, no matter how much I gained from it personally.

CONCLUSION

SO . . . WHERE TO FROM HERE?

I WISH I COULD TELL YOU THAT THE QUOTE I'M ABOUT
to give you is from some courageous new media critic. I wish I could point
to it and say, See, someone gets it. We're going to be OK. Hell, I wish *I'd*
said it.

> *Fake news. I don't mean fake news in the Fox News sense. I mean the*
> *fake news that clogs up most newspapers and most news websites, for*
> *that matter. The new initiative will go nowhere. The new policy isn't*
> *new at all. . . . The product isn't revolutionary. And journalists pre-*
> *tend that these official statements and company press releases actu-*
> *ally constitute news. . . . Fake news, manufactured; hyped, rehashed,*
> *retracted—until at the end of the week you know no more than at the*
> *beginning. You really might as well wait for a weekly like the Econo-*
> *mist to tell you what the net position is at the end of the week.*[1]

I was hoping to be able to go out on a hopeful note. But I'm not able do
that. Because the person who said it is Nick Denton, one of the biggest
topics of this book.

In an interview with *The Atlantic* magazine, Denton claimed he was on
a "jihad" inside *Gawker* "against fake news." It's an irony almost too much
to bear, from him or from virtually all other bloggers. It's like Kim Kar-
dashian complaining about how fake reality TV shows are. Not that there
is any question about a media jihad. As I have shown in this book, there
is one, only it is a war with you, against you. It's me against them, against
you. By proxy we fight countless battles for your attention, and we'll go to
any length to get it.

The result is a loop of incentives that cannot be escaped.

More than twenty-five years ago, in *Amusing Ourselves to Death*, Neil
Postman argued that the needs of television, then our culture's chief mode

of communicating ideas, had come to determine the very culture it was supposed to represent. The particular way that television stages the world, he wrote, becomes the model for how the world itself is to be staged.

Entertainment powered television, and so everything that television touched—from war to politics to art—would inevitably be turned into entertainment. TV had to create a fake world to fit its needs, and we, the audience, watched that fake world on TV, imitated it, and it became the new reality in which we lived. The dominant cultural medium, Postman understood, determines culture itself.

Well, television is no longer the main stage of culture. The Internet is. Blogs are. YouTube is. Twitter is. And their demands control our culture exactly as television once did. Only the Internet worships a different god: Traffic. It lives and dies by clicks, because that's what drives ad revenue and influence. The central question for the Internet is not, Is this entertaining? but, Will this get attention? Will it spread?

You've seen the economics behind the spread of news online. It's not a pretty picture (although if it was, it'd be a slideshow). Rather than turn the world into entertainment, these forces reduce it to conflict, controversy, and crap. Blogs have no choice but to turn the world against itself for a few more pageviews, turning you against the world, so you'll read them. They produce a web of mis-, dis-, and un-information so complete that few people—even the system's purveyors—are able to tell fact from fiction, rumor from reality. This is what makes it possible for manipulators like me to make our living.

What does it mean when Nick Denton, the innovator behind nearly every trend that has come to define blogging today—the man who fed and raised the monster more than anyone—can't stand the final product? What does it mean when he doesn't realize that his sites created the very market for fake news he claims to hate?

I guess it brings us full circle. He is unhappy. I am unhappy—both with the system and my own role in it. We're right back to where we started, and now we have another chance to decide how the story ends. Only this time you should be involved, now that you know how the media works.

I could have confessed a thousand more violations, felonies I have committed against a media system that practically invited me to perpetrate them. But what I have disclosed is more than enough to show you what goes on behind the scenes and the sickening secrets by which blogs and their millionaire publishers operate. There is more, and the appalling splendor only gets more stunning the deeper you dig.

Bloggers lie, distort, and attack because it is in their interest to do so. The medium believes it is giving the people what they want when it simplifies, sensationalizes, and panders. This creates countless opportunities for manipulation and influence. I now know what the cumulative effect of this manipulation is: Its effect is unreality. Surrounded by illusions, we lash out at our fellow man for his very humanness, congratulate ourselves as a cover for apathy, and confuse advertising with art. Reality. Our lives. Knowing what is important. Information. These have been the causalities.

My mission was to rip back the curtain and expose a problem that thus far everyone else has been too intimidated or self-interested to discuss openly: Our dominant cultural medium—the web—is hopelessly broken. I did so at considerable risk to my own livelihood and reputation. Despite those costs, I intended to make it impossible for you to read this book and conclude anything other than this: All aspects of our society suffer because of these economics.

I wish there was an easy solution to all of it. It would help me answer my critics and the defensive bloggers who will invariably whine: Well, what are we supposed to do about it? Or, Okay, wise guy, tell us how to fix it. Well, I don't know the answer, and I don't put any stock in that kind of chatter. My job was to prove that something was massively, massively wrong and to come clean about my role in it. To prove that we've all been feeding the monster. What exactly to do about it will be the work of those who come after me.

If I saw bright spots or green sprouts, I would have pointed them out. If there were solutions, I would give them to you. But currently I don't see any. In fact, I object to using the word "solution" at all. To seek a solution implies and confirms that this problem needs to even exist. It takes for granted the bad assumptions at the root of blogs—assumptions that are deeply mistaken.

Take the frantic chase for pageviews, for example. This wrongly assumes that the traffic blogs generates is worth anything. It isn't. Sites sell only a fraction of their inventory each month, essentially giving the rest away for pennies, yet they attempt to grow their traffic above all else. As I write this the TMZ.com tab in my browser has refreshed dozens of times even though I have not looked at it in nearly an hour. Many sites do this: *Drudge Report, Huffington Post, Search Engine Journal*, and so on. Free pageviews! The advertisers who paid for those impressions were robbed, and the blogs that charged for them are no more than crooks.

Meanwhile, smaller sites that have built core audiences on trust and loyalty sell out their ad space months in advance. They have less total inventory, but they sell all of theirs at higher prices and are more profitable, sustainable businesses. Blogs scramble for a few thousand extra pageviews, and manipulate their readers to do so, because they value the wrong metrics and the wrong revenue stream. They follow short-term and short-sighted incentives.

But incentives can be changed, just as the *New York Times* showed in switching from the one-off to a subscription model under Adolph Ochs. In order to survive as a quality publication, the *New York Times* is redefining its economics once again. The recent implementation of their controversial pay wall (which limits readers to twenty free articles a month before requiring them to pay for more access) is a lesson in great incentives. According to economist Tyler Cowen, it means that "the new NYT incentive is to have more than twenty must-read articles each month."[2] How absurd that under the current model—the one that most publishers are sticking with and believe in—there is no imperative to produce these must-read articles, only must-clicks.

As Ed Wallace, the *BusinessWeek* writer, reminds us: "The first job of the journalist is to ask, 'Is this information true?'" Bloggers refuse to accept this mantle. Instead of getting us the truth, they focus on one thing, and one thing only: getting their publisher pageviews. I don't care that finding the truth can be expensive, that iterative news is faster, or that it's too hard not to play the pageview game. Find another business if you don't like it. Because your professional's *true* purpose is to serve the best interests of your readers—doing anything else is to misread your own long-term interests. Advertisers pay you to get to readers, so screwing the readers is a bad idea.

Readers hold equally exhausting assumptions of their own. The current system of delegated trust and deferred responsibility exists because readers have tacitly accepted the burden that blogs have abdicated. We've assumed it was our duty to sort through the muck and garbage to find the occasional gem, to do their fact-checking for them, to correct their mistakes and call ourselves contributors, when actually we're cogs. We never asked the critical question: If we have to do all the work, what are we paying you guys for?

When intelligent people read, they ask themselves a simple question: What do I plan to do with this information? Most readers have abandoned even pretending to consider this. I imagine it's because they're afraid of the answer: There isn't a thing we can do with it. There is no practical purpose in our lives for most of what blogs produce other than distraction. When readers decide to start demanding quality over quantity, the economics of Internet content will change. Manipulation and marketing will immediately become more difficult.

It took me a long time to get to this point, but I know that I am a large part of the problem as well. Nobody forced me to do what I did. I was a bad actor, and I created many of the loopholes I now criticize. Both I and my clients profited greatly from the manipulations I confessed here: Millions of books were sold, celebrity was created, and brands were reinvigorated and built. But we also paid very heavily for those gains with currency like dignity, respect, and trust. Deep down I suspect that the losses may not have been worth the cost. Marketers need to understand this. Social media is an industry that now employs thousands of people, and you may just be starting out in it. All I will say is that if you chase the kind of attention I chased, and use the tactics I have used, there will be blowback. Consider that seriously.

As a society, we don't need to submit to the rule of an abusive media system, as though those who control it are in charge and not us or our laws. In other countries, libel and defamation laws require a "conspicuous retraction" by the publisher if proven. A lame update at the bottom of a blog wouldn't cut it there and shouldn't cut it anymore *anywhere*. Colonial newspapers at various points in British history were required to post a security bond in order to enter the publishing business. It was intended to secure payments in the event of a libel action and to ensure some responsibility by the press. It gave the public (and the state) some recourse against publishers who often had few assets to pay for the damage they could potentially inflict. There is precedent for these types of protections—

which blogs show us we desperately need once again. We have simply forgotten about them.

We must rid ourselves of the false beliefs that caused so much of this. Publicity does not come easily, profits do not come easily, and knowledge does not come easily. The delusion that they could was what fed the monster most heartily. It is what propelled us past so many of the warning signs that this was simply not working.

You cannot have your news instantly *and* have it done well. You cannot have your news reduced to 140 characters or less without losing large parts of it. You cannot manipulate the news but not expect it to be manipulated against you. You cannot have your news for free; you can only obscure the costs. If, as a culture, we can learn this lesson, and if we can learn to love the hard work, we will save ourselves much trouble and collateral damage. We must remember: There is no easy way.

The current system cannot stand without these faulty assumptions. My contribution was to expose the problem, because once seen for all its contradictions and selfishness, it begins to fall apart. What is known can't jerk us around unwittingly. Before anything can be resolved, the implicit must be made into the explicit.

This may seem simplistic. But I have repeatedly used the metaphor of a feedback loop or arms race in this book—a company hires an online hitman like me, and so their rival does too; a blog tricks their readers with an exaggerated story, and their next post must deceive their skeptical audience more boldly. Opting out of this cycle, choosing not to feed the monster, is not some thankless favor I am asking for. It has massive and immediate implications for the rest of the chain.

Every new invention brings new problems with it. This is true for every medium and every communication method in history. For instance, in only the last thousand years of Latin were spaces inserted between words—a direct result of the spreading of books and scrolls that drowned people in so much text that they couldn't read. Blogs have created their own problems. We too are drowning in information that bleeds together into an endless blur. Someone has to stand up and say the emperor has no clothes—the words have no spaces between them, and godammit, that's ridiculous—because only after the problem is identified and the new ideal articulated can creative solutions can be found.

235

Part of writing this book was about a controlled burn of the plays and scams I had created and used along with the best of them. They have become constant dangers to me and the people I care about—to culture itself, in some ways. I not only want to render the tricks useless by exposing how they work, but I want to opt out of doing them myself. I want to force everyone else to opt out as well. Hopefully clearing this ominous pile of debris will make it easier to start fresh.

Of course, I know some of you might ignore that part and use this book as an instruction manual. So be it. You will come to regret that choice, just as I have. But you will also have fun, and it could make you rich.

To those of you who I have burned in this book, who I have hurt or taken aim at or criticized or made fun of, I'm sorry. Trust me, I'm lying when I say that. It's just that you deserve better. And the second you stop and walk away, the monster will start to wither, and you will be happy again.

I confess all I have confessed in order to make that an option.

ACKNOWLEDGMENTS

TO MY MENTORS: TUCKER MAX, ROBERT GREENE, Aaron Ray, and Dov Charney. I learned these lessons on your dime and patience. You taught me a craft and a profession and imbued me with the humility and responsibility not to let it corrupt me or go to my head. Thank you for shaping me into the person I am today—in every sense of the word.

Tucker, as a clueless eighteen-year-old I felt there was a lot I could learn from you. Who would have thought that the most valuable of those lessons would be how to be a loyal and generous friend? Thank you for everything.

Dov, you made me feel loved and cared about in a way that goes far beyond the obligations of a "boss." No one deserves the punishment that the monster mercilessly inflicted on American Apparel, least of all you. They'll get theirs. You have supported me, been my patron, and given me immense resources. I hope I have made you proud.

Thank you to my literary agent, Stephen Hanselman, whom I called on October 9 with the unsolicited manuscript of this book and by November 15 had more offers on it than I knew what to do with. Thank you to Julia for your tireless work behind the scenes. More important, thank you to Tim Ferriss (so glad we met all these years ago) for introducing us and paving the way.

Thank you to the wonderful staff at Portfolio—my excellent editor Niki Papadopoulos, publicist Amanda Pritzker—and to Adrian Zackheim.

Thank you to Erin Tyler for an amazing cover and graphic design.

Thank you to my employees, who were often tasked with participating in the escapades detailed in this book. I was training you in the dark arts whether you knew it or not. Use that power responsibly.

Thank you to everyone who has e-mailed me from my site and asked me thought-provoking questions. It was in trying to answer them that I developed many of the ideas described here. Thanks to everyone who read a draft of this book and gave great notes: Nils Parker, Derek Kreindler, Neil Strauss, Andrew McMillen, Amy Holiday, Sep Kamvar, Jeff Waldman, Ian Claudius, Ben Bartley, Drew Curtis, and Milt Deherrera. Thanks to those (everyone else I know) who didn't read a draft but endured my many rants about the subject.

Sammy. My rule has always been to keep the crazy at home. You got stuck with the crazy and supported and loved me anyway. I could not have done this—or anything—without you. Thank you. Hi Hanno.

Here's to books.

NOTES

INTRODUCTION

1. Tucker Max e-mailed Daulerio in June 2009 about a *Deadspin* story that incorrectly guessed the identity of someone in one of Tucker's exploits. Daulerio's candor was breathtaking. In addition to his line about gossip blogging being "professional wrestling," he said, about the speculative errors, "Honestly, I could give a fuck who it is, intrepid reporter or not, so cover your ass, their ass, as much as you feel is necessary for this. You keep doing whatever it is you're doing, and I'll do the same."

I: BLOGS MAKE THE NEWS

1. Jeremy W. Peters, "Political Blogs Are Ready to Flood Campaign Trail," *New York Times*, January 29, 2011, http://www.nytimes.com/2011/01/30/business/media/30blogs.html.

II: HOW TO TURN NOTHING INTO SOMETHING IN THREE WAY-TOO-EASY STEPS

1. Lindsey Robertson, "The Do's and Don'ts of Online Publicity, For Some Reason," last modified January 12, 2010, http://lindsayrobertson.tumblr.com/post/330892541/the-dos-and-donts-of-online-publicity-for-some.
2. "National Survey Finds Majority of Journalists Now Depend on Social Media for Story Research," January 20, 2010, http://us.cision.com/news_room/press_releases/2010/2010-1-20_gwu_survey.asp.
3. Ibid.
4. NPR staff, "The Music Man Behind 'Entourage' Shares His Secret," last modified November 20, 2011, http://www.npr.org/2011/11/20/142558220/the-music-man-behind-entourage-shares-his-secret.
5. Tina Dupoy, "Tucker Max: America's Douche," last modified September 24, 2009, http://www.mediabistro.com/fishbowlla/tucker-max-americas-douche_b9479; Dakota Smith, "LA Not Particularly Welcoming to Tucker Max," last modified September 24, 2009, http://la.curbed.com/archives/2009/09/la_not_particularly_welcoming_to_tucker_max.php.
6. Mackenzie Schmidt, "16 Angry Women Attempt to Protest the World's Biggest Douche. Or, The Anti–Tucker Max Story, 'I Hope They Serve Subpoenas in Hell,'" last modified October 1, 2009, http://blogs.villagevoice.com/runnin scared/2009/10/16_angry_women.php.
7. Dan Shanoff, "Brett Favre on 'Dancing With the Stars?' No. Not Even a Rumor," last modified February 11, 2011, http://www.quickish.com/articles/brett-favre-on-dancing-with-the-stars-no-not-even-a-rumor; Barry Petchesky, "From Bleacher Report to ProFootballTalk: A Brett Favre Non-Rumor Goes National," last modified February 11, 2011, http://deadspin.com/5757958/from-bleacher-report-to-profootballtalk-a-brett-favre-non+rumor-goes-national.

8. Steve Myers, "Florida Quran Burning, Afghanistan Violence Raise Questions About the Power of Media Blackouts," last modified April 7, 2011, http://www.poynter.org/latest-news/making-sense-of-news/126878/florida-quran-burning-afghanistan-violence-raise-questions-about-the-power-of-media-blackouts; Jeff Bercovici, "When Journalism 2.0 Kills," last modified April 7, 2011, http://www.forbes.com/sites/jeffbercovici/2011/04/07/when-journalism-2-0-kills.

III: THE BLOG CON: HOW PUBLISHERS MAKE MONEY ONLINE

1. TMZ Staff, "TMZ Falls For JFK Photo Hoax," last modified December 28, 2009, http://www.thesmokinggun.com/documents/celebrity/tmz-falls-jfk-photo-hoax.
2. Forest Kamer, "Gawker's March Editorial Review Memo: Essentially 'Stop Writing Shitty Headlines.' Also 'MOAR SEX CRIMES PLZKTHX,' " last modified April 7, 2010, http://blogs.villagevoice.com/runninscared/2010/04/gawkers_march_e.php.

IV: TACTIC #1: BLOGGERS ARE POOR; HELP PAY THEIR BILLS

1. Ben Parr, "What Do the Big Tech Blogs Such as Techcrunch or Mashable Look for When They Hire Writers?" last modified December 28, 2010, http://www.quora.com/What-do-the-big-tech-blogs-such-as-TechCrunch-or-Mashable-look-for-when-they-hire-writers.
2. Darren Rowse, "Weblogs Inc. Pays $4 per Post to Bloggers," last modified August 27, 2005, http://www.problogger.net/archives/2005/08/27/weblogs-inc-pays-4-per-post-to-bloggers.
3. David Kaplan, "Updated: Seeking Alpha On Track to Pay Its Bloggers $1.2 Million This Year," last modified July 5, 2011, http://paidcontent.org/article/419-seeking-alpha-on-track-to-pay-its-bloggers-1.2-million-this-year; Joe Pompeo, "The Awl to Start Paying its Writers in January," last modified December 14, 2010, http://news.yahoo.com/blogs/cutline/awl-start-paying-writers-january-20101214-111403-891.html.
4. Henry Blodget, "More Than You Ever Wanted to Know About the Economics of the Online News Business—A TWEETIFESTO," last modified March 27, 2010, http://www.businessinsider.com/henry-blodget-more-than-you-ever-wanted-to-know-about-the-economics-of-the-online-news-business-a-tweetifesto-2010-3.
5. Jenni Maier, "Tucker Max Proves You Can Pay Celebrities to Tweet Whatever You Want," last modified February 9, 2012, http://crushable.com/entertainment/tucker-max-pay-celebrities-to-tweet-213.
6. Nate Silver, "The Economics of Blogging and the Huffington Post," last modified February 12, 2011, http://fivethirtyeight.blogs.nytimes.com/2011/02/12/the-economics-of-blogging-and-the-huffington-post.
7. Victoria Barret, "Is Pure Journalism Unaffordable?" last modified February 17, 2011, http://www.forbes.com/sites/victoriabarret/2011/02/17/is-pure-journalism-unaffordable; Blodget, "More Than You Ever Wanted To Know."

V: TACTIC #2: TELL THEM WHAT THEY WANT TO HEAR

1. "A Study of the News Ecosystem of One American City," last modified January 11, 2010, http://www.journalism.org/analysis_report/how_news_happens.
2. Taylor Buley, "Tech's Would-Be Takeover Con Artist," last modified October

27, 2010, http://www.forbes.com/2009/10/27/fraud-stockbrocker-google
-technology-Internet-takeover.html.

3.   Robert Scoble, last modified July 28, 2010, https://profiles.google.com/
111091089527727420853/buzz/EsMhJvooEWv.

VI: TACTIC #3: GIVE THEM WHAT SPREADS, NOT WHAT'S GOOD

1.   Nicole Hardesty, "Haunting Images of Detroit's Decline (PHOTOS)," last
modified March 23, 2011, http://www.huffingtonpost.com/2011/03/23/detroit
-decline_n_813696.html; Stephen McGee, "Detroit's Iconic Ruins," http://
www.nytimes.com/slide show/2010/03/06/us/0306_STATION_7.html; Andrew Moore, "Slide Show: Detroit, City of Ruins," last modified April 8, 2010,
http://www.nybooks.com/blogs/nyrblog/2010/apr/08/slide-show-detroit-city
-of-ruins; *The Observer*, "Detroit in ruins," last modified January 1, 2011,
http://www.guardian.co.uk/artanddesign/gallery/2011/jan/02/photography
-detroit#; Bruce Gilden, "Detroit: The Troubled City," last modified May 6, 2009,
http://blog.magnumphotos.com/2009/05/detroit_the_troubled_city.html.

2.   Noreen Malone, "The Case Against Economic Disaster Porn," last modified
January 22, 2011, http://www.tnr.com/article/metro-policy/81954/Detroit
-economic-disaster-porn.

3.   Adrianne Jeffries, "Interview With Jonah Peretti, on BuzzFeed's Move Into
News," last modified January 18, 2012, http://www.betabeat.com/2012/01/18/
interview-with-jonah-peretti-on-buzzfeeds-move-into-news.

4.   Jonah Berger and Katherine L. Milkman, "What Makes Content Viral?" 2011,
Wharton School.

5.   Annie Lang, "Negative Video as Structure: Emotion, Attention, Capacity and
Memory," *Journal of Broadcasting & Electronic Arts* (Fall 1996): 460.

VII: TACTIC #4: HELP THEM TRICK THEIR READERS

1.   Venkatesh Rao, "The Greasy, Fix-It 'Web of Intent' Vision," last modified August 17, 2010, http://www.ribbonfarm.com/2010/08/17/the-greasy-fix-it-web
-of-intent-vision/.

VIII: TACTIC #5: SELL THEM SOMETHING THEY CAN SELL
(EXPLOIT THE ONE-OFF PROBLEM)

1.   Jacqui Cheng, "Why Keeping Up with RSS Is Poisonous to Productivity, Sanity," http://arstechnica.com/web/news/2011/09/why-keeping-up-with-rss-is
-poisonous-to-productivity-sanity.ars.

IX: TACTIC #6: MAKE IT ALL ABOUT THE HEADLINE

1.   Kenneth Whyte, *The Uncrowned King: The Sensational Rise of William Randolph Hearst.* Berkeley, Cal.: Counterpoint, 2009.

2.   Upton Sinclair, *The Brass Check: A Study of American Journalism.* Champaign,
Il.: University of Illinois Press, 1919.

3.   Jenna Sauers, "American Apparel's Rejected Halloween Costume Ideas," last
modified October 18, 2010, http://Jezebel.com/5666842/exclusive-american
-apparels-rejected-halloween-costume-idea.

4.   Eric Schmidt, "How Google Can Help Newspapers," *Wall Street Journal*, December 1, 2009, http://online.wsj.com/article/SB1000142405274870410710457
4569570797550520.html.

5. Carr, "Taylor Momsen," *New York Times*.

6. E. B. Boyd, "Brains and Bots Deep Inside Yahoo's CORE Grab a Billion Clicks," *Fast Company*, August 1, 2011, http://www.fastcompany.com/1770673/how -yahoo-got-to-a-billion-clicks.

X: TACTIC #7: KILL 'EM WITH PAGEVIEW KINDNESS

1. http://www.businessinsider.com/the-aol-way#-17.

2. http://www.newyorker.com/online/blogs/susanorlean/2.html.

3. Brandon Mendelson, "Mashable Continues to Cash In on Death," last modified September 6, 2011, http://ph.news.yahoo.com/mashable-continues-cash -death-173201323.html.

4. Bryan C. Warnock, "Re: RFCs: Two Proposals for Change," last modified August 7, 2000, http://www.nntp.perl.org/group/perl.bootstrap/2000/08/ msg1127.html.

5. Nate Silver, "The Economics of Blogging and the Huffington Post," last modified February 12, 2011, http://fivethirtyeight.blogs.nytimes.com/2011/02/12/ the-economics-of-blogging-and-the-huffington-post.

XI: TACTIC #8: USE THE TECHNOLOGY AGAINST ITSELF

1. Justin Hall, last modified January 10, 1996, http://links.net/daze/96/01/10.

2. "The Gawker Job Interview," last modified January 12, 2008, http://www .nytimes.com/2008/01/12/fashion/13gweb.html.

3. S. Kim, "Content Analysis of Cancer Blog Posts," *Journal of the Medical Library Association* (October 2009) 97: 260–66.

4. Jakob Nielsen, "Long vs. Short Articles as Content Strategy," last modified November 12, 2007, http://www.useit.com/alertbox/content-strategy.html.

5. Jack Fuller, "Public Inauthenticity: a Crisis of Falling Expectations," May 12, 1999, http://newsombudsmen.org/fuller.html.

XII: TACTIC #9: JUST MAKE STUFF UP (EVERYONE ELSE IS DOING IT)

1. "Seeing Non-existent Things," *Washington Post*, June 18, 1899, accessed July 30, 2011, ProQuest Historical Newspapers.

2. Meranda Watling, "Where to Find Original, Local Story Ideas Online," last modified May 31, 2011, http://www.mediabistro.com/10000words/where-to -find-original-local-story-ideas-online_b4352.

3. MG Siegler, "Content Everywhere, But Not a Drop to Drink," February 12, 2012, http://parislemon.com/post/17527312140/content-everywhere-but-not -a-drop-to-drink.

4. Maysa Rawi, "Has American Apparel Gone Too Far with 'Creepy' Controversial New Campaign?" last modified January 11, 2011, http://www.dailymail.co .uk/fe-mail/article-1346138/Has-American-Apparel-gone-far-creepy -controversial-new-campaign.html.

5. Nate Freeman, "Gawker Editor Remy Stern Talks Approach to O'Donnell Story," last modified October 28, 2010, http://www.observer.com/2010/media/ gawker-editor-remy-stern-approach-odonnell-story?utm_medium=partial -text&utm_campaign=media.

XIII: IRIN CARMON, *THE DAILY SHOW,* AND ME: THE PERFECT STORM OF HOW TOXIC BLOGGING CAN BE

1. Irin Carmon, "*The Daily Show*'s Woman Problem," last modified June 23, 2010, http://Jezebel.com/5570545.
2. Jennifer Mascia, "A Web Site That's Not Afraid to Pick a Fight," *New York Times,* July 11, 2010, http://www.nytimes.com/2010/07/12/business/media/12Jezebel.html.
3. "Women of *The Daily Show* Speak," http://www.thedailyshow.com/message.
4. Dave Itzkoff, "'The Daily Show' Women Say the Staff Isn't Sexist," *New York Times,* July 6, 2010, http://www.nytimes.com/2010/07/07/arts/television/07daily.html.
5. Irin Carmon, "5 Unconvincing Excuses For Daily Show Sexism," last modified June 24, 2010, http://Jezebel.com/5571826/5-unconvincing-excuses-for-daily-show-sexism.
6. Irin Carmon, "Female Employees of the Daily Show Speak Out," http://Jezebel.com/5580512/female-employees-of-the-daily-show-speak-out.
7. Emily Gould, "Outrage World," last modified July 6, 2010, http://www.slate.com/articles/double_x/doublex/2010/07/outrage_world.html.
8. Irin Carmon, "Judd Apatow Defends His Record On Female Characters," last modified November 10, 2010, http://Jezebel.com/5686517/judd-apatow-defends-his-record-on-female-characters.

XV: CUTE BUT EVIL: ONLINE ENTERTAINMENT TACTICS THAT DRUG YOU AND ME

1. Peter Kafka, "YouTube Steps Closer to Your TV With 'Leanback,'" last modified July 7, 2010, http://allthingsd.com/20100707/youtube-steps-closer-to-your-tv-with-leanback.
2. Tamar Lewin, "If Your Kids Are Awake, They're Probably Online," *New York Times,* January 20, 2010, http://www.nytimes.com/2010/01/20/education/20wired.html; "Social Media Report: Q3 2011," http://blog.nielsen.com/nielsenwire/social.
3. Ricky Link, "Demand Meda—Breaking the Bank," access date January 17, 2012, http://www.onlinemba.com/demand-media-breaking-the-bank.
4. Sean Blanda, "Back to the Drawing Board," last modified March 10, 2010, http://emediavitals.com/blog/16/back-drawing-board.
5. Paul Lazarsfeld and Robert Merton, "Mass Communication, Popular Taste, and Organized Social Action," *The Communication of Ideas* (1948).

XVI: THE LINK ECONOMY: THE LEVERAGED ILLUSION OF SOURCING

1. Mark Schneider, "Delegating Trust: An Argument for an 'Ingredients Label' for News Products," October 2005, http://journalismethics.info/online_journalism_ethics/index.htm.
2. Adrianne Pasquarelli, "American Apparel Likely to Shed Some NY Stores," last modified August 18, 2010, http://www.crainsnewyork.com/article/20100818/REAL_ESTATE/100819812; Mercedes Cardona, "10 Big Retailers Closing Stores," last modified August 20, 2010, http://www.dailyfinance.com/2010/08/20/10-big-retailers-closing-stores.
3. Shawn Pogatchnik, "Student Hoaxes World's Media on Wikipedia," last updated May 12, 2009, http://www.msnbc.msn.com/id/30699302/ns/technology

_and_science-tech_and_gadgets/t/student-hoaxes-worlds-media-wikipedia/
#.Tz7D1iOHeYc.

XVII: EXTORTION VIA THE WEB: FACING THE ONLINE SHAKEDOWN

1. Antonio Regalado, "Guerrilla Webfare," *Technology Review* (2010), http://
   www.technologyreview.com/business/26281.
2. Michael Arrington, "Why We Often Blindside Companies," last modified June
   20, 2011, http://techcrunch.com/2011/06/20/why-we-often-blindside-companies.
3. Tom Mulraney, "An Open Letter to the Luxury Watch Industry—Help Us,
   Help You," last modified November 13, 2010, http://thewatchlounge.com/an
   -open-letter-to-the-luxury-watch-industry-%E2%80%93-help-us-help-you.

XVIII: THE ITERATIVE HUSTLE: ONLINE JOURNALISM'S BOGUS PHILOSOPHY

1. Erik Wemple, "Joe Paterno Dies On Sunday, Not Saturday," last modified January 22, 2012, http://www.washingtonpost.com/blogs/erik-wemple/post/joe
   -paterno-dies-on-sunday-not-saturday/2012/01/22/gIQATznwIQ_blog.html.
2. David Sternman, "American Apparel: In Deep Trouble," last modified January
   12, 2012, http://seekingalpha.com/article/319135-american-apparel-in-deep
   -trouble; John Biggs, "Paypal Shreds Ostensibly Rare Violin Because It Cares,"
   last modified January 4, 2012, http://techcrunch.com/2012/01/04/paypal
   -shreds-ostensibly-rare-violin-because-it-cares.
3. Joe Weisenthal, "NYT's Big David Paterson Bombshell Will Break Monday,
   Governor's Resignation to Follow," last modified February 7, 2010, http://www
   .businessinsider.com/source-nyts-david-paterson-bombshell-to-break
   -tomorrow-governors-resignation-to-follow-2010-2; Joe Weisenthal,
   "SOURCE: The NYT's Big David Paterson Bombshell Will Break Soon, Governor's Office Denies Resignation In Works*," last modified February 7, 2010,
   http://articles.businessinsider.com/2010-02-07/news/29968588_1_governor
   -paterson-david-paterson-resignation.
4. Henry Blodget, "Apple Denies Steve Jobs Heart Attack Report: 'It Is Not
   True,'" last modified October 3, 2008, http://www.businessinsider.com/
   2008/10/apple-s-steve-jobs-rushed-to-er-after-heart-attack-says-cnn-citizen
   -journalist.
5. Josh Duboff, "Paterson Reportedly to Resign Monday Following Times Story,"
   last modified February 7, 2010, http://nymag.com/daily/intel/2010/02/paterson
   _reportedly_to_resign.html.

XIX: THE MYTH OF CORRECTIONS

1. Howard Kurtz, "Clinton Aide Settles Libel Suit Against Matt Drudge—at a
   Cost," *Washington Post*, May 2, 2001, http://www.washingtonpost.com/ac2/
   wp-dyn/A30046-2001May1.
2. Shirley Brady, "American Apparel Taps Drew Carey for Image Turnaround,"
   last modified September 6, 2010, http://www.brandchannel.com/home/
   post/2010/09/06/American-Apparel-Drew-Carey.aspx.
3. Brendan Nyhan and Jason Reifler, "When Corrections Fail: The Persistence of
   Political Misperceptions." *Political Behavior* 32: 303–30.
4. Jeffrey A. Gibbons, Angela F. Lukowski, and W. Richard Walker, "Exposure
   Increases the Believability of Unbelievable News Headlines via Elaborate Cognitive Processing." *Media Psychology* 7 (2005): 273–300.

XX: CHEERING ON OUR OWN DECEPTION

1. Staci Kramer, July 7, 2010, https://twitter.com/#!/sdkstl/statuses/17994359302.

XXI: THE DARK SIDE OF SNARK: WHEN INTERNET HUMOR ATTACKS

1. Philip Petrov, "Why Are College Students—and Bwog—So Clever?" last modified March 8, 2009, http://www.columbiaspectator.com/2009/03/08/why-are-college-students-and-bwog-so-clever.

XXII: THE 21st-CENTURY DEGRADATION CEREMONY: BLOGS AS MACHINES OF HATRED AND PUNISHMENT

1. Dov Charney, "Statement from Dov Charney, Founder and CEO of American Apparel," *The Guardian*, May 18, 2009, http://www.guardian.co.uk/film/2009/may/18/american-apparel-woody-allen.

XXIII: WELCOME TO UNREALITY

1. Henry Blodget, "DEAR PR FOLKS: Please Stop Sending Us 'Experts' and 'Story Ideas'—Here's What to Send Us Instead," last modified April 15, 2011, http://www.businessinsider.com/pr-advice-2011-4.
2. "Conservative Media Silent on Prior Publication of Leaks Favorable to White House," last modified June 30, 2006, http://mediamatters.org/research/200607010007.

CONCLUSION: SO . . . WHERE TO FROM HERE?

1. John Hudson, "Nick Denton: What I Read," last modified February 6, 2011, http://www.theatlanticwire.com/entertainment/2011/02/nick-denton-what-i-read/17870.
2. Tyler Cowen, "What's the new incentive of The New York Times?" last modified March 18, 2011, http://marginalrevolution.com/marginalrevolution/2011/03/whats-the-new-incentive-of-the-new-york-times.html.

WORKS CITED

Alterman, Eric. *Sound and Fury: The Making of the Washington Punditocracy*. New York: Cornell University Press, 2000.

Baker, Jesse. "Gawker Wants to Offer More Than Snark, Gossip," January 3, 2011, http://www.npr.org/2011/01/03/132613645/Gawker-Wants-To-Offer-More-Than-Snark-Vicious-Gossip.

Blodget, Henry. "Post Hate Mail About Our Link to Steve Jobs Heart Attack Report Here," *Business Insider*, October 4, 2008.

Brown, Scott, and Steven Leckart. "*Wired's* Guide to Hoaxes: How to Give—and Take—a Joke, *Wired*, September 2009.

Campbell, W. Joseph. *Yellow Journalism: Puncturing the Myths, Defining the Legacies*. Westport, CT: Westport Praeger, 2001.

———. *Getting It Wrong: Ten of the Greatest Misreported Stories in American Journalism*. Berkeley: University of California Press, 2010.

Carmon, Irin. "What Went Wrong with Sarah Palin?" *Jezebel*, May 10, 2011.

Carr, David. "Taylor Momsen Did Not Write This Headline," *New York Times*, May 16, 2010.

Chomsky, Noam, and Edward S. Herman. *Manufacturing Consent: The Political Economy of the Mass Media*. New York: Pantheon, 1988.

Crouthamel, James L. *Bennett's New York Herald and the Rise of the Popular Press*. Syracuse, NY: Syracuse University Press, 1989.

Curtis, Drew. *It's Not News, It's Fark: How Mass Media Tries to Pass Off Crap as News*. New York: Gotham, 2007.

Del Signore, John. "Choire Sicha, Ex-Gawker Editor," *Gothamist*, December 5, 2007.

Denby, David. *Snark*. New York: Simon & Schuster, 2009.

Epstein, Edward Jay. *News from Nowhere: Television and the News*. New York: Random House, 1973.

———. *Between Fact and Fiction: The Problem of Journalism*. New York: Vintage, 1975.

Farhi, Paul. "Traffic Problems," *American Journalism Review*, September 2010.

Fishman, Mark. *Manufacturing the News*. Austin: University of Texas Press, 1980.

Gawker Media. *The* Gawker *Guide to Conquering All Media*. New York: Atria Books, 2007.

Goldstein, Tom. *The News at Any Cost: How Journalists Compromise Their Ethics to Shape the News*. New York: Simon & Schuster, 1985.

Greene, Robert. *The 48 Laws of Power*. New York: Viking, 1998.

Haas, Tanni. *Making it in the Political Blogosphere: The World's Top Political Bloggers Share the Secrets to Success*. Cambridge. Lutterworth Press: 2011

Huffington, Arianna. *The Huffington Post Guide to Blogging*. New York: Simon & Schuster, 2008.

Kierkegaard, Søren. *The Present Age*. New York: Harper Perennial, 1962.

Lanier, Jaron. *You Are Not a Gadget: A Manifesto*. New York: Alfred A. Knopf, 2010.

Lippman, Walter. *Public Opinion*. New York: Free Press, 1965.

Lizza, Ryan. "Don't Look Back," *The New Yorker*, January 24, 2011.

McCarthy, Ryan. "Business Insider, Over-Aggregation, and the Mad Grab for Traffic," Reuters, September 22, 2011.

Morozov, Evgeny. *The Net Delusion: The Dark Side of Internet Freedom*. New York: PublicAffairs, 2011.

Mulkern, Anne C., and Alex Kaplun. "Fake Reporters Part of Climate Prankersters' 'Theater,'" www.enews.net, October 20, 2009.

Munsterberg, Hugo. "The Case of the Reporter," *McClure's*, Volume 28: November 1910–April 1911.

Orlin, Jon. "If It's On the Internet, It Must Be True," *TechCrunch*, August 14, 2010.

Owyang, Jeremiah. "Crisis Planning: Prepare Your Company for Social Media Attacks," March 22, 2010, http://www.web-strategist.com/blog/2010/03/22/prepare-your-company-now-for-social-attacks.

Pariser, Eli. *The Filter Bubble: What the Internet Is Hiding from You*. New York: The Penguin Press, 2011.

Postman, Neil. *Technopoly: The Surrender of Culture to Technology*. New York: Alfred A. Knopf, 1992.

———. *Amusing Ourselves to Death: Public Discourse in the Age of Show Business*. New York: Viking, 1985.

Rosenberg, Scott. *Say Everything: How Blogging Began, What It's Becoming, and Why It Matters*. New York: Crown, 2009.

Rowse, Darren. "'If You Had a Gun Against Your Head to Double Your Readership in Two Weeks, What Would You Do?'—An Interview with Tim Ferriss," *Problogger*, July 25, 2007.

Rutten, Tim. "AOL? HuffPo. The Loser? Journalism," *Los Angeles Times*, February 9, 2011.

Schudson, Michael. *Discovering the News: A Social History of American Newspapers*. New York: Basic Books, 1978.

Silverman, Craig. *Regret the Error: How Media Mistakes Pollute the Press and Imperil Free Speech*. New York: Union Square Press, 2007.

Sinclair, Upton. *The Brass Check: A Study of American Journalism*. Chicago: University of Illinois Press, 2002.

Strauss, Neil. "The Insidious Evils of 'Like' Culture," *Wall Street Journal*, July 2, 2011.

Trow, George W. S. *Within the Context of No Context*. New York: Atlantic Monthly Press, 1997.

Walker, Rob. http://murketing.tumblr.com/post/4670139768.

Wasik, Bill. *And Then There's This: How Stories Live and Die in Viral Culture*. New York: Penguin, 2009.

White, Charlie. *Bloggers Boot Camp: Learning How to Build, Write, and Run a Successful Blog*. Waltham, MA: Focal Press, 2011.

WORKS CITED

FURTHER READING

I firmly believe that I still have much learn about this subject, and I have not slowed down my research since turning in the manuscript for this book. To continue this journey along with me, and to get monthly recommendations of books (on this topic and all others) sign up for my reading list e-mail. It currently has nearly five thousand subscribers, and it's a great and lively place to discuss books. I would love to hear your recommendations on it as well. Sign up at: **ryanholiday.net/reading-newsletter**

For a list of books that changed my life, check out the Ryan Holiday reading list: **ryanholiday.net/reading-list**

Some recommendations for books that greatly influenced what you just read are the following:

The Image a Guide to Pseudo-Events in America by Daniel Boorstin

If there was one book I wish I could force into more people's hands, it would be *The Image* by Daniel Boorstin. In 1960, before talk radio, before Fox News or blogs, he wrote a scathing indictment of the deliberately false reality molded around us by our media culture. Boorstin's book will shake you to your core. It made me want to write this book.

Amusing Ourselves to Death: Public Discourse in the Age of Show Business and *Technopoly: The Surrender of Culture to Technology* by Neil Postman

These are the spiritual sequels to *The Image*. Postman wants us to realize that there is something inherently inferior about the information we consume through visual media. As far TV producers are concerned, the worst thing that it could possibly do is inspire or provoke you, two horrible emotions that risk having you get up and leave your living room and miss the imminently scheduled set of commercials. You realize that the last thing we have to fear is a malicious Orwellian political censorship, because what we have already is so much worse: culture incentivized to be as shallow, fabricated, and captivating as possible—at the expense of what is actually real or true or meaningful. *Technopoly* is equally compelling; it tells us why the inventors of a technology are the absolutely worst people to listen to when it comes to deciding how to use it.

The Brass Check: A Study of American Journalism by Upton Sinclair

You probably don't know this but in 1920 Upton Sinclair self-published a muckraking exposé of the corrupt and broken press system in America. Not only did he self-publish it—at the height of his fame, no less—but he refused to copyright it, hoping to pass through the media blacklist a critical book like his faced. It went on to sell more than 150,000 copies. This fascinating and deeply personal analysis of the media was the model for what I aspired to while writing my own. Sinclair deeply understood the economic incentives of early-twentieth-century journalism and thus could predict and analyze the manipulative effect it had on The Truth. Today those incentives and pressures are different, but they warp our information in a similar way.

News from Nowhere: Television and the News; Between Fact and Fiction: The Problem of Journalism; The Big Picture: Money and Power in Hollywood by Edward J Epstein

I used economic reasons to explain why bloggers act the way they do. I could not have done this without the father of this line of thinking, Edward Jay Epstein. From his 1973 Harvard thesis, which was later published as *News from Nowhere*, that pioneered the study of network news (the first and last person to get access to their inner sanctum) to his wonderful books on the movie business, Epstein finds, exposes, and explains the hidden economic factors that determine the courses of entire industries. I followed in his footsteps for this book at almost every turn. I had the privilege of meeting him recently, which only increased my advocacy for his methods. I am morally obligated to press his books into your hands just as they were pressed into mine by my mentors when I entered the entertainment business.

INDEX